JAMES DOUGLAS CAMPBELL

LIFE-WORLD AND POLITICS

LIFE-WORLD AND POLITICS
BETWEEN MODERNITY AND POSTMODERNITY

Essays in Honor of Fred R. Dallmayr

Edited by Stephen K. White

UNIVERSITY OF NOTRE DAME PRESS
NOTRE DAME, INDIANA

"The Politics of Exclusion: On the Chronic Mental Patient and the Politics of Community" is reprinted in revised form from James M. Glass, *Private Terror/Public Life: Psychosis and the Politics of Community,* copyright © 1989 by Cornell University. Used by permission of the publisher, Cornell University Press.

Library of Congress Cataloging-in-Publication Data

Life-world and politics : between modernity and postmodernity : essays in honor of Fred R. Dallmayr / edited by Stephen K. White.
   p. cm.
  Includes bibliographical references.
  ISBN 0–268–01289–X
  1. Political science—Philosophy. 2. Dallmayr, Fred R. (Fred Reinhard), 1928– .   I. Dallmayr, Fred R. (Fred Reinhard), 1928– . II. White, Stephen K.
JA71.L54   1989
320.01—dc20   89–40017

CONTENTS

PREFACE

One of the most dramatic adventures of philosophy in our century has been the discovery, as Fred Dallmayr puts it, "of the unthought within or of our thought, the unreason of our reason, the unconscious of our conscious." The present volume is an exploration of this theme from its appearance in Edmund Husserl's notion of the "life-world" to contemporary efforts clustering around the topic of postmodernism. Two subthemes predominate among the contributors. First is the conviction that discussions of modernity's "others" must be directed in ways that speak more cogently to the concerns of ethical and political life. Second is a reluctance to be satisfied with comfortable positions in the debates between defenders of modernity and celebrators of postmodernity. The most fertile ground for thinking today is the disputed territory between the two camps.

Our sustained exploration of these common concerns is the most appropriate way to honor a scholar such as Fred Dallmayr on his sixtieth birthday. His contributions to political science, philosophy, and sociology over the last thirty years have provided a continuing source of insight not only to us but also to many others.

My introduction is divided into two parts. The first is an intellectual biography of Dallmayr, the trail of which leads directly into the central themes of the volume. The second introduces the individual essays. The reader who is impatient to "get to the issues" may want to jump immediately to the second part. The effect of this strategy of reading will not be fatal, but it will mean a certain loss in depth of understanding that emerges as one follows the development of these issues over the course of Dallmayr's work.

I would like to thank the Alexander von Humboldt Foundation and the Center for Programs in the Humanities at Virginia Polytechnic Institute and State University for supporting me during the preparation of this volume. I would also like to thank Richard Bernstein for his thoughtful comments on an earlier version of the Introduction.

INTRODUCTION

STEPHEN K. WHITE

I

Over the last fifty years, political philosophy in the United States has been indelibly marked by the influence of German émigrés who fled the Nazi regime. The individuals involved are familiar; to name but a few: Theodor Adorno, Hannah Arendt, Max Horkheimer, Herbert Marcuse, Leo Strauss, and Eric Voegelin. Fred Dallmayr also emigrated from Germany, but he is of a later generation. And although his work has drawn heavily from that of some of these earlier émigrés, it nevertheless exhibits distinctive qualities that have their roots in somewhat different experiences.

Dallmayr was born in Ulm in 1928 and grew up in Augsburg. His mother was of Protestant background, his father a Catholic with agnostic leanings. He was too young to serve in the German army during World War II, but the effects of the war were vivid enough. His older brother died on the Russian front; moreover, in the last stages of the war, Dallmayr was drafted into the home guard, which had the almost fruitless task of trying to control the fires caused by Allied air raids.

When the war ended, Dallmayr attended a gymnasium in Augsburg run by the Benedictine Order. There he was introduced to classical Greek and Roman literature. The experience of attending this school had a profound influence, but it was an influence that had less to do with academic or religious learning per se than with the environment—the "world"—that the school and the Benedictine teachers provided him. The peace he found there and the quality of

1

human care or concern stood in stark contrast to the surrounding destruction and desolation.

During this immediate postwar period, as well as his years studying law at the University of Munich (1949–53), the intellectual atmosphere was suffused with French existentialism, especially the works of Sartre, Camus, and Cocteau. Their books, plays, and films spoke in a direct way to a generation for whom old social structures and traditions seemed exhausted.

After completing his law dissertation, he spent some time in Belgium and Italy and finally decided instead to emigrate to the United States. He was attracted both by the idea of seeing the country and by the American way of studying politics, a way that seemed less tightly bound to jurisprudence and traditional *Staatslehre*. Southern Illinois University gave him a fellowship to study political science. There he earned his masters degree; met his future wife, Ilse; and made the decision to remain in the United States.

In 1957, Dallmayr received a doctoral fellowship to Duke University. There he worked closely with a constitutional scholar, Robert Rankin, and one of the leading political theorists of the time, John Hallowell. His doctorate was granted in 1960. In the following years, Dallmayr taught at Purdue University and University of Georgia and was a visiting professor at the University of Hamburg and a research fellow at Oxford University. Since 1978, he has been Packey Dee Professor of Government at Notre Dame University.

During the late 1950s and 1960s, Dallmayr wrote on a variety of subjects: comparative law and politics, history of political thought, constitutional law, and philosophy of the social sciences. In regard to the last of these, he argued, as did many others at the time, against what he felt was an increasingly narrow behavioral orientation in American political science, an orientation that tended to disparage or neglect historical, interpretive, phenomenological, and ontological reflection in the realm of political inquiry.[1] The real distinctiveness of Dallmayr's thinking, however, emerged when he began to concentrate on exactly what sort of philosophical orientation was appropriate for political thinking in the late twenti-

eth century. It is his persistent search for this new orientation, as well as his refusal to be satisfied with answers many
of us find at least temporarily comfortable, that gives Dallmayr's thought some of its most attractive characteristics. He
refers to his books as "exercises" or "journeys" or "encounters"; the thinking is always *unterwegs*, never comfortably
at its destination.

It would be misleading to present this philosophical endeavor as primarily a response to behavioralism in social science. Certainly it did respond to those concerns. But it also, in
a sense, was a response to the dominant orientation of political theory in the United States at that time as manifested in
the work of individuals such as Strauss, Voegelin, and Hallowell. Although he has always remained attuned to the history
of political thought, Dallmayr nevertheless became disen-
chanted with the doctrinaire flavor sometimes evident in
these authors' treatment of classical works, as well as with
their overly retrospective search for answers to the dilemmas
of the contemporary world. This shift of emphasis is clearly
evident in his 1969 essay "Hobbes and Existentialism: Some
Affinities."[2] Whereas other theorists focused on Hobbes's
atheism and lamented his destruction of the natural law tradition, Dallmayr probed some of the affinities between Hobbes's description of the human condition and that offered by
French existentialism. For present purposes, the particulars
of this argument are less important than the new orientation
it signaled.

But we will still misconstrue this departure if we understand it primarily as a strategic shift along theoretical fronts.
Its roots are deeply practical and personal. But these terms
must be correctly understood. By *practical*, I mean an unre-
lenting commitment always to return complex philosophical
discussions back to the questions: what is the point of human
existence, what modes of intersubjectivity or "co-being"
should we foster, and how can we reconstruct politics around
our answers to the first two questions?[3] Presumably, these
should be the concerns of any political philosopher. However,
these questions have an intensity and a radicality in Dallmayr's
work that are distinctive. It is this quality I allude to as "per-

sonal." The intense and radical persistence of these questions is, I think, grounded in his life experience, in particular the experience of fragile, but sustaining human bonds in his youth, juxtaposed with the experience of thoroughgoing destruction and desolation. And yet to call this experience "personal" is to risk missing its broader significance: the sense in which it reflects the predicament of contemporary life. How do we rethink and provide normative orientation to intersubjectivity without traditional metaphysical or religious foundations, all the while threatened with unprecedented powers of destruction?

So it is both a set of questions and his intensity of commitment to them that define Dallmayr's philosophical journey. Guidance on this journey came first from existentialism, although it was not so much that of Sartre and Camus as the variant developed by Maurice Merleau-Ponty. Despite their insights, the former exhibited a tendency to analyze human subjectivity in ways that still abstracted too strongly from everyday life. Merleau-Ponty's thought, on the other hand, tried to keep subjectivity closer to its natural and intersubjective constituents. It was only from the sustained analysis of this everyday life-world, coupled with an awareness of radical "contingency," that thinking about reason, freedom, and politics could take on a new cast.[4]

Joining the resources of phenomenology to existentialism was not, however, sufficient for reconstructing the normative basis of politics. Dallmayr saw in the work of the Frankfurt School, especially Jürgen Habermas, a rich source for rethinking intersubjectivity. Critical theory and existential phenomenology, he thought, provided the two necessary moments of insight for his project, which he now called "critical phenomenology." The strength of the former was its normative analysis, but its Marxian and Enlightenment heritage still required correction from the latter with its emphasis on the concrete, everyday life-world and its accentuation of "man's precarious and incongruous status in the world."[5]

By about 1980 rethinking had begun on this project. Critical theory continued to be an influence, but now more in the person of Adorno. In a distinctively radical way Adorno sought to pursue the problem of destruction and domination in Western civilization to its deepest sources. The influence of *Dialectic of Enlightenment* (with Horkheimer) and *Negative Dialectics* increasingly convinced Dallmayr that Habermas's analysis of rationality and intersubjectivity and Merleau-Ponty's analysis of "embodied subjectivity" were themselves still too entangled in conceptual modes that Adorno saw as participating in an underlying logic of destruction and domination.[6] The notion of "embodied subjectivity" had been embraced with the thought that it could provide a reorientation away from views of political life revolving around individuals conceived abstractly and action conceived instrumentally, in terms of mastery. But to found analysis on "subjectivity" of any sort means that one has already presupposed the validity of that binary distinction, so basic to Western thought, between subject and object. And that separation itself already orients philosophical reflection on politics in precisely those directions Dallmayr wanted to avoid.

The concern here can be elaborated in terms of different conceptions of the life-world. When subjectivity is given too prominent a role, the accompanying conception of the life-world will necessarily be too thin or "weak," in the sense of being too easily penetrable by the rational subject. The otherness of what is beyond the horizon of the rational subject is allowed to be too easily drawn into the foreground, an operation carrying overtones of progressive mastery. This weak version of the life-world originally appeared in Husserl, but it has been even more influential in social theory, first in the social phenomenology of Alfred Schutz, and more recently in Jürgen Habermas's work.[7] Dallmayr still admires Habermas's writings, particularly their exposure of how functional reason, embodied in modern economies and administrative states, fosters a destructive "colonization of the life-world."[8] But Habermas's attempt to defend the life-world is undermined from within; his weak conception of it allows subjectivity to participate in a less conspicuous, but parallel, form of colonization.[9]

The most important source of a "strong" conception of the life-world is Heidegger. It is his analysis of being-in-the-world that reveals a dimension that is ontologically prior to the subject-object dichotomy. Dallmayr's turn toward Heidegger has proceeded slowly and deliberately. Not only must Heidegger's involvement with nazism be a persistent concern for a German émigré, but one must also remember how deeply critical Adorno was of him.[10] It is in confronting Adorno's critique that Dallmayr shows why he now refers to his investigation as being guided by the notion of a "practical ontology."[11]

Despite Heidegger's own claims to the contrary, Adorno saw him as engaged in a "theoretical ontology," whose claims ultimately assumed the status of a traditional metaphysics, in the sense of some absolute grasp in thought of fundamental structures of the world; and, moreover, this grasp sometimes seemed wedded to the promise of some unmediated stance of authentic being in the world. For Adorno, both these orientations threatened to eliminate the gap or space of "negativity" between concept and world that must be preserved by any postmetaphysical philosophical reflection. Now Dallmayr shares Adorno's concern here, and he is aware that Heidegger can be read in this way, but he is also convinced that one can read him "against the grain" in such a way as to allow that concern to be philosophically developed in a fruitful fashion. Under this latter description, Heidegger provides significant insights toward a practical ontology, that is, one centered around action and intersubjectivity or co-being.

What fascinates Dallmayr about Heidegger is the way in which he analyzes the contextual embeddedness of action, or rather its nexus with being. This analysis is perhaps the most deeply radical challenge to the predominant ways of conceptualizing action in terms of subject-centeredness and the linear linking of means and ends.[12] By referring to Heidegger as the most prominent exponent of a "strong" view of the life-world, Dallmayr wishes to draw attention to the irreducible embeddedness of action, the impossibility of making all our horizons of otherness into a surveyable and comforting foreground. Now there are certainly others whose work pushes forward this strong view of the life-world. Much of recent French thought, Dallmayr observes, presents the life-world as "a multilayered arena fraught with ruptures and discontinuities; ... human life itself appears as permeated by otherness and absence—where absence does not denote a simple negativity but a present absence or the absence of a present, the invisible of the visible."[13] Although there are thus many companions in the move toward a strong conception of the lifeworld, Dallmayr's development of the key insights of practical ontology relies quite heavily on Heidegger, especially the later writings. In what follows I want to sketch out some of these insights.

Following Heidegger, Dallmayr portrays "genuine action as participation in an ontological event or happening: the disclosure of the 'truth' of being."[14] The force of "genuine" here is to mark out certain modes of action as particularly revealing of both the character of human being and its relation to being. Genuine action has the possibility of drawing us away from a purely cognitive-instrumental orientation to the world, which merely pushes us further from the only true insight about being of which we are capable. Ontological reflection "never completely surveys or grasps its field; ... [it] inevitably yields partial and discontinuous insights or glimpses."[15] The most profound insight available to such reflection is, as Heidegger expresses it, that all "lighting" or disclosure is simultaneously a "concealing." The distinctiveness of human being lies in its capacity to participate actively in this "lighting and concealing"; our action or, more specifically, our ability to speak allows us "to make appear, set free, that is, to offer and extend what we call World. ... "[16]

Genuine action can now be understood as a mode of linguistic interaction that keeps us attentive to this lighting-concealing, and also to the intersection of doing and suffering (or passion). Dallmayr often speaks of such action as having poetic, creative, and playful dimensions.[17] Here, of course, his position is close to that of many poststructuralists. But it is also at this point that Dallmayr begins to turn toward the question of intersubjectivity and ethics in a way that departs from these thinkers. First of all, he expresses concern that Jacques Derrida, although emphasizing the poetic, creative, playful dimensions of language, sometimes tends toward a mere "celebration of difference" resulting in "a potential indifference or apathy" to a whole range of issues tied up with understanding and intersubjectivity. In his "deconstructive zeal" he and his followers put themselves in an ironic posture: in their deconstructive performances intended to extol the play of difference and multiplicity, they run the risk of excessively celebrating their own artistry (and thus their own subjectivity), as if they were the ringmasters of otherness. This tendency threatens to undermine a strong conception of the life-world.[18] And it is only from a persistent adherence to such a conception that an appropriate orientation for ethics can be won. Dallmayr speaks here of a "recollective ethics" whose judgments are always attentive to the finitude and contextuality of human being, its embeddedness in the "opacity" of being.[19]

The ethical direction Dallmayr is seeking also comes through in his second criticism of deconstruction: the latter manifests a certain inattention to the "nurturing and sustaining quality" of genuine human action. Such interaction allows a relationship between self and others that nurtures and respects "the multidimensionality and unfathomable plurivocity of their various idioms."[20] (By differentiating his views from deconstruction in this way, Dallmayr seems to move rather close to the insights of a number of contemporary feminist thinkers, such as Jean Elshtain, although he continues to draw his direct inspiration on this score from Heidegger.)[21] Here Dallmayr reads Heidegger's thinking about authenticity as urging an attitude of "emancipatory care" for the other. The sustaining and nurturing quality of this attitude can be emphasized by contrasting it with a Kantian one. The postulate to treat others as ends rather than means still contains "instrumentalist traces," as each ego rationally locates others abstractly within the purview of its moral goals. Liberating care, on the contrary, approaches otherness at the level of concrete, embodied being (here Merleau-Ponty's presence remains important) and manifests respect for others' "potentiality for being," for participating in the lighting and concealing.[22]

There is a final difference between Dallmayr and prevalent variants of deconstruction, as well as other poststructuralist modes of thought. It gives his work one of its most significant qualities, and it anchors all of his ethical concerns. I spoke previously of Dallmayr's analysis of the embeddedness of action in an ontological context, but stated in such a straightforward way, this claim loses perhaps its fullest resonance. When one listens to that resonance, one senses a deep reverence for "being." Action is not merely ontologically structured, but "submerged in goodness itself (that is, in being or the divine)."[23] Now this sort of reverence should not necessarily be taken in a conventional religious sense.[24] One can think, for example, of the reverential attitude toward nature that one often finds in radical ecologists. But whatever sense we should attribute to this reverence (and Dallmayr has not explicitly said much here), it plays a subtle but essential role in his thinking about attentive care or concern. The difference from many poststructuralists on this matter can be gauged if one also listens for the undertones of Foucault's ontological insights. There one hears only the "distant roar" of warfare, of clashes in relation to which Heideggerian metaphors of "belonging together" and "homecoming" seem radically inappropriate.[25]

Turning back now to the problem of interaction, Dallmayr's task is to find modes that have the "structural attributes" necessary for an attitude of attentive care or concern.[26] But this task must remain in touch with the world of politics. We must rethink interaction in such a way that we can recognize its place in political life. Without this problem to contend with, we could perhaps remain content with an illumination of "poetic modes of colloquy or dialogue," for they represent the most unalloyed challenge to the "linguistic sclerosis" that closes off access to otherness.[27] But politics remains intrinsically tied to a responsibility to act in some form of binding coordination with others. (It is of course precisely this existential quality that often misleads us into thinking of politics solely in terms of subject-centered, strategic concepts.) Dallmayr's task is to rethink action so as not to sever this connection entirely, but at the same time leave an opening to the world-disclosing voice of poetry. Part of this problem can be relieved by simply sorting out various "moments" of political life and the differentiated character of interaction at those stages. Thus Dallmayr suggests that the real problem is re-thinking action in relation to citizen dialogue and deliberation in the public sphere. How is this moment of politics to be en-visioned such that each actor does not freeze the other (or himself/herself) into a routinized script, for example, into sim-ply a rational bargainer or a recalcitrant in the path of realiz-ing a particular conception of the good?

Hans-Georg Gadamer's analysis of "conversation" or, more specifically, hermeneutical conversation in *Truth and Method,* is considered by Dallmayr to be one useful place to start this rethinking.[28] This model of conversation has two es-sential elements. First, there is a dimension of intention and minimal morality that links it to a will to understand the other, to generate a "fusion of horizons," and thus possibly coordinate future action. But this kind of teleology has to be counterbalanced if otherness is to be allowed to flourish. It is precisely here that Dallmayr has reservations about the way Habermas has tried to accomplish similar overall goals with his notion of "communicative action." Gadamer, unlike Haber-mas, stresses that even ordinary discourse carries with it po-etic qualities, a "play" of conversation that can alternate with its intentional qualities. At root, Gadamer's insights here re-flect his own strong conception of the life-world. It is only with such a conception that one will obtain a "deflated" enough notion of human being to urge that in genuine con-versation one must always allow "slack" in intentionality, and by so doing express "respect for the indefinite and unregi-mented character of the discussed subject matter and the lin-guistic medium."[29]

Dallmayr would be the first to admit the tentative char-acter of his speculations here. But about one thing he is any-thing but tentative:

> Much, perhaps everything, will depend on our ability to find a mode of interaction balancing hermeneutics and counter-hermeneutics, cumulative self-understanding and self-aban-donment, identity and transformation.[30]

For political theory a reconceptualization of communicative interaction is crucial, because it constitutes the axis around which a postmodern or postmetaphysical revision of our basic political concepts will revolve. Dallmayr has initiated some trains of thought in this regard that attest to the suggestiveness of this reconceptualization. The notion of community, for example, would now have to be rethought as the sharing of an "anticipative-emancipatory practice" based on "an attitude dedicated to letting others be—a distinctive and peculiar mode since it is lodged at the intersection of activity and passivity."[31] It is so lodged because this sort of letting be is not the simple abandonment of all strategies of actively "appropriating" the other, to be replaced by the purely passive attitude of ignoring or simply tolerating the other. Similarly, the notion of freedom, while retaining its "negative" sense relating to concrete political liberties, would also be given a "positive" sense, but not the traditional one associated with the claims of rational autonomy, which has so often lent itself to authoritarian projects.[32] This new sense would be of freedom to participate in the ontological event of disclosure, or "to move toward" human beings' own "ontological ground—a ground which is always already implicit in everyday existence."[33]

The task of trying to find a postmodern or postmetaphysical form for political dialogue and new ways of conceptualizing political life is formidable. Given the dimensions of this endeavor, we are all only beginners, swimming with difficulty in very deep waters. One characteristic that makes Dallmayr's thought so helpful here is its extraordinary interpretive sensitivity. No one is better at drawing out the heart of different contributions in the postmodernity debate, and then carefully nudging that debate forward.

In that spirit of sensitivity and tentativeness, I want finally to raise a couple of questions about the specific guidance Dallmayr provides us for traversing the borderland of modernity and postmodernity. The first question is related to the turn to Heidegger. Do difficulties not arise at one point where Dallmayr follows Heideggerian insights rather than those of contemporary poststructuralists? And not just any difficulties, but precisely the sort he wishes to avoid. In aligning oneself with the more reverential posture of Heidegger's ontology, where action is "submerged" in goodness or being, does one not also thereby define a "proper" for human being? And does this in turn not threaten to produce, as Derrida has pointed out, a subtle reinflation of the figure of man, a focal point for a new "We" that stands beyond critical reflection?[34] (Compare here the essay by Shapiro on the problems of "We" and the essay by Connolly that raises doubts generally about philosophies of "attunement.")

Dallmayr would likely reply here that a posture of attunement does not necessarily require a simple, harmonious conception of being. He would point to themes in Heidegger that are not so far from those in Foucault: the emphasis on "ontological . . . contest, or . . . strife between being and non-being, presense and absence."[35] It is only when *both* orientations—reverence and care, as well as contest and strife—supplement one another that we will be able to move toward more adequate modes of praxis.

Dallmayr stresses repeatedly that there can be no simple derivation of practice from ontological or other theoretical insights. At best such insights give one intimations for guiding political life. Following the intimations of his own twofold ontology, Dallmayr endorses what he calls a "postmodern pluralist polity." Such a polity would involve a more radical attentiveness to the agonal quality of public life than the old "end of ideology" pluralism.[36] At the same time, the orientation toward care would be expressed in a renewed commitment to the "politically and socially dispossessed."[37]

A twofold vision of politics thus reflects a twofold ontology. This political vision has, at least for me, a strong appeal. But my attraction is tempered by a lingering concern. As mentioned earlier, one of Dallmayr's great strengths is the way he blends perceptive interpretations of other thinkers with progressive elaborations of his own thought. In this fashion Dallmayr encounters and works through one problem after another on the terrain of modernity and postmodernity. The question I want to raise involves a possible tension between the singular character of these encounters and the more general vision that emerges as one looks back over their course. An ethical and political vision aimed at helping to orient our practice must relate its parts to one another in a systematic way. On the other hand, in a series of encounters this demand is relatively weak. My concern is whether the parts of Dallmayr's vision (for example, the themes of attunement and discord), which have been joined in a persuasive series, really hold together as well when placed under a stronger, retrospective demand for coherence. My hope is that Dallmayr will address this need somewhat more directly in his future work.

II

In following Dallmayr's project, one is led, as I have said, into a terrain between modernity and postmodernity. It is the taking up of this "in between" position that provides the primary similarity among the essays in this volume. Being in this "in between" means that one refuses a dichotomous choice: either to endorse postmodernity wholeheartedly, waving a happy farewell to those still struggling in the tangles of the discourse of modernity; or to hunker down in the bunkers of modern discourse, hoping that a steady field of fire will soon annihilate the new nihilists of postmodernity.

The essays also share that concern of Dallmayr's with the life-world. As his own contribution indicates, although the notion of the life-world has been variously conceived, these variations all constitute efforts to come to terms with "the unthought within our thoughts." These efforts have not been spurred by epistemological interests alone, but have rather reflected a growing awareness that this unthought is linked with the dark political underside of Western reason. Put simply, the blindness and urge to infinitude of modern reason make the discourses it licenses hostile to a whole range of "others": all manner of experience that has fallen on the wrong side of the confident distinctions: between Western/non-Western, mind/body, normal/abnormal, male/female, central/peripheral, and so on. Each of the contributions in this volume struggles with such distinctions. Each tries to deconstruct them in some way; but, as I have said, they do so in ways that are unsettling to fervent members of either the modern or the postmodern camp.

The Unthought within Our Thought: The Other of Modern Reason

The first essays by Dallmayr and Bernhard Waldenfels open up the question of the life-world and the history of its development from Husserl to Foucault and Derrida. This history can be grasped, Dallmayr argues, as a "progressive radicalization of the life-world perspective." Radicalization here means "stronger" conceptualizations of the life-world; and stronger means ones that better illuminate why reason cannot solve its sight problems once and for all by a strategy of progressively shifting its horizon or background into the foreground, so that everything is eventually foreground. Such an insistent strategy merely provides new evidence of our reason's tendency to seek a panoptic or infinite vision. Waldenfels's essay focuses specifically on the dilemmas of such a strategy of "appropriation" of the "other." It also exposes the weakness of mirror-image, postmodern counterstrategies of pure "disappropriation." It suggests, as an alternative, strategies of what Merleau-Ponty called "enlacement" (*entrelacs*). Here the border between own and alien, self and other, is to be rethought in new ways that "mean neither fusion in the sense of non-distinction nor separation in the sense of sharp differentiation." This means thinking of own and alien as existing in a pattern whose components are neither submerged in synthesis nor capable of being sharply separated without destroying the pattern.

Loosening Rationality: Reasoning toward the Other

The thrust and leading metaphor of Waldenfels's essay find resonance in the contribution of Calvin Schrag. He seeks ways of "loosening up" the standard criteria of rationality so as to make them more open to otherness, without relinquishing a minimal universalism resistant to dissolution in the radical multiplicity of "local narratives" so emphasized by postmodern thinkers. Schrag recommends a "refiguration of rationality," understood now as "a social practice . . . that involves the telling of a story, laden with interpretation, containing resources and strategies for critique." This refigured, communicative rationality operates within a "space of transversality," between self and other, between "our" life-world and "theirs." Within this space, universals are not projected confidently from one side, but built up in a play of challenge and response.

Schrag thus seeks a new appreciation of particularity without losing the possibility of universalism. How exactly is this universalism to be preserved? If I understand him correctly, he looks to shared, general features in the background practices or life-world of different local narratives or forms of life.

Although Schrag draws heavily from Continental philosophers, such as Merleau-Ponty, it is important to keep in mind that current attempts to refigure rationality can also draw upon the resources of Anglo-American philosophy. John O'Neill's contribution reexamines Peter Winch's ideas about rationality and social science, using Alfred Schutz's phenomenology as a guide to finding some new implications. Two ideas of Schutz's are drawn upon: first, his thematization of the life-world as the everyday world of common sense; and, second, his "postulate of adequacy" for the social sciences, stating that concepts spawned within the expert culture of social science must be understandable in the language of the everyday life-world. O'Neill argues that one can read Winch as implicitly moving in a similar direction, with the effect that his much-debated relativism can now be seen as an "insistence that *common sense knowledge of persons and society is a structure of ethical competence* that could not be replaced by social science programmes." The broad critical implication here is that social scientists lose their privileged status vis-à-vis citizens. They lose it not because, as Winch wrongly claimed, there are no causal explanations of action, but rather because the explanations of action that are discovered must be brought into everyday discourse.

O'Neill explicitly aims his reading of Winch toward a rethinking of the relation of science and citizenship in a democratic culture. In doing so, he seems, however, to endorse a somewhat stronger mode of universalism than Winch. Every world of common sense may indeed be a "structure of ethical competence" deserving respect, but O'Neill wants to accord special place to cultures with a high "degree of reflexivity in individuals and . . . openness of . . . institutions to . . . critical appraisals." We must, he says, think here of a standard somewhat like Habermas's ideal speech situation.

This raises a key question for the Schrag essay: In his proposal for loosening the criteria of modern reason, can he convincingly retrieve standards that are nevertheless strong enough to preserve some special validity for democratic values?

Tripping Rationality: Strategies for Seeing What Is Too Close by Looking from Afar

The foregoing proposals for loosening rationality provide guidelines according to which we can improve our conversations with others and thus consistently become more aware of our unthought. Michael Shapiro and William Connolly would probably endorse such efforts to a degree, but argue nevertheless that our consciousness often needs rougher treatment. Following more in the spirit of Derrida and Foucault, they seek strategies that force us to trip over metaphors and other figures of thought buried so deeply in our modern life-world that they are shared by both expert and citizen. Failure to unearth such assumptions means failure to comprehend adequately the roots of our modern pathologies and thus continued coproduction of the sorts of disciplines and normalization about which Foucault has spoken so eloquently.

Shapiro suggests that we must pay more attention to methods of distancing ourselves from the conversational mode, improved or otherwise. What we must seek is "not improving our conversations but the construction of counterdiscourses, modes of writing which oppose the terms of power and authority circulated and recirculated in prevailing modes of discourse." Shapiro illustrates at length how a literary strategy can perform such a task by demythologizing foundational codes, in this case a complex economic-political code carried in the Robinson Crusoe story.

Connolly takes a complementary tack when he shows that there is an underlying "phenomenology of life and death" that is shared by what are usually taken to be alternative modern perspectives on contemporary politics: individualist, collectivist, and communitarian. The structure of basic assumptions provided by this common phenomenology functions as a "compensatory code of secular reassurance" for a world in which God is dead "or at least severely injured." Individualists and collectivists reassure us with the promise of "mastery" of nature and society. Communitarians reassure us with the promise of "attunement" to the world. The inconspicuous effect of these codes on efforts to theorize about politics is one of blindness to the accelerating emergence of radical contingency in late modernity. It is not that the menace of contingency is not experienced; it is. Individual life projects seem to find that the institutional contexts in which they are to unfold all too easily erode away, and nation-states seem to master internal problems only at the cost of globalizing contingency.

Connolly's point is that the dynamics of contingency and freedom are inadequately understood, and thus our responses to contingency tend to tie us ever more tightly into a spiral of increasing discipline to master it, matched by a growing "generalized resentment" at the persistent failures of such efforts. Connolly argues that the only way out of this self-defeating spiral is to recognize that at the heart of all variants of our compensatory code of secular reassurance is the unthought "insistence" that "the world, at least in the last instance, must be FOR US in one way or another." He concludes with suggestions for rethinking freedom and contingency once we have given up this insistence.

Mapping the Terrain in Political Analysis:
Sites of Normalization and Resistance

The last two contributions focus on more concrete, contemporary political phenomena, more specifically on categories of individuals who occupy the status of "other" to the rational, public, disembodied self of modernity. James Glass looks at mental patients and the recent U.S. policy of deinstitutionalization. His findings provide fertile ground for reflection on the whole problem of otherness and public life. Deinstitutionalization could be interpreted as the embodiment of a postmodern freeing of the "other" from therapeutic discipline. But Glass paints a more sobering picture of halfway houses "halfway to nowhere." The public spaces made available by our late modern life-world are generally more inhospitable than we tend to think. The ex-patient can find no place in them. Thus Glass raises in a specific way the general problem of the self's having a sense of its own efficacy in the public world. As Dallmayr and Waldenfels remind us, "letting-be" is not a simple passive, disappropriating gesture toward the "other." It implies new modes of relationship, community, and fostering of one another.

Finally, Jean Elshtain broaches questions relating to the leavening role that women and other "others" of modern reason can have on contemporary politics. This essay continues her previous efforts at developing a feminist identity that eschews what she sees as an illegitimately constrained choice: either the liberal alternative of the "fully modern" woman who fits seamlessly into a normalized economic and political life or that mode of radical redefinition that cuts women's identity off both from the available "public" identities as well as their traditional "private" identities. In the context of this volume, one might draw a loose analogy between these alternatives and the ones noted earlier: a comfortable modernism versus a postmodernism that slashes all ties to established discourse. Thus, Elshtain would seem as well to be situated in a peculiar "in between," just as is Sophocles' Antigone, about whom she has written so provocatively. Here she continues her reflections on Antigone and finds the same spirit evident in the Mothers of the Plaza de Mayos, whose intransigent demands for an accounting of the "disappeared" ones played such a significant role in eroding the power of an authoritarian regime in Argentina. The language of the Mothers "was double." It was both the "other" language of a "mother's love" that is normally organized out of accepted political discourse and the language of universal human rights; "acceptable," but in fact often just as effectively shunted aside.

This analysis raises an intriguing question. Are the best values of modernity—ones that we both want to affirm as universally valid and yet separate from scientism, logocentrism, and the sources of societal normalization—today often finding their most moving advocacy in the voices of those who have been modernity's "others," but who now situate themselves on the border?

NOTES

Dallmayr's books will be abbreviated as follows:

DD: *Beyond Dogma and Despair: Toward a Critical Phenomenology of Politics* (Notre Dame, Ind.: University of Notre Dame Press, 1981).

TS: *Twilight of Subjectivity: Contributions to a Post-Individualist Theory of Politics* (Amherst, Mass.: University of Massachusetts Press, 1981).

LP: *Language and Politics: Why Does Language Matter to Political Philosophy?* (Notre Dame, Ind.: University of Notre Dame Press, 1984).

PP: *Polis and Praxis: Exercises in Contemporary Political Theory* (Cambridge, Mass.: MIT Press, 1984).

CE: *Critical Encounters: Between Philosophy and Politics* (Notre Dame, Ind.: University of Notre Dame Press, 1987).

1. *DD*, pp. 21–42.
2. *DD*, pp. 120–38.
3. *TS*, pp. 40–41, 65–71.
4. Cf. *DD*, pp. 120–38.
5. *DD*, pp. 3, 7.
6. *TS*, "Preface," "Introduction," 127–43, and chap. 4.

7. "Life-World: Variations on a Theme," in this volume; and *CE*, pp. 91 ff.

8. Jürgen Habermas, *The Theory of Communicative Action*, vol. 2: *Lifeworld and System: A Critique of Functionalist Reason*. Trans. Thomas McCarthy (Boston: Beacon Press, 1987), chap. 8.

9. For a defense of Habermas against this charge, see my *The Recent Work of Jürgen Habermas: Reason, Justice and Modernity* (Cambridge: Cambridge University Press, 1988), pp. 102–3.

10. Cf. *PP*, pp. 104–32; *CE*, pp. 130–58.

11. On "practical ontology," see *TS*, p. 5; *PP*, pp. 3–5; *LE*, pp. 2–3.

12. *CE*, pp. 205–6; *PP*, "Introduction."

13. "Life-World," pp. 57–58.

14. *PP*, p. 3.

15. *PP*, p. 5.

16. Martin Heidegger, "The Nature of Language," *On the Way to Language*, trans. Peter D. Hertz (New York: Harper and Row, 1971), p. 93.

17. *LP*, pp. 165–66, and chap. 7; *PP*, chap. 7.

18. *CE*, pp. 153–56. This criticism should not be taken as unqualified. Dallmayr shows great respect for other aspects of Derrida's work; cf. *TS*, pp. 107–14.

19. *TS*, p. 251; *CE*, p. 156. Dallmayr is careful to differentiate "recollection" as anamnesis here from a Platonic view of innate ideas.

20. *LP*, p. 179.

21. Cf. Jean Elshtain, "Antigone's Daughters," *Democracy* 2 (April 1982); Sara Ruddick, "Material Thinking," *Feminist Studies* 6 (1980); and Carol Gilligan, *In a Different Voice: Psychological Theory and Women's Development* (Cambridge, Mass.: Harvard University Press, 1982).

22. *TS*, pp. 67–69. A chapter in *PP* is entitled "Ontology and Freedom: Heidegger and Political Philosophy," a focus that deliberately offsets Heidegger's customary linkage with fascism.

23. *CE*, pp. 205–6.

24. Cf. the interesting remarks in Dallmayr, "Politics of the Kingdom: Pannenberg's Anthropology," *Review of Politics* 1 (Winter 1987), p. 104. See also, Martin Heidegger, *Identity and Difference*, trans. Joan Stambaugh (New York: Harper and Row, 1969), p. 72. Dallmayr's reference to the divine, one should note, is very subdued, ecumenical, and devoid of fundamentalist zeal; his comments are closer to "negative theology" than to any positive doctrine.

25. Michel Foucault, *Discipline and Punish* (New York: Random House, 1977), pp. 139, 307–8; and *Power/Knowledge: Selected Interviews and Other Writings 1972–1977*, ed. Colin Gordon (New York: Pantheon, 1980), p. 208. Martin Heidegger, *Erläuterungen zu Hölderlins Dichtung* (Frankfurt: Klosterman, 1971 ed.); and *Identity and Difference*. In *TS*, Dallmayr emphasizes that "homecoming" should not be read in the sense of a return to familiar ground; *TS*, p. 7.

26. *TS*, p. 67.

27. *PP*, p. 216.

28. Hans-Georg Gadamar, *Truth and Method* (New York: Continuum, 1975), pp. 310–51.

29. *CE*, p. 156; *TS*, p. 31; *PP*, pp. 199–200. On the notion of "slack," see William Connolly, "Discipline, Politics and Ambiguity," *Political Theory* (August, 1983), pp. 337–40.

30. *CE*, p. 157.

31. *TS*, pp. 142–43.

32. Isaiah Berlin, "Two Concepts of Liberty," *Four Essays on Liberty* (London: Oxford University Press, 1969).

33. *PP*, p. 114; *LP*, pp. 190–91.

34. Jacques Derrida, "The Ends of Man," *Margins of Philosophy*, trans. Alan Bass (Chicago: University of Chicago Press, 1982). But note Dallmayr's comments on *"reductio hominis"* in *TS*, pp. 29–37.

35. On the contested character of being, see *LP*, pp. 1, 166–67, 192; *PP*, pp. 3–5, 9; and *CE*, pp. 2, 70–71.

36. "Democracy and Post-Modernism," *Human Studies* 10 (1986), pp. 163–65; and *PP*, p. 9. In the emphasis on the agonal quality of political life, one sees the influence of both Foucault and Hannah Arendt.

37. "Life-World," p. 60.

PART I

The Unthought within Our Thought: The Other of Modern Reason

LIFE-WORLD: VARIATIONS ON A THEME

Fred R. Dallmayr

The age of discoveries, we are sometimes told, is nearly over, at least on our inhabited globe; with all parts of this globe neatly mapped out and recorded, little or no room is left for open frontiers or the lure of a *terra incognita*. Although this may be true in a narrow geographical sense, the assumption is refuted in other fields. Irrespective of the presumed closure of frontiers, our century—perhaps more than the last—remains an age of adventure and discovery, not only in the vastness of outer space and the inner recesses of physical matter. One of the most dramatic adventures of our century, I believe, occurs in the midst of our inhabited and "civilized" world and involves the discovery of the unfamiliar within the familiar, of the unthought within our thoughts. I am not referring here to simple dichotomies, some of which are traditional enough, such as the dichotomies between reason and passion, between the rational and the irrational, between knowledge and belief. What I have in mind is something more startling and unsettling, namely, the discovery of the unthought within or of our thought, the unreason of our reason, the unconscious of our consciousness. In large measure, this discovery eludes the categories and conceptual arsenal of traditional philosophy; hence the difficulty of naming and articulating the new terrain. In the confines of the phenomenological movement, the terrain has tended to be thematized under the labels "world of everyday life," "commonsense world" or—more frequently—"life-world." The exploration of this terrain has been aided and abetted

25

by another innovative thrust of our century: the move to language (provided the latter is not viewed as a means of information exchange or as a purely internal faculty or competence). The proper significance of language, however, emerges only in light of the previously mentioned discovery; to this extent, the so-called linguistic turn is (in my view) ancillary to the turn to the life-world.

As in all hazardous ventures, the exploration of the life-world has been slow and halting, sometimes fraught with setbacks; occasionally, initial advances were nearly canceled or reversed, only to be resumed later with fresh strength and vigor. Generally speaking, I believe, one can distinguish between a "weak" and a "strong" conception of the life-world, with a spectrum of intermediary positions between the two. In the weak conception, the life-world is basically viewed as a preamble to reason or rational reflection, as a non- or prerational antechamber to cognition—but an antechamber that pliantly submits to thought (as the result of an inherent affinity between prereason and reason). In the strong version, by contrast, the life-world functions no longer as a mere precursor of reason or as its relatively immature or embryonic modality, but rather emerges as an integral dimension of thought, a dimension impinging powerfully on the status of rational or cognitive claims (not by nullifying them, but by changing their sense). By and large, intellectual developments in our century can be grasped as a progressive radicalization of the life-world perspective. In the following I shall not attempt to recount this unfolding story in all details; instead, I intend to focus on some exemplary highlights (mainly in the context of the phenomenological movement, broadly conceived). My presentation opens within a discussion of Husserl's path-breaking foray into the life-world terrain, a foray still largely indebted to traditional philosophical categories. Turning to the immediate aftermath of Husserl's work, I next comment briefly on Schutz's inauguration of a phenomenological social science and also on subsequent sociological adaptations of the life-world theme (including Habermasian critical theory). To show incipient modes of radicalization, I

shift attention then to Heideggerian ontology, chiefly as outlined in *Being and Time*. From Heidegger the path of radicalization leads me to French phenomenology and finally to
recent trends of postphenomenology and poststructuralism—
trends in which classical phenomenology is both transcended
and *aufgehoben*. By way of conclusion, I comment on the linkage between life-world and politics.

I

As is commonly recognized, a philosophically rigorous
treatment of the "life-world" (under this or cognate labels)
was first initiated by Husserl and on the basis of his phenomenological program. To be sure, the term itself was not invented by Husserl but can be traced to various writers of his
period. In his own work, preoccupation with the life-world
theme emerged slowly or haltingly and frequently under the
guise of different designations (such as "natural world" or
"surrounding world").[1] Nevertheless, despite terminological
and conceptual quandaries, the problem posed by the theme
can be seen as a constant concern in Husserl's evolving opus.
As he wrote a few years before his death, the issue of the relation of man and world, or of objects and their appearance
in human consciousness, constituted always the driving motor
of his investigations. "The first breakthrough of this universal
a priori of correlation between experienced object and manners of appearance," we read, "affected me so deeply that my
whole subsequent lifework has been dominated by the task of
systematically elaborating on this a priori of correlation."[2] For
present purposes I shall not trace in detail the emergence of
the theme in Husserl's publications; instead, I want to concentrate on the last and culminating work of his career, *The Crisis
of European Sciences and Transcendental Phenomenology*. More
than in any other Husserlian writing, I believe, the life-world
occupies a central place in the arguments of that work; moreover, it was chiefly as a result of these arguments that the
term was transformed into popular currency.

In Husserl's final study, the life-world was introduced basically as an antidote or corrective to the "crisis of European sciences," that is, the crisis of modern empirical science and its epistemological foundations from Galilei and Descartes to Kant. Although applauding Descartes's radical turn to the *cogito,* Husserl found Cartesian epistemology defective because of its psychological misconstrual of cognition, a misconstrual promoting an "objectivism" no longer grounded in cognitive acts. In his "haste" to ground objective knowledge, he observed, Descartes neglected to investigate the "pure ego" with regard to "its acts and capacities" and especially with regard to the "intentional accomplishments" enabled by the former. For this reason, Descartes was unable to face up to an "immense problem": namely, the question "through which demonstrable immanent accomplishments of the ego the world actually acquires its meaning (*Seinssinn*)." Despite the more emphatically "transcendental" character of Kantian philosophy, Husserl saw Kant's system marred by a similar, quasi-objectivist flaw: the tendency to rely on abstract conceptual categories and a priori faculties without an exploration of cognitive experience. As a result, we read, Kant was ultimately unable as a philosopher to penetrate to "a clear understanding of himself as the primordially functioning subjectivity." Although relentlessly insisting on a priori conditions of possibility, Kant for his own part had "no idea that his philosophizing stands on unquestioned presuppositions and that the undoubtedly great discoveries contained in his theories are present there only in disguise, that is, not as finished results"—a fact that accounts for the nearly "mythical" character of some of his concepts and formulations.[3]

In Husserl's presentation, what was missing in Kant (and in modern epistemology in general) was a recourse to the concrete underpinnings of cognition; these underpinnings, however, could only be found on the level of ordinary, precognitive experience. "Clearly," Husserl stated, "what is presupposed from the start in Kant's inquiries is the everyday surrounding life-world as already existing—a world in which all of us (including myself as philosopher) consciously have their existence together with the sciences, as cultural facts in this world, with their scientists and theories." Despite the persistent inquisitiveness of the modern mind, inquiry always stopped short of probing this presupposed domain—a failure that in the end accounts for the lack of grounding or "crisis" of modern science. From Husserl's perspective, scientific and philosophical reasoning invariably starts from the taken-for-granted premise "that there is a world as always already existing" and that every correction of an opinion presupposes this existing world as a horizon of unquestioned givenness. In exploring this domain Husserl's study had all the earmarks of high adventure, of crossing over into a genuine *terra incognita*. As soon as, starting from Kant, we trace our steps back to taken-for-granted premises, "we discover to our growing amazement an infinity of ever new phenomena belonging to a new dimension, coming to light only through consistent penetration into the meaning and validity implications of what was thus taken for granted—an infinity, because continued penetration shows that every phenomenon attained through this unfolding of meaning and presupposed in the pregiven life-world, contains itself meaning and validity implications whose exploration leads again to new phenomena, and so on." As Husserl added, "no objective science, no psychology . . . and no philosophy has ever thematized and thus actually discovered this realm of the subjective—not even Kantian philosophy which, after all, sought to go back to the subjective conditions of the possibility of an objectively experienceable and knowable world." It is a realm that has "never been held in view, never been grasped and understood."[4]

In attempting to describe or map out the new terrain, Husserl's formulations were inevitably somewhat groping or vacillating, accentuating now this and now that prominent feature. In the study the life-world is initially introduced as a "realm of subjective phenomena which have remained 'anonymous'," but also as a mode of "the sense-world, the world of sense perception or of sensual appearances." Somewhat later, the life-world is presented as a "pregiven world"—prior to all science and philosophical reflection—a world that forms the context of all our concrete activities and life-praxis. In Husserl's words, this world is "pregiven to us all quite naturally, as persons living within the horizon of our fellowmen, that is, in every actual connection with others, as 'the' world common to us all. Thus, it is ... the constant ground of validity, an ever available source of what is taken for granted—a source to which we readily lay claim whether as practical people or as scientists." As a pregiven context, the life-world is said to have always already existed for mankind "prior to science," just as its existence continues "in the epoch of science"; consequently, it is possible to concentrate specifically on "the problem of the mode of being of the life-world" and to place oneself completely upon "the ground of this straightforwardly perceived and lived world." Still a bit later, the life-world is portrayed as a world of "subjective-relative" phenomena or of "subjective-relative" experience, an experience that is linked with the traditional domain of opinion or *doxa*. "What is really first or primary," Husserl writes, "is the 'merely subjective-relative' perception and experience of pre-scientific world-life. For us, to be sure, this 'merely' has—as an old inheritance—the disdainful coloring of *doxa*. In pre-scientific life, however, it has nothing of this; there it is a realm of valuable experiential testing and, based on this, of well-grounded insights and secure truths in precise measure as this is demanded by the practical life projects which govern their sense."[5]

In the preceding descriptions, the life-world retains a somewhat amorphous or ambivalent character, including cultural, natural, and perhaps imaginary features. In subsequent discussions of the theme, however, this ambivalence is reduced and replaced by a more stable focus; despite the cited references to "practical life projects" or an ongoing life-praxis, the accent is increasingly placed on visual perception and on perceived objects and artifacts. The life-world, we read, is "a realm of original self-evidence. What is self-evidently given is, in perception, experienced as the 'thing itself' in immediate presence or, in memory, remembered as that thing; and every other manner of experience is a 'presentification' (rendering present) of the thing." Still more clearly the accent is manifest in the passage describing the life-world as "the spatio-temporal world of things or objects as we experience them in our pre- and extra-scientific life and as we know them to be experienceable beyond the immediately given. We have a world-horizon as a horizon of possible object-experience"— where objects include "stones, animals, plants, even human beings and human artifacts (all in a subjective-relative mode)." The focus on things or objects is justified by Husserl by the (normal) primacy of visual perception in human experience. More importantly, the focus in his view is able to surmount or undercut cultural or idiosyncratic variability and to lay bare generic or universal structures of the life-world. In his words, the dilemma of variability vanishes once we take in account "that the life-world in all its relative features possesses none-theless a *general structure*. This general structure, to which everything that exists relatively is tied, is not itself relative; we can attend to it in its generality and, with sufficient care, pin-point it once and for all in a way equally accessible to all." Once this task is undertaken, the life-world can in fact be shown to exhibit the "same" structural ingredients as the world examined by empirical science—in such a manner that the life-world actually figures as a preamble (though a neces-sary preamble) to science as well as philosophical reflection. "As life-world," we read, "the world has pre-scientifically the 'same' structures that the objective sciences . . . presuppose as a priori structures and systematically unfold in a priori sciences. . . . The categorial features of the life-world have the same names (as in science) but are not concerned, so to speak, with the theoretical idealizations and hypothetical con-structions of the geometrician and physicist." To this extent, objective-scientific knowledge refers to a corresponding life-world experience, and every "objective a priori" to an experi-ential premise: "A certain idealizing accomplishment is what brings about the higher-level meaning-formation and validity of the mathematical and objective a priori, on the basis of the a priori of the life-world."[6]

Husserl's accent on thing-perception, one should note, does not in any way obviate his simultaneous reliance on sub-jective experience; on the contrary, life-world experience al-ways involves a prescientific (or precognitive) subject-object correlation. On the level of the life-world, he states, we are "objects among objects," but at the same time we are also

"subjects for this world, namely, as the ego-subjects experiencing, contemplating, valuing, and purposefully relating to
it—subjects for whom this surrounding world has only the
meaning given to it by our experiences, thoughts, and valua-
tions." To be sure, the term *ego-subjects* at this point does not
refer to empirical psychological processes, nor to an arena of
pure self-reflection. As Husserl emphasizes, the "anonymous"
phenomena of the life-world are subjective—not in the sense
of "psycho-physical processes" or factual "sense data" but of
"innermental" (*geistig*) occurrences. With this proviso, the life-
world from his perspective is always a subjective or "surrounding" world—one that surrounds experiencing subjects.
These subjects, moreover, are not merely abstract concepts
but concretely embodied creatures—provided the body is construed not as a mere physical entity but as a living or lived
organ. In the words of the study: "The living body is in a
unique way constantly and quite immediately present in the
perceptual field, with a completely unique meaning, precisely
the meaning indicated by the word 'organ'. . . . In my perceptual field I find myself operative as ego through my organs
and generally through everything belonging to me as an ego
in my ego-acts and faculties." Once the embodiment and situ-
atedness of the subject are taken into account, the life-world
emerges as the universe of embodied experiences and complementary life-situations: "Thus we exist as concretely embodied, though not only as bodily but as full ego-subjects, as
the full-fledged 'I-the-human-being' in the perceptual field
and, more broadly, the field of consciousness. Therefore, in
whatever way world as universal horizon, as coherent universe
of existing objects becomes conscious to us, we—each 'I-the-
human-being' and all of us together—belong to the world as
living jointly in the world, which is our consciously acknowledged world precisely through this 'living together'."[7]

Husserl's study does not limit itself to the simple description of the life-world, but pursues an ulterior aim: namely, the
aim of transcendental elucidation and meaning-constitution.
Before turning to this goal, I want to point briefly to a crucial
aspect of his description: the basic or "foundational" status of
the life-world. This aspect is repeatedly expressed in different

formulations. Thus, at one point, anonymous life-world experience is portrayed as the "ground" or basis of all objective (including scientific) knowledge. Has it not been the pervasive thrust of modern philosophy, Husserl asks, to show that "science is possible only as universal philosophy involving . . . a totality of all knowledge domains, and did this not imply that they all repose upon *one* single ground, to be investigated in advance of all others—and can this ground, I add, be any other than that of anonymous subjectivity?" Shortly afterward, the same domain is singled out as an arena of "truly apodictic certainty," that is, as "a universal ground which finally can be revealed as the apodictically necessary and ultimate ground of all scientific objectivity" and the "source of all ultimate concepts of knowledge." In a slightly different formulation, the life-world appears as the foundation of experiential self-evidence, a stratum that is anterior to scientific and mathematical types of proof: "From objective-logical evidence . . . the path leads back here to the primary self-evidence (*Urevidenz*) in which the life-world is ever pregiven." Adopting the terminology of surface and depth layers, Husserl at another point categorizes the life-world as the inner "core" or nucleus of all knowledge and experience. Prior to the clarification of scientific inquiry and all other kinds of human endeavor, he notes, it is imperative "to pay heed to the concrete life-world in terms of its truly concrete universality whereby it embraces directly and as horizons all the diverse layers of validity accumulated by men for their common life and whereby the totality of these layers is related in the end to a world-core (*Weltkern*) reflectively to be distilled: namely, the world of simple intersubjective experiences."[8]

To be sure, despite its grounding status, the life-world harbors its apodictic evidence initially only in an unreflective and taken-for-granted manner. As indicated, the goal of Husserl's study is to penetrate this taken-for-grantedness and to raise the life-world to the level of broadly "scientific" or philosophical inquiry. To accomplish this goal, the study invokes the phenomenological method of *epoché* or "bracketing," basically in a two-stage sequence. The first stage involves the bracketing of the field of empirical-scientific knowledge—a step that initially brings the life-world into view (together with its grounding role for empirical science). What is at issue at this point is not a mere mental abstraction or a fictive ignorance but a cessation of "all participation in the cognitive endeavors of the objective sciences, an *epoché* of any critical position-taking vis-à-vis their truth or falsity." Even after this initial cessation, however, the life-world persists as a taken-for-granted arena experienced in the "naive and natural straightforward attitude." To move to the level of radical reflection or reflexivity, a second step is required—one that leads to a "completely different sort of waking life," in fact, to a "transformation of the thematic consciousness of the world which breaks through the normalcy of straightforward living." This is the stage of the second or "transcendental" *epoché*, a step that, in Husserl's terms, uncovers a previously "completely unknown" and "never envisioned" field or topic: the field of "universal constitutive life" in and through which the world "comes into being as constantly 'pregiven' for us." Differently phrased, the step inaugurates a new type of inquiry, namely, a "novel universal science of subjectivity as the agency 'pregiving' the world," a philosophical science focusing centrally on the "all-encompassing unity of an ultimately functioning and constitutive subjectivity which accounts for the existence of the world (the world for us as natural life-horizon)." To underscore the radicalness of this step, the study speaks of a "*total change* of the natural attitude, such that we no longer live straightforwardly in natural existence": of the need for a "*total* reversal, for a *unique, universal epoché*." Once inaugurated this change even is said to carry in its train the possibility of a "radical transformation of all human existence" effected through a bracketing touching its core.[9]

Basically, what opens up at this stage is the field of pure or transcendental phenomenology, which is the heart of Husserl's lifework. For present purposes I can only highlight a few points as they are developed in his *Crisis*. In the study, the second *epoché* yields the discovery of "transcendental subjectivity," which in turn entails a liberation or emancipation from the simple givenness of the world and the achievement of a higher, reflective standpoint: a standpoint "above" the pregivenness of the world and "above" natural, straightforward existence: "I stand *above* the world which now has become for me in a unique sense a phenomenon." To be sure, reflexivity does not terminate natural existence as such, but only changes its mode of relevance: the world in its ordinary sense, we are told, "does not vanish; but in the wake of a consistently effected *epoché*, it confronts our gaze purely as a correlate of meaning-giving subjectivity through whose validation the world 'is' at all." As a result, a new correlation corresponding to the unreflective subject-object nexus operative in the life-world emerges: the correlation between "world" and "world-consciousness," between beings and meanings of every sort, on the one hand, and "absolute" meaning-constituting subjectivity, on the other. Husserl speaks in this connection of a "universal a priori of correlation" involving the relationship between world and its subjective modes of appearance or, more radically, between the *cogito* (and its thoughts or *cogitationes*) and the *cogitatum* (referring to the modes of appearance of phenomena). Elaborating on these dualisms and sharpening them into correlated fields of inquiry, the study differentiates between an "object-pole" of intentional objects or appearing phenomena, on the one hand, and an "ego-pole" as the source of intentional meaning-constitution and the "identical performer of all validation," on the other. Ultimately, we read, "everything is centered in the ego-pole— including the modalities of ontic certainty, the 'crossing-out' as illusion, the readiness to decide about uncertainties, doubt, etc. . . . These and similar matters point to special depth analyses of the ego as ego-pole."[10]

Much of the remainder of Husserl's discussion in the *Crisis* moves in the direction of such depth analyses. The subject emerging from the radical *epoché* is presented as a detached or "fully disinterested" spectator of the world, concerned only with its subjective modes of appearance. Yet, while being an onlooker, the subject also discovers itself (and subjectivity in general) to be the mainspring of "foundational" accomplishments, namely, as source of that meaning-constitution that allows a world to exist for us. These constitutive acts are addressed at all perceptual and intended objects (the "object-pole"), first of all in their immediate presence but further in the manner in which they are retained from the past or projected into the future. To this extent, constitutive consciousness always involves a mode of "temporalization" or attribution of a "time-form," but it is only in the "all-inclusive, universal synthesis" of basic world-constitution that these temporalities converge into the "unity of one time." Moreover, meaning-constitution or transcendental synthesis is not the accomplishment of an isolated, idiosyncratic consciousness, but rather somehow the product of a community or plurality of subjects. However meaning-constitution is conceived, Husserl observes, it is clear "that we are dealing with a multidimensional intentional accomplishment of the subjectivity in question—not of an isolated subject but of a collectively united constitutive intersubjectivity." Probing and sifting the different layers of constitution we finally are said to arrive at a "universal unity of synthesis" through which "the objective universe or the world comes into being"; in this regard "we speak of the 'intersubjective constitution' of the world." At this point, it is true, Husserl is embroiled in a troubling paradox or dilemma: the problem how mankind as plural or collective subject can be both an object in the world and the source of meaning-constitution for the world—a paradox that is ultimately resolved in the *Crisis* in favor of "ego constitution," where "ego" signifies not a concrete individual subject but rather a transcendental or "primal I" (*Ur-Ich*) emerging through reduction to the "absolutely unique, ultimately functioning ego." Having arrived at the ego in this apodictic sense, Husserl concludes, "one becomes aware of standing within a sphere of self-evidence of such a nature that any attempt of inquiring behind it would be absurd."[11]

Having reviewed the discussion in the *Crisis*, I want to mention briefly some of the chief problems or quandaries besetting Husserl's arguments. One issue, frequently noted in the literature, concerns the perceptual model pervading these arguments, that is, the distinct privileging of visual perception and perceived objects in the welter of life-world experiences. This aspect is intimately related to the subject-object nexus stipulated as central feature of natural existence. As one ob-

server has remarked, this stipulation is not so much an experiential given as a construct surreptitiously imported from
transcendental analysis.[12] It is mainly on the basis of this privileging of object-experience (or perception of nature) that
Husserl is able to screen out cultural variability and to arrive
at the postulate of universal and invariant life-world structures. The mentioned issues are all closely tied in with the
central quandary beleaguering Husserlian phenomenology:
the privileged centrality assigned to subjectivity and ego-
constitution. If meaning-constitution is indeed happening in
the world, why is it mandatory that this feature be an inner-
subjective accomplishment, and why should radical philosophical inquiry be arrested at the "sphere of self-evidence" of the
ego? In addition, if the ego is truly a "disinterested" spectator,
how can it simultaneously function as the constitutive agency
of meaning—a question that conjures up the broader topic of
the relation between constitution and life-world. If the life-
world is really a close-knit subject-object nexus, how can the
subject (no matter how much transformed or reduced) simultaneously distance that world into a target of transcendental
analysis, without dissolving its basic fabric? Differently
phrased: how can the life-world be "pregiven" to reflection
and yet, at the same time, be the product of constitutive consciousness? This constitution of pregivenness is particularly
puzzling if it extends—as Husserl finally notes—to the domains of language and social institutions; to gender differences, mental illness, and the unconscious; and even to the
experiences of "birth and death" as "world occurrences."[13]

In a sense, however, Husserl's weaknesses are also his
strengths. Before departing from Husserlian phenomenology,
I want to accentuate rapidly these strengths. A primary asset
or virtue, in my view, is the immense integrity of his work, an
integrity evident in the careful and painstaking character of
his investigations. The same quality attaches to the "transcendental" ambitions of his thought, ambitions that, in his case,
never congealed into a school doctrine and always remained
synonymous with radical philosophical inquiry. A case in point
is his "foundational" treatment of the life-world. Despite the
emphasis on its "grounding" status for both science and phi-

losophy, the *Crisis* repeatedly points to the tenuous character of this ground. The distinctive trait of radical philosophizing, we read, is the fact that "instead of having in advance a taken-for-granted ground of things, . . . it excludes in principle a ground of this or any other sort; thus, its beginning must initially be groundless." Even when gaining valid insights, such philosophizing realizes that "every acquired ground points to new grounds, every discovered horizon to new horizons." The same considerations apply to subjective meaning-constitution. Irrespective of its "apodictic" status, subjectivity in Husserl's presentation always retains an element of "facticity" and thus of ultimate contingency. To this extent, transcendentalism designates not so much a definite solution as an open-ended probing of unresolved issues. "From the beginning," Husserl states, "the phenomenologist lives in the paradox of having to regard the obvious as questionable or enigmatic, and henceforth of being unable to have any other theme than that of transforming the universal obviousness of the world—for him the greatest of all riddles—into something intelligible." At another point he portrays the constitutive ego as "a paradox and indeed the greatest of all enigmas," with "much and perhaps everything for philosophy turning upon this enigma."[14] As it seems to me, formulations of this kind provide a yardstick for the subsequent phenomenological (and postphenomenological) movement. As a minimum, one may ask to which extent Husserl's successors have remained faithful to his approach: the task both of clarifying paradoxes and of preserving the riddle as a riddle.

II

Husserl's discovery of the life-world was not and could not be restricted to philosophy seen as a specialized discipline or field of inquiry. Precisely because of its precarious character of (nonempirical) pregivenness, the life-world theme quickly radiated into adjacent human and social studies, frequently being modified, sometimes radically changed, in the process of adaptation. In the context of the social sciences, the newly discovered terrain was particularly significant as a result of the prevalent sway of scientific objectivism in these fields, which was a direct outgrowth of the "crisis of European sciences" Husserl had thematized. The possibility of a mundane-social or nontranscendental treatment of the life-world was recognized and underscored by Husserl on repeated occasions. Referring to the "constituted" life-world as the "universe of life-world objects," the *Crisis* states at one point: "Even without any transcendental interest—that is, within the 'natural attitude' . . . the life-world could readily have become the subject matter of a science of its own, an ontology of the life-world purely as an experiential world." While rejecting the notion of a "descriptive" science of transcendental meaning-constitution, Husserl willingly made room for a descriptive analysis of natural experience: even transcendental philosophers, he wrote, "can at any time return to and restore the natural attitude and, within it, inquire after the invariant structures of the life-world."[15]

Among Husserl's students, no one has been more persistent and influential in implementing these suggestions than Alfred Schutz, whose lifework bridges not only philosophy and social science, but also the Old World and the New. Although devoted to his teacher and mentor, Schutz's writings from the beginning were both faithful and unfaithful to Husserl's program. This dual aspect was already evident in his early work, called *Phenomenology of the Social World* (dating from 1932), a work aiming to forge a link between phenomenology and Weberian sociology. From Schutz's perspective, Weber's opus, though correct in its goals, was marred by the lack of properly philosophical or epistemological moorings, a defect that could only be remedied by a transcendental analysis of the process of meaning-constitution. While thus maintaining, in a sense, Husserl's deeper intentions, the turn to Weber was bound to modify other aspects of the former's teachings, mainly by shifting the accent of inquiry from visual perception to practical interaction. In Weber's account, sociology was basically a discipline concerned with "social action" seen as carrier of an actor's subjectively intended meanings in his relations with other actors. Taking its bearings from this frame of reference, Schutz's "phenomenology of the social world" from the start carried less a cognitive-epistemological than a practical or pragmatic cast. The same shift affected the investigation of the "invariant structures" of experience (recommended by Husserl): structures that, in Schutz's treatment, acquired variable and culturally conditioned (rather than a priori and universal) connotations. Over time, these initial modifications deepened and accumulated into a distinct divergence of views, with Schutzian phenomenology's increasingly taking on hues of philosophical anthropology and existentialism.

Irrespective of evolving modifications, a constant aim of Schutz's writings was the investigation of the concrete-social "life-world," though not always under this label. This was true already in his early work, where the topic was thematized under the loose heading of "social world," defined as a "realm of intersubjectivity" or a world "experienced by the individual as shared by his fellow creatures." Following Weber, Schutz portrayed society as a network of social relations or interactions, with subjectively constituted meanings functioning as purposive goals or "in-order-to" motives of human activities. Departing from and moving beyond Weber, his study embarked on a phenomenological description of the "multiform" or multidimensional structures of social life as experienced by participants in varying degrees of proximity. Noting the difficult status of society in pure phenomenology, Schutz at this point abandoned transcendental analysis in favor of the "natural attitude" or the "attitude of the natural standpoint," a decision that in large measure determined the course of social (or sociological) phenomenology. In his early study, the social world basically emerged as an array of concentric layers, centered around a nucleus of direct acquaintance and familiarity and spreading out into the margins of typicality and anonymity. The inner core of this structured web was the realm of "directly experienced social reality," also termed the immediately "surrounding world" (*Umwelt*), a domain marked by face-to-face encounters and a direct "we-relationship" with fellow beings. The transition from this nucleus to adjacent and outer layers followed, in Schutz's words, a "spectrum of decreasing vividness." The first layer encountered in this way was the world of "contemporaries" (*Mitwelt*), that is, of people who "coexist with me in time but whom I do not experience immediately." Still further outlying are the provinces of predecessors (*Vorwelt*) and successors (*Folgewelt*), where even temporal coexistence is canceled. Genuine intersubjective "understanding" was said to be possible only in case of direct encounter; with growing distance, sociological inquiry had to rely increasingly on typifications or "ideal-typical" constructs of behavior, constructs that, at least in the case of contemporaries, included mutual role assignments and expectations. Although grounded in experience, social science was concerned primarily with typified meaning structures, on a level where the participant's perspective shaded over into the observer's stance (congruent with Weber's postulate of neutral-objective analysis).[16]

Despite numerous changes and reformulations, the scheme of concentric layers was never really abandoned in Schutz's subsequent writings. To this extent, his work maintained Husserl's conception of the subject-object nexus as structuring model of the life-world. On the side of subjective experience (the "ego-pole"), this model manifested itself in portrayals of the social agent's biographical situation and lived encounters, portrayals that often exuded a tragic-existential pathos. On the side of the experienced world (the "object-pole"), the model gave rise to a complex mundane ontology of social relationships and typified meaning structures. These features are amply present in a number of essays written by Schutz after the war (and later assembled in his *Collected Papers*). Thus, commenting on the world of "commonsense" experience, Schutz observes at one point: "I, the human being, born into the social world, and living my daily life in it, experience it as built around my place in it, as open to my interpretation and action, but always referring to my actual biographically determined situation. Only in reference to me does a certain kind of my relations with others obtain the specific meaning which I designate with the word 'We'." Elaborating specifically on face-to-face encounters as grounding of other relationships, another passage states: "The '*hic*' (here) is the zero point of the system of co-ordinates in terms of which the individual groups the *Lebenswelt* into zones within actual and potential reach, each of which carries along open horizons of undetermined determinability." Accentuating the pragmatic rather than purely cognitive thrust of mundane phenomenology, an essay on "multiple realities" presents the social world as in the first place "not an object of our thought but a field of domination. We have an eminently practical interest in it, caused by the necessity of complying with the basic requirements of our life." Since we cannot equally be concerned with all dimensions of life, our interest, according to Schutz, organizes the world "into strata of major or minor relevance." The ordering principle for this stratification derives ultimately from an existential motive: namely, our "fundamental anxiety," the realization "that I shall die and I fear to die"; from this fundamental motive "spring the many interrelated systems of hopes and fears, of wants and satisfactions, of chances and risks which incite man . . . to attempt the mastery of the world, to overcome obstacles, to draft projects, and to realize them."[17]

Although centered around the individual—and thus initially a "surrounding world" (*Umwelt*)—the domain of commonsense or everyday life is not simply a private or biographical world, but always permeated from the beginning by preconstituted social meanings and typifications. In Schutz's words: "The world, as has been shown by Husserl, is from the outset experienced in the prescientific thinking of everyday life in the mode of typicality"—in the sense that objects and events appearing to us are "unique within a horizon of typical familiarity and pre-acquaintanceship." Differently phrased, the commonsense world appears from the start as "an intersubjective world of culture": it is "intersubjective" because we experience it "as men among other men, bound to them through common influence and work," and it is "of culture" because it emerges from the outset as a "universe of significations," a "framework of meaning which we have to interpret, and of interrelations of meaning which we institute only through our action in this life-world." In interpreting this web of significations, the individual actor commonly does not in-vent meanings, but instead relies on socially sedimented meanings and typical behavior patterns enshrined in role structures. To this extent, social action and interpretation presuppose a basic "stock of knowledge at hand," that is, a "stock of previous experiences" of the world, either our own or those "handed down to us by parents or teachers"; properly distributed these stocks of knowledge function as a "system of reference" and general orientation—especially on those more anonymous levels of social life not amenable to direct face-to-face encounter. Elaborating on the topic, Schutz finds everyday knowledge socialized in at least three respects: it is "structurally socialized" because it permits a "reciprocity of perspectives" on the basis of typical behavior patterns; it is "genetically socialized" because it is mostly socially derived and this "in socially approved terms"; and it is socially distributed in the form of complementarity, with actors differing as to "its distinctness, clarity, acquaintanceship, or mere belief."[18]

The same subject-object nexus can still be found in one of Schutz's later essays, devoted specifically to "some structures of the life-world" (and written a few years before his death). Replicating the scheme of concentric layers, the essay notes that "there is, to begin with, a stratum of the life-world experienced or experienceable which is now within my actual reach, a world of which I have or can have direct perception with or without the aid of instruments of all sorts." Next, there is a layer that "formerly was, though no longer is, within my reach," but that through various means, especially acts of remembering, can be brought back within my grasp. A third zone is the segment that neither was nor is now in my actual grasp but which can be actualized in the future by relying on a degree of historical continuity. This arrangement of the world into zones of "actual, restorable and obtainable reach" is said to reflect basic modes of temporality and their subjective correlates (such as retention and protention). In terms of social relationships, the inner core of this structure is the sphere of face-to-face contacts that is "surrounded" by the world of contemporaries "whose subjects co-exist with me in time without, however, being with me in reciprocal spatial

reach"; further layers are those of predecessors and successors. Whereas the inner core is accessible to direct understanding, the outer zones require complex interpretive
schemata relying on typical meaning structures and behavior
patterns "prevailing in the group to which we belong." Regarding systems of relevance ordering the interpretation of a
given social situation, the essay sketched a dual perspective,
one compatible with subject-object or inner-outer categories.
"Closer analysis shows," Schutz writes, "that the concept of a
situation to be defined contains two principal components:
The one originates from the ontological structure of the
pregiven world." The other component "originates from the
actual biographical state of the individual, a state which includes his stock of knowledge in its actual articulation. What
belongs to the former, the ontological component of the situation, is experienced by the individual as imposed upon, and
occurring to him, as a condition imposed from without upon
all possible free manifestations of spontaneity. The biographical state determines the spontaneous definition of the situation within the imposed ontological framework."[19]

As inaugurated by Schutz, mundane phenomenology has
had a profound influence on the social sciences, spawning or
reshaping a host of investigative approaches from ethnomethodology over symbolic interactionism to the sociology
of knowledge. The chief virtue of the Schutzian legacy, in my
view, resides in its attentiveness to detail and its stress on diverse modes of experience. As in Husserl's case, however, his
legacy is fraught with troubling dilemmas and predicaments,
aggravated further by the restrictive focus on everyday life (as
seen from the "natural standpoint"). Particularly troublesome
and dubious is the system of concentric layers, presented as
taken-for-granted and near-universal feature of the life-world;
given the stress on "reach" or degrees of reachability, this presentation sometimes carries overtones of possessive individualism. Precisely in view of Schutz's incipient "pragmatic turn,"
the contingent and historically variable character of this structure would surely have deserved closer scrutiny. Closely associated with the model of layers—arranged along the spectrum
of closeness-distance, familiarity-anonymity—is the problem

of social-scientific methodology. Throughout his life, Schutz basically defended a dual-level methodology or a "dual vision" of approaches: a combination of subjective-interpretive understanding and objective sociological explanation (along Weberian lines).[20] To this extent, Schutz's work replicates Husserl's juxtaposition of objective science and life-world thematization, the latter becoming possible essentially through a bracketing of scientific idealizations and typifications. What is lacking in Schutz's (and other forms of) mundane phenomenology is any trace of the second *epoché* or what Husserl called "philosophical-phenomenological radicalism": that is, the radical investigation of the enigma of the life-world.

Instead of delving into the array of post-Schutzian approaches, I want to highlight his impact briefly by alluding to one of the most prominent recent adaptations of his legacy: Habermas's critical sociology. In the latter's opus, the life-world theme (under this or related titles) always has occupied an important place. His early epistemological writings referred to a diffuse "life-praxis" construed as a sphere of taken-for-granted meanings and interactions, while differentiating this sphere from the "praxis of inquiry," where cognitive and scientific validity claims are examined. The notion of the "life-world" was specifically introduced in *Legitimation Crisis* as a label designating the subjectively and intersubjectively experienced dimension of social life. We speak of "life-world," the study noted, when focusing on patterns of institutions that are "symbolically structured" and "in which speaking and acting subjects are socially integrated." In contradistinction to this symbolic domain, the term *system* was used to denote a society's capacity for self-maintenance, and particularly the instrumental-rational efficiency of its institutions. Thus, whereas the life-world perspective was said to accentuate social meaning patterns as well as "normative structures (values and institutions)," systemic analysis was designed to concentrate on "a society's steering mechanisms and the extension of the scope of contingency," in a loose variation of the Schutzian "dual-vision" methodology. The same dual method resurfaces in more elaborate fashion in Habermas's *Theory of Communicative Action* (first published in 1981). Differentiating

between two modes of "integration," one symbolically or com-
municatively mediated and the other obeying instrumental or
cybernetic imperatives, the study observes: "If we grasp the
integration of society exclusively as 'social integration', we opt
for a methodology which, relying on communicative action,
construes society as a life-world. Tied to the internal perspective of members of social groups, this approach requires the
hermeneutical mediation of the analyst's and the participants'
understanding." On the other hand, "if we define integration
as 'system integration', we opt for a conception of society patterned on the model of a self-regulated system; in this case
social analysis is governed by the external perspective of the
empirical observer."[21]

In *Theory of Communicative Action*, the life-world theme is
first introduced with explicit reference to Schutz's legacy,
especially his concept of "mundane" or commonsense reasoning. Relying on the insights of social phenomenology, Habermas portrays the life-world as an "intersubjectively shared" or
"collective life-context" comprising the "totality of interpretations which are presupposed as background knowledge by
members of society." Regarding background knowledge, the
study artfully combines Schutz's "stocks of knowledge at
hand" with Polanyi's notion of "tacit" or implicit familiarity. As
a counterpoint to rational or scientific cognition, the life-
world is said to be a fabric of "implicit knowledge," that is, a
collection of "more or less diffuse, always unproblematical
background convictions" providing a source of action orientations. Schutzian teachings, including his model of concentric
circles, are also present in the depiction of the actor's perspective and its role in social understanding. Invoking Schutz's distinction between situation and context, Habermas writes: "A
situation is a thematically focused, action-pertinent segment of
patterns of relevance in the life-world which are concentri-
cally ordered and whose anonymity and diffuseness increases
with growing social and spatio-temporal distance." For actors
or participants, he adds, the concrete situation is "always the
center of their life-world; but it has a moving horizon because
it points to the complexity of the life-world," a life-world that
is constantly "present" but only as "background of actual

events." Noting a certain subjective-symbolic accent or bias in Schutz's work, Habermas seeks to correct this defect through recourse to hermeneutics and ordinary language analysis, a modification that transforms the life-world into an arena of prereflective communicative or linguistic "practices." Under hermeneutical and post-Wittgensteinian auspices, we are told, the life-world appears as "a culturally transmitted and linguistically organized reservoir of meaning patterns."[22]

The turn to language, no doubt, might have been the occasion of a reversal rather than simple modification of Schutz's model. In fact, Habermas's formulations sometimes move toward, or hover at the brink of, a "strong" (or structuring) view of the life-world. This is the case when he depicts implicit knowledge as entering "into cooperative efforts of interpretation *a tergo*" and the life-world itself as an arena operating "in the back of communicative participants." Even more clearly the same tendency emerges in the portrayal of life-world experience as something "not at our disposal insofar as we are unable to render it conscious or subject it to doubt at our discretion." On the whole, however, formulations of this kind remain without effect on the general framework. This is evident in the methodological bifurcation alluded to earlier. Linking Schutz's familiarity—distance scheme with participant and observer perspectives, the study contrasts the internally accessible "life-world of a group" to functional-cybernetic "systems of behavior" as seen from the vantage point of an "outsider": a contrast reducing the life-world to a domain of subjective (or intersubjective) meanings, irrespective of its linguistic character. The latter aspect is underscored in a passage identifying the life-world with a "subject-writ-large," in the sense that members of a group or collectivity typically rely on it "in the first person plural." Schutzian (and Husserlian) motives are particularly manifest in the treatment of the life-world as an embryonic matrix of reflective and scientific categories and "idealizations." Seeking to map out the internal terrain of everyday life, Habermas differentiates among three "structural components," labeled respectively "culture," "society," and "personality," with culture denoting a reservoir of shared knowledge and preunderstandings, society a fabric of normative rules, and personality a set of faculties (or "competences") enabling individuals to speak and to act. This differentiation is closely connected with the process of social development or modernization outlined in the study, a process that, anchored in the progressive replacement of implicit by explicit or rational meaning patterns, leads to the modern segregation of three categorial "worlds"—the objective, social, and subjective worlds—in which reflective and scientific "validity claims" can be thematized. To this extent, the life-world (in its various dimensions) functions as a pliant experiential premise or preamble to modern "communicative rationality."[23]

III

In some of its key features, Habermas's approach illustrates a conception widely accepted in the social sciences, but one that has not been unchallenged or unopposed; its prevalence, in fact, is startling given the long string of criticisms leveled against it. In large measure, the beginnings of the challenge can be traced to Heidegger's *Being and Time*. Presenting human *Dasein* as a "being-in-the-world" (or a being in integral union with the world), *Being and Time* from the outset countered the phenomenological construal of the life-world as an incipient subject-object correlation; also, by concentrating on everyday routine activities, the study—more resolutely than the work of Schutz—inaugurated a practical or "pragmatic" shift from cognitive or epistemological modes of analysis. As one should add, Heidegger's work was only a first step on a lifelong journey—his protracted exodus from traditional metaphysics—a journey that led him to steadily radicalized reformulations of language and human praxis, and also to a view of everyday life as part of a decentered (nonsubjective) happening or event.

In *Being and Time*, the life-world theme (or "world" theme) is introduced and silhouetted against the backdrop of modern philosophical developments, in a manner reminiscent of, or rather anticipating, Husserl's arguments. Concentrating

on Cartesian "ontology," Heidegger finds the conception of
the universe as "extended matter" or *res extensa* completely
inadequate, and in fact an insurmountable barrier to a proper grasp of "world." For Descartes, access to external or
extended things was granted through pure cognition, a cognition closely approximated to apodictic-mathematical knowledge. "Mathematical knowledge," Heidegger comments, "is
viewed here as that type of cognition which provides us with a
sure grasp of the 'being' of perceived things; anything that
measures up to the level opened up by mathematical insight
qualifies as 'being' in a genuine sense." Given that mathematics focuses on things or entities "which always are what they
are," extended matter emerges as an arena of permanent objects in space and time, or of substances with fixed attributes
or properties. On the basis of this presupposed but entirely
unexamined ontology, Heidegger argues, Descartes "pre-
scribes" to the universe its essential character or mode of being, namely, the mode of permanent objective givenness or of
a constant "presence-at-hand" (*Vorhandenheit*). The same "ontologically defective" view, in turn, prompts Cartesian philosophy in the end to "*leap over*" the phenomenon of the "world"
as well as the experience of those beings or things with which
Dasein is most directly involved or that are "ready-to-hand"
(*zuhanden*). From Cartesianism the study moves on to Kant,
whose "a priori categories" reformulated and deepened the
presuppositions of *res extensa*, thereby embroiling him in the
noted ontological deficiency. "In taking over Descartes's ontology," we read, "Kant shared the former's essential omission:
the omission to provide an ontology of *Dasein*." The aim of
the Cartesian *cogito* as well as Kant's transcendental consciousness was "to put philosophy on a new and firm grounding.
But what was left undetermined in this 'radical' start was the
nature of the *res cogitans* or, more precisely, the ontological
meaning of the *sum*."[24]

Seeking to correct this omission, *Being and Time* accentuates initially and first of all *Dasein's* basic status as "being-in-
the-world." In Heidegger's words: "The compound expression
'being-in-the-world' indicates already in its phrasing that it
stands for a *unitary* (or unified) phenomenon," a fact that is

particularly highlighted in the component "being-in" or the notion of "in-being" (*In-Sein*). The latter notion, he emphasizes, has nothing whatever in common with a mere spatial coordination or the placement of one thing in another. In normal usage, it is true, the phrase "being-in" suggests vaguely a containerlike image, on a par with the way "water is 'in' the glass or a garment 'in' the cupboard; by 'in' we mean here the relation of two spatially extended things with regard to their location in space." Differently put: the phrase refers to a simple spatial coexistence or juxtaposition, to a simultaneous "presence-at-hand" of things. In the case of "being-in-the-world," however, the spatial image is completely misplaced. Involving as it does the ontological status of *Dasein,* the phrase does not designate the presence of one thing—specifically a corporeal thing (the human body)—inside another; nor does it mean the "juxtaposition of one entity called *Dasein* and another entity called 'world'." As intended in the phrase, world does not denote an external adjunct or accidental property but a constitutive premise of *Dasein;* accordingly, "in-being" pinpoints not a spatial location but rather a mode of dwelling, in-dwelling or residing, a mode that manifests itself in *Dasein's* essential "care" or "concern" for world and everything encountered in it. "As an infinitive of 'I am'," Heidegger writes, "being signifies 'to reside with', 'to be familiar with'. Thus, in-being is the formal-existential expression for the being of *Dasein* which is essentially constituted as being-in-the-world."[25]

Elaborating on the theme, *Being and Time* rejects various interpretations of being-in-the-world, especially its misconstrual as a simple "correlation" (where world would be something added on to *Dasein* "by itself"). "Man," we read, "does not exist as such and then maintains additionally and occasionally a relationship to world. *Dasein* is not initially a world-free entity, so to speak, which sometimes 'feels like' relating to a world." The critique of the correlational view applies to the construal of *Dasein* as a mental-spiritual creature placed, through its body, into a spatial-corporeal universe. More importantly, the critique is a frontal attack on everyday life seen as a subject-object correlation. In Heidegger's presentation, the latter model is an outgrowth and import from modern epistemology and the "metaphysics of knowledge." In that tradition, he comments, "what would be more obvious than that a 'subject' is related to an 'object' and vice versa—and that a 'subject-object correlation' must hence be presupposed?" Yet, in application to everyday being-in-the-world, the import is basically misleading. Though customary and even prevalent today, he adds, the reliance on cognition as a relation between subject and object is a procedure "which harbors as much 'truth' as vacuity; subject and object in any case do not coincide with *Dasein* and world." According to *Being and Time*, the subject-object nexus is basically a synonym or stand-in for other metaphysical dualisms, such as the mind-nature or inside-outside bifurcations. Relying on these dualisms, modern epistemology arrives finally at quandaries like the following: "How does the knowing subject exit from its inner 'sphere' into an 'other and external' realm; how can knowing have any object at all; and how must the object be construed so that the subject knows it eventually without having to venture a leap outside?" In Heidegger's view, what is left unasked in these puzzles is the question regarding the ontological status of cognition. Once traditional epistemology is put aside, however, knowing or cognition emerges as a particular "ontological mode of being-in-the-world," namely, as a "deficient" mode where ordinary activities or everyday concerns are temporarily suspended: "In refraining from all acts of producing, manipulating and the like, care or concern shifts into the sole remaining mode of in-being, the mode of 'just-tarrying-alongside'. It is only on the basis and as a type of this in-being—where mundane beings are encountered only in their pure appearance (*eidos*)—that an explicit inspection or investigation of these encountered beings is possible."[26]

Digging beneath epistemology, *Being and Time* proceeds to uncover a primary, nondeficient mode of being-in-the-world and its corresponding form of worldliness or "worldhood" (*Weltlichkeit*). As Heidegger insists, access to this primary mode can only be gained in the horizon of "average everyday life," and particularly of the concrete activities and concerns occupying *Dasein* on that level. "The closest world of everyday

Dasein," we read, "is the environing or surrounding world (*Umwelt*). . . . We seek to probe the worldhood of this surrounding world via an ontological interpretation of the most directly encountered beings in this world." For Heidegger, the most direct way of encountering and dealing with the world is not perceptual cognition, but rather a concern "that handles or manipulates things and puts them to use." In Greek, such things used to be called *pragmata,* that is, matters or items with which one deals in a concerned or purposeful manner; Heidegger applies to them the term "gear" or "equipment" (*Zeug*), as it is used in "fishing gear" or "hunting gear," and tries to determine the gear-character of such things. As he notes, gear or equipment never exists by itself, but always belongs into a purposive framework—a use context (or "in-order-to"context)—in which it can properly function. It is only in the use or handling of gear or equipment that its essential gear-character or ontological status becomes manifest: namely, its status as "readiness-to-hand" (*Zuhandenheit*). In Heidegger's portrayal, this character remains inaccessible to mere external inspection or cognitive perception, since "readiness-to-hand" is not a simple property or contingent aspect added on to preexisting things or objects; rather, gear is usable only because of its intrinsic ontological status. In addition to pointing to a purposive framework or use context, gear also refers always to users, carriers, or agents for whom the equipment is ready-to-hand; moreover, together with users and carriers gear brings into view their concrete everyday world in its worldliness or worldhood. In the words of *Being and Time:* Along with the works (produced through gear), "we encounter not only ready-to-hand things but also beings of the nature of *Dasein* for whom products are ready-to-hand items of daily concern; and simultaneously we encounter the world in which wearers and users live and which is also ours."[27]

These arguments lead Heidegger finally to a discussion of the "phenomenon of world" or an ontological exploration of worldliness. As he observes, everyday concern with gear regularly also involves world, but only implicitly; an explicit awareness of world arises only when gear turns out to be unusable or when its use frame is somehow disrupted or disturbed. "A tool is unusable," he writes, "which means: the constitutive reference frame linking gear to its purpose is disturbed. . . . In the *disturbance of reference,* the unusability of equipment for (something), the reference frame becomes explicit." Together with this reference frame, however, the phenomenon of world announces itself or comes into view, not as another object or equipment but as the always pregiven grounding of being-in-the-world. Heidegger enters at this point into a detailed examination of reference frames, and especially of "signs" or signals as distinctive media of reference. Signs as signals, he argues, are a special kind of gear and a preeminent mode of reference because they render explicit a reference frame that otherwise remains latent or implicit. A sign, we read, is "not something which stands to another thing in a relationship of pointing; rather, it is a means which expressly brings a totality of gear to circumspect awareness so that simultaneously the world-character of gear can emerge." Differently phrased: signs reveal the central "point" or coherent significance (*Bewandtnis*) of a life context; thus, they pinpoint "the ontological structure of gear," together with its reference frame and "worldliness." In revealing this structure, signs ultimately point beyond the usefulness of equipment to something that is no longer usable, the purposiveness of *Dasein* itself: "The primary 'what-for' is a purposive directedness; the latter always pertains to *Dasein* for which its own being is essentially at stake." The directedness of *Dasein,* Heidegger concludes, always refers to and opens up a frame of significance in which gear and other things can appear in their different modes of being. This opening up of a space of encounter with beings and things "is the phenomenon of world; and the structure of the frame to which *Dasein* refers constitutes the *worldhood* of the world."[28]

Despite its general boldness and innovative flair, *Being and Time* is clearly marred by unevenness and an occasional halfheartedness in staking out its novel terrain. Its primary strength resides no doubt in its assault on the subject-object nexus and its portrayal of *Dasein* as an integral being-in-the-world, where world functions not merely as external adjunct or pliant preamble but as constitutive *vis a tergo* for human actions and designs. Probably one should also note the antiobjectivist thrust of the argument, evident both in the critique of epistemology and in the attention to negativity: in caring about its own being, *Dasein* is also exposed to nothingness and its nihilating impact.[29] Strengths or virtues of this kind, however, are counterbalanced by at least a partial reendorsement of traditional metaphysics or the "philosophy of consciousness." Notwithstanding its ontological ambitions, *Being and Time* pays tribute to this legacy in a number of ways, primarily in the portrayal of everyday world as basically a "surrounding world" enveloping *Dasein* (if not spatially, at least existentially). Closely connected with this portrayal is the emphasis on the essential intimacy of world experience, on the "primordial familiarity with world" that is said to be constitutive for *Dasein*. This intimacy, in turn, is linked with the possibility of understanding, that is, with a certain pragmatic (though not cognitive) "transparency" or intelligibility of the world that sustains *Dasein's* interpretive grasp. Terming the total meaning frame of ordinary life "significance," Heidegger describes the latter as "the structure of the world in which *Dasein* finds itself from the outset." What these and similar arguments neglect is the simultaneous strangeness and unfamiliarity of the world, the mixture of transparency and nontransparency of meanings (a feature that is not simply due to *Dasein's* untamed or "uncanny" potential). Ontologically dubious and disconcerting is also the focus on gear and on instrumental or manipulative behavior, a focus largely bracketing or overshadowing other modes of activity or praxis. As it seems to, even the discussion of "time" carries metaphysical overtones, with temporality chiefly designating an experiential mode of *Dasein* (in a manner reminiscent of Husserl's retention-protention scheme).[30]

On all these points, Heidegger's subsequent writings introduced decisive modifications and shifts of accent; central among these shifts was the progressive decentering of *Dasein* coupled with the relative distancing or defamiliarization of world. A crucial marker along this road, in my view, can be found in the essay on "The Origin of the Art-Work" (composed roughly a decade after *Being and Time*). In that essay, *Dasein* is no longer the fountain of meanings, given that the artist is said to emerge only through and as a result of the artwork. More importantly, artworks are sharply differenti- ated from use objects or from products of instrumental care; instead of serving *Dasein's* purposes, they manifest or encap- sulate an ongoing happening or "disclosure of truth," a hap- pening in which the artist creatively participates (but in a manner radically distinct from instrumental behavior). The meaning frame disclosed by artworks is still termed "world," but the latter is now seen as intimately linked with the opacity and nontransparency of "earth" (a notion granting new dignity and ontological status to those things "in themselves" still deprecated in *Being and Time*). From the "artwork" essay, the road points fairly directly to Heidegger's later studies on language and ontological "linguisticality," studies in which lan- guage appears no longer as the expressive medium of speak- er's intentions but as a matrix radically overarching intended meanings (chiefly due to its depth structure of metaphoricity). The same journey leads to a basic, nonmetaphysical reformu- lation of "time" and finally to the conception of both time and being as outgrowth or features of an ontological hap- pening or event (*Ereignis*), an event bringing into view the fourfold constellation of "mortals and immortals, earth and sky" (which now, in a still more complicated sense, is called "world").[31]

IV

Heidegger's innovative impulses have radiated widely in recent philosophy and intellectual life. It cannot be my pur- pose here to survey this complex scene. With regard to the life-world theme, I believe, some of his radical initiatives have been picked up and developed particularly in the French con- text, in that cauldron of intellectual tendencies ranging from existential phenomenology to postphenomenology and post- structuralism. A linchpin in this broad development is the work of Maurice Merleau-Ponty, to which at least brief attention should be given. Comparable loosely to *Being and Time*, Merleau-Ponty's early writings revealed an uneasy blend of ontology and subjectivity, an amalgam effected chiefly through the medium of "embodiment." His *Phenomenology of Perception* contained a long chapter on "the world as perceived" (a formulation still paying tribute to the visual-perceptual model). Once the focus is placed on embodiment, the study argued, the subject-object nexus of traditional thought is liable to be eroded. From the angle of situated awareness, body and world are no longer "objects co-ordinated together by the functional relationships that physics establishes," nor are they "spread out before me and ranged over by a constituting consciousness"; rather: "I *have* the world as an incomplete individual, through the agency of my body as the potentiality of this world." Body and world, moreover, are not simply externally or spatially correlated but are entangled with each other through mutual "implication," a linkage reflecting our basic "inherence in things." Grasped as a "third genus of being" between subject and object, Merleau-Ponty observed, perceptual experience "loses its purity and transparency"; along with sensory fields and the world itself as "the field of all fields," it adumbrates "the opacity of a primary past." Torn from epistemological moorings, consciousness was no longer a pure mirror; stripped of constitutive functions, it had to be grasped as "perceptual consciousness, as the subject of a pattern of behavior, as being-in-the-world or existence, for only thus can another appear at the top of this phenomenal body and be endowed with a sort of 'locality'."[32]

Following roughly Heidegger's journey, Merleau-Ponty's later writings were marked by radical defamiliarization, by the insertion of embodiment in an ontological frame that was no longer a frame of familiar meanings (derived from situated awareness). Exploring the sense of this insertion, *The Visible and the Invisible* insisted on the open-ended, transformative character of embodied experience, its tendency to transgress its own boundaries. In the words of the study: "We are not implicating in 'our experience' any reference to an *ego* or to a certain type of intellectual relation with being . . . ; we are interrogating our experience precisely in order to know how it opens us to what is not ourselves. *This does not even exclude the possibility that we find in our experience a movement toward what could not in any event be present to us in the original and whose irremediable absence would thus count among our originating experiences.*" From the perspective of such experience, the life-world could no longer appear as a "surrounding world" safely enveloping *Dasein* whose purposes provide basic orientation signals or a system of relevance. Merleau-Ponty's final "Working Notes" speak cryptically of the "infinity of the *Lebenswelt*," which is not the infinity of rational or metaphysical "idealization"; eluding descriptive delimitation, its character was that of "negative infinity, therefore—meaning or reason which *are* contingency." Regarding the possibility of philosophical inquiry against the backdrop of the life-world, the same "Working Notes" portrayed their relationship as one of mutual entwinement or implication, a portrayal militating against the reduction of the life-world to a preamble for reason or a target of positive research. "In a sense," we read, the life-world is "still involved as non-thematized by the very statements that describe it: for the statements as such will in their turn be sedimented, 'taken back' by the *Lebenswelt*, will be comprehended in it rather than they comprehend it—are already comprehended in it insofar as they imply a whole *Selbstverständlichkeit*."[33]

When he wrote these notes, Merleau-Ponty had moved quite a distance beyond traditional phenomenology and was already deeply embroiled in newer intellectual currents in France, currents such as structuralism, semiotics, and Freudianism that ultimately paved the way to contemporary poststructuralism or postphenomenology. Although not frequently cited by his successors or heirs, his thought (I believe) left an indelible imprint on all these currents, as is evident in the pervasive decentering of the ego, the resolute turn toward "otherness," and the preoccupation with entwinement or "difference." To the extent that it is thematized in recent literature, the life-world no longer is *Dasein's* safe abode or a seamless web of significations, but rather a multilayered arena fraught with ruptures and discontinuities; instead of revealing an unfolding story, human life itself appears as permeated by otherness or absence, where absence does not denote a simple negativity but a present absence or the absence of a present, the invisible of the visible.[34] In somewhat accentuated language, the life-world emerges also as a "death world," not in the sense of a gloomy ending or termination, but as indication of *Dasein's* dispossession or final inability to manage or master the world. As Michel Foucault observed, at one point: in probing *Dasein's* boundaries we arrive not at the "heart" of man but at "the brink of what limits him—a region where death prowls, where thought is extinguished, where the promise of the origin interminably recedes." In another context, commenting on Nietzsche's notion of history and its implications for our being-in-the-world, Foucault portrays the same region as a chiasm of meaning and nonmeaning, as a web of tangible metaphors. "The world we know," he writes, "is not this ultimately simple configuration where events are reduced to accentuate their essential traits, their final meaning . . . ; rather, it is a profusion of entangled events. If it appears as a 'marvelous motley, profound and totally meaningful', this is because it began and continues its secret existence through a 'host of errors and phantasms'."[35]

To illustrate this view of the life-world further, let me briefly turn to another poststructuralist writer: Jacques Derrida. In his "Otobiographie," an essay devoted to Nietzsche and more specifically to the "politics of the proper name" in Nietzsche's work, Derrida elaborates on the "logic of the living," focusing on the intertwining on subject and object, life and life-context, author and work. Pleading for a new approach to biography and authorial signatures he states: "Neither the 'immanentist' construals of philosophical systems . . . nor the external empirical-genetic treatments have ever properly examined the *dynamis* of that margin between 'work' and 'life', between system and subject of system. This margin—I call it *dynamis* because of its power, its virtual and mobile potency— is neither active nor passive, neither inside nor outside. Above all it is not a thin line, an invisible or indivisible dash between the domain of philosophemes, on the one hand, and the life of an author identified by his signature, on the other." According to Derrida, focusing on biography and authorial signatures does not mean pinpointing an author's identity or encapsulating him in a smoothly unfolding narrative (congruent with a descriptive life-philosophy); rather, through his work (and our work as well) life is already multiplied and dispersed—more importantly, it is marginalized by being placed at the margin of life and death, presence and absence. Turning to Nietzsche's *Ecce Homo*, the essay picks out particularly these lines from the prologue: "Not in vain have I buried my forty-fourth year today, I was entitled to bury it—what there was of life in it is rescued. . . . And so I tell myself my life." And Derrida comments: Nietzsche's birthday celebrates also the birth of his name but in a double sense, because it originates in "a unique pair: life and death, the dead and the living, father and mother." But the outcome is joyful affirmation: "To receive one's life as a gift and to be grateful to life, our life; more precisely to be grateful to life for the gift of what can be written and underwritten by a name. . . . all this is comprehended and conjoined in the strange gift of this autobiographical narrative."[36]

In his essay, Derrida moves from biography and authorship directly to politics or political life—and this for good reasons. Once life is seen neither as an unfolding intentionality nor as an external chain of causation, living, both individual and collective, acquires the connotations of a struggle or *agon*, of an ongoing creative (though not willful) praxis. It is through this *agon* that individual and collective identities emerge and are changed, together with the life-contexts circumscribing these identities; it is in the same *agon* that meaning is constantly contested by nonmeaning, social order by conflict. This, in my view, does not mean an abdication of responsibility or a lapse into apathy or indifference. In the context of French poststructuralism, the interplay of presence and absence is sometimes portrayed as an ultimate "undecidability" or a suspension of choice, as if living were still basically a matter of decision or nondecision. Although life may be an interplay of presence and absence, it is not a play subject simply to our control or *mise-en-scène;* rather, its plots and counterplots have long been stirring and gathering momentum. As it seems to me, the view of the life-world sketched in these pages does have a practical (though not an arbitrary) implication: namely, what today is called the "preferential option for the poor," the poor of the world. A life-world marked by decentering and dispossession appears to me particularly congenial to the politically and socially dispossessed, those who have never presumed to be "in charge," provided their hopes are not in turn channeled or manipulated in the direction of possession. Struggling with and for the dispossessed, I believe, involves a peculiar kind of struggle: namely, a struggle for an affirmation of life on the other side of hostility and the spirit of revenge. This was certainly Zarathustra's longing when he said, "For that man be delivered from revenge, that is for me the bridge to the highest hope, and a rainbow after many storms."

NOTES

1. For a discussion of the genealogy of the term in nineteenth-century literature and the slow emergence of the theme in Husserl's work, see Rüdiger Welter, *Der Begriff der Lebenswelt: Theorien vortheoretischer Erfahrungswelt* (Munich: Fink Verlag, 1986), pp. 13–17, 78–79. For general background compare also Gerd Brand, *Die Lebenswelt: Eine Philosophie des Konkreten Apriori* (Berlin: de Gruyter, 1971); Paul Janssen, *Geschichte und Lebenswelt* (The Hague: Martinus Nijhoff, 1970), James M. Edie, Francis H. Parker, and Calvin O. Schrag, eds., *Patterns of the Life-World: Essays in Honor of John Wild* (Evanston, Ill.: Northwestern University Press, 1970).

2. Edmund Husserl, *The Crisis of European Sciences and Transcendental Phenomenology: An Introduction to Phenomenological Philosophy*, trans. David Carr (Evanston, Ill.: Northwestern University Press, 1970), p. 166, note. (In this and subsequent citations I have slightly altered the translation for purposes of clarity.)

3. *Crisis*, pp. 82, 99, 103, 114.

4. *Crisis*, pp. 104, 110, 112.

5. *Crisis*, pp. 106, 111, 122–23, 125. (I translate *Anschauung* as "perception and experience" or "lived perception" rather than as "intuition," mainly because of the idiosyncratic overtones of intuition.)

6. *Crisis*, pp. 127–28, 138–40. Husserl's object-focus casts a certain shadow on his notion of "world." The world, he states at one point (p. 142), is "the universe of things which are distributed in the world-form of space-time and 'localized' in a dual sense (spatially and temporally)—the spatio-temporal *onta*." At the same time, however, he distinguishes between objects and world as their (nonobjectifiable) "horizon" (p. 143): "Every object has its possible variable modes of validity and ontic certainty. The world, on the other hand, exists not as an entity or object, but rather in such uniqueness as to render the application of the plural meaningless."

7. *Crisis*, pp. 104–5, 107–8, 114.

8. *Crisis*, pp. 113–15, 128, 133.

9. *Crisis*, pp. 135, 144–48, 151. At one point (pp. 154–55), Husserl formulates the task of transcendental inquiry as the "task of a special science (a peculiar science, to be sure, since it concerns the disparaged *doxa* which now suddenly claims the dignity of a foundation for science or *episteme*)."

10. *Crisis*, pp. 150–53, 159, 165, 167, 170–71. In discussing the "universal" correlation, Husserl repeatedly emphasizes the novel and startling character of discovered terrain. "The naively accepted fact," he writes (p. 165), "that each person sees things and the world in general as they appear to him, concealed, as we now realize, a vast horizon of amazing truths whose uniqueness and systematic interconnection never entered the purview of philosophy. The correlation between world (the world of which we always speak) and its subjective modes of givenness never evoked philosophical wonder (that is, prior to the first breakthrough of 'transcendental phenomenology' in the *Logical Investigations*), despite the fact that it had made itself felt already in pre-Socratic philosophy and among the Sophists (though here only as a motive for skeptical argumentation)." Somewhat later (p. 169), the charge effected by the *epoché* is said to yield the result that "the theoretical interest grows quickly and one becomes more and more amazed at each step by the endless array of emerging problems and important discoveries to be made."

11. *Crisis*, pp. 157, 167–69, 185–86, 188. Compare also the statement (p. 184): "*I* am the one who performs the *epoché*, and even if there are others and if they practice the *epoché* in direct community with me, and all other human beings with their entire act-life are included, for me within my *epoché*, in the world-phenomenon which, in my *epoché*, is exclusively mine."

12. In the words of Alexandre Métraux: "Although taking as
its point of departure quite correctly the 'world of the natural attitude', Husserl's account continues to be permeated by a dualist conception of the relationship between subject and world which finds
no warrant in everyday experience." See his Preface to Aron Gurwitsch, *Die mitmenschlichen Begegnungen in der Milieuwelt* (Berlin and
New York: de Gruyter, 1977), p. xx.

13. Husserl, *Crisis*, pp. 187–88. The problem of constitution
also includes the world of children, of animals, and of history. For
an instructive discussion of the quandaries inherent in Husserl's life-
world conception see Bernhard Waldenfels, *In den Netzen der Lebenswelt* (Frankfurt-Main: Suhrkamp, 1985), pp. 15–54. Regarding
the issue of intersubjectivity compare especially Michael Theunissen, *The Other: Studies in the Social Ontology of Husserl, Heidegger, Sartre, and Buber,* trans. Christopher Macann (Cambridge: Mass.: MIT
Press, 1984).

14. Husserl, *Crisis,* pp. 80, 170, 180–81. Another passage (p.
96) speaks of "the world-engima in the deepest and ultimate sense,
the riddle of a world whose being is being through subjective constitution." Compare also the statement (p. 131) "The paradoxical
correlations of 'objectively true world' and 'life-world' render enigmatic the mode of being of both. Thus, the idea of a true world in
any sense, and within it our own being, becomes a riddle in respect
to the sense of this being."

15. *Crisis,* pp. 173, 178.

16. Alfred Schutz, *The Phenomenology of the Social World,* trans.
George Walsh and Frederick Lehnert (Evanstan, Ill.: Northwestern
University Press, 1967), pp. 97, 139–43, 177, 181, 215–24. Compare
also my "Phenomenology and Social Science," in *Beyond Dogma and
Despair* (Notre Dame, Ind.: University of Notre Dame Press, 1981),
pp. 111–12.

17. Alfred Schutz, *Collected Papers,* vol. 1: *The Problem of Social
Reality,* ed. Maurice Natanson, 2d ed. (The Hague: Nijhoff, 1967),
pp. 15, 147, 227–28. Compare also the statement (p. 134): "This
world, built around my own I, presents itself for interpretation to
me, a being living naively within it. From this standpoint everything
has reference to my actual historical situation, or as we can also say,
to my pragmatic interests which belong to the situation in which I
find myself here and now. The place in which I am living has not
significance for me as a geographical concept, but as my home. The
objects of my daily use have significance as my implements, and the
people to whom I stand in relationships are my kin, my friends, or

strangers. . . . My social world with the *alter egos* in it is arranged, around me as the center, into associates (*Umwelt*), contemporaries (*Mitwelt*), predecessors (*Vorwelt*), and successors (*Folgewelt*)." Regarding systems of relevance see also Schutz, *Reflections on the Problem of Relevance,* ed. Richard M. Zaner (New Haven, Conn.: Yale University Press, 1970).

18. *Collected Papers,* vol. 1, pp. 7, 59–61, 133.

19. Schutz, "Some Structures of the Life-World," in *Collected Papers,* vol. 3: *Studies in Phenomenological Philosophy,* ed. Ilse Schutz (The Hague: Nijhoff, 1966), pp. 117–19, 122. Compare also Schutz and Thomas Luckmann, *The Structures of the Life-World,* trans. Richard M. Zaner and H. Tristram Engelhardt (Evanston, Ill.: Northwestern University Press, 1973); Maurice Natanson, "Alfred Schutz on Social Reality and Social Science," *Social Research* 35 (1968), pp. 217–44; Aron Gurwitsch, "The Common-Sense World as Social Reality: A Discourse on Alfred Schutz," *Social Research* 29 (1962), pp. 50–72. Welter in *Der Begriff der Lebenswelt* (pp. 168–77) distinguishes among five different meanings of "life-world" in Schutz's writings— thus, in my view, overcomplicating the issue.

20. See Robert A. Gorman, *The Dual Vision: Alfred Schutz and the Myth of Phenomenological Social Science* (London: Routledge & Kegan Paul, 1977).

21. Jürgen Habermas, "A Postscript to *Knowledge and Human Interests,*" *Philosophy of the Social Sciences,* 3 (1975), p. 181; *Legitimation Crisis,* trans. Thomas McCarthy (Boston: Beacon Press, 1975), pp. 4–5; *Theorie des kommunikativen Handelns* (Frankfurt-Main: Suhrkamp, 1981), vol. 2, pp. 226–27.

22. Habermas, *The Theory of Communicative Action,* vol. 1: *Reason and the Rationalization of Society,* trans. Thomas McCarthy (Boston: Beacon Press, 1984), p. 13; *Theorie des kommunikativen Handelns,* vol. 2, pp. 187–89, 192.

23. Basically, from Habermas's perspective, modernization occurs on two levels, those of life-world and system. In his words, society in its broad sense means "an entity which in the course of evolution is increasingly differentiated both as system and as life-world. Systemic evolution is measured by the growth of a society's steering capacity, while the segregation of culture, society, and personality indicates the evolutionary stage of the symbolically structured life-world." See *The Theory of Communicative Action,* vol. 1, pp. 335–36; *Theorie des kommunikativen Handelns,* vol. 2, pp. 179, 200, 228. For a critique of Habermas's conception of the life-world see Ulf Matthiesen, *Das Dickicht der Lebenswelt und die Theorie des kommu-*

nikativen Handelns (Munich: Fink Verlag, 1983); also my "Life-World and Communicative Action," in *Polis and Praxis* (Cambridge, Mass.: MIT Press, 1984), pp. 223–53; and Waldenfels, *In den Netzen der Lebenswelt*, pp. 107–17.

24. Martin Heidegger, *Being and Time*, trans. John Macquarrie and Edward Robinson (New York: Harper & Row, 1962), par. 6, 21, pp. 46, 128–29. Turning to post-Kantian developments Heidegger states that the critique of extended matter also applies to the neo-Kantian notion of "value-related" things (p. 132): "Values are properties of a thing which are present-at-hand." (In these and subsequent citations I have altered the translation slightly for purposes of clarity.)

25. *Being and Time*, par. 12, pp. 78–81, 83–84.

26. *Being and Time*, par. 12–13, pp. 84, 86–88. According to Heidegger, such investigation can take the form of scientific inquiry or of a cognitive thematization of being-in-the-world. "In cognition," he writes (p. 90), "*Dasein* acquires a new ontological status vis-à-vis the world which was already pre-discovered in *Dasein*. This new possibility can be separately developed, be transformed into a distinct task and as scientific knowledge take on the lead for being-in-the-world."

27. *Being and Time*, par. 14–15, pp. 94–98, 100.

28. *Being and Time*, par. 16–18, pp. 105, 110–11, 114, 116–17, 119. The disturbance of everyday frames of reference is a well-known technique of contemporary ethnomethodology.

29. On nothingness, nullity, and "notness" see esp. *Being and Time*, par. 58, pp. 330–31. The theme is more fully developed in Heidegger's "What is Metaphysics?" trans. R. F. C. Hull and Alan Crick, in *Existence and Being* (Chicago: Regnery, 1949), pp. 325–61.

30. *Being and Time*, par. 18, pp. 118–20. Regarding temporality as the essential meaning of "care," see esp. par. 65, pp. 374–75.

31. Heidegger, "The Origin of the Work of Art," *Basic Writings*, ed. David F. Krell (New York: Harper & Row, 1977), pp. 149–87; *On the Way to Language*, trans. Peter D. Hertz and Joan Stambaugh (New York: Harper & Row, 1972); *On Time and Being*, trans. Joan Stambaugh (New York: Harper & Row, 1972); "Das Ding," *Vorträge und Aufsätze*, 3d ed. (Pfullingen: Neske, 1967), vol. 2, p. 52.

32. Maurice Merleau-Ponty, *Phenomenology of Perception*, trans. Colin Smith (London: Routledge & Kegan Paul, 1962), pp. 350–51.

33. Merleau-Ponty, *The Visible and the Invisible*, ed. Claude Lefort, trans. Alphonso Lingis (Evanston, Ill.: Northwestern University Press, 1968), pp. 159, 169–70. In the same context (p. 170) Merleau-

Ponty also describes the life-world or the "perceived world" as "the brute or wild being."

34. In Merleau-Ponty's words (*The Visible and the Invisible*, p. 254): "The negative here is not a positive that is elsewhere (a transcendent)—It is a true negative, i.e., an *Unverborgenheit* of the *Verborgenheit*, an *Urpräsentation* of the *Nichturpräsentierbar*, an original mode of elsewhere, a *Selbst* that is an Other, a hollow." On Merleau-Ponty's later works compare the sensitive comments by Waldenfels, *In den Netzen der Lebenswelt*, pp. 68–73.

35. Michel Foucault, *The Order of Things: An Archaeology of the Human Sciences* (New York: Vintage Books, 1973), pp. 382–83; *Language, Counter-Memory, Practice*, trans. Donald F. Bouchard and Sherry Simon (Oxford: Blackwell, 1977), pp. 155. According to another passage in the latter work (p. 32), "the death of God does not restore us to a limited positivistic world, but to a world exposed by the experience of its limits, made and unmade by that excess which transgresses it." (The citations in Foucault's text are from Nietzsche, *Human, All Too Human*.)

36. Jacques Derrida, "Nietzsches Otobiographie oder Politik des Eigennamens: Die Lehre Nietzsches," *Fugen, Deutsch-Französisches Jahrbuch für Text-Analytik* (Freiburg: Walter Verlag, 1980), pp. 71, 76–77, 80.

EXPERIENCE OF THE OTHER: BETWEEN APPROPRIATION AND DISAPPROPRIATION

BERNHARD WALDENFELS

The modern disintegration of any notion of order that might be grounded in the nature of things calls for the existence of someone who creates order. Whether this ordering force is a divine being or only a human being who appears as God's representative or successor is not crucial. The essential pont is rather the gesture of domination and appropriation that arises from this situation. We find this gesture in Descartes, who nominates human beings as "maîtres et possesseurs de la nature." However, domination and appropriation of nature presuppose some kind of self-domination and self-appropriation that constitutes the site from which domination and appropriation can be carried out. For a long time signs have been appearing that lead one to suspect that this endeavor is about to be foiled by its own success. When Freud proclaims that man is not master in his own house, let alone in the domain of stars and animals, not much seems left of the proud project of modernity. But does this mean that the pendulum merely swings in the opposite direction? Is domination going to be replaced by a new kind of servitude, appropriation by mere disappropriation, with the effect that the modern subject will fall back into the simple role of subordinate, of a "subject" in the sense of being "subjected" to heteronomous powers? This is the question I shall try to explore. From the beginning it should be made clear that my inquiry into the "subject" has nothing to do with an epistemological game of hide-and-seek. We don't have to ask how the subject can surprise itself in its hiding place, how it can look into itself and from there into others. These cognitive maneuvers have been overcome by Husserl as well as by Wittgenstein. The subject to be questioned is the *subjectum* that underlies everything. It not only participates in everything *in a certain way* as the Aristotelian soul does, but also gathers everything in itself *in a central way*. The crisis of modern reason and the crisis of the modern subject are intimately connected.[1]

Thus a field of problems opens up where philosophy and psychoanalysis, that is, Husserl's and Freud's heirs, come together, and on either side this problematic has a certain political impact. I do not want to speak prematurely of a convergence between the two sides nor of a simple confrontation such as phenomenology of consciousness versus psychoanalysis of the unconscious. There is movement back and forth on both sides. On the one side the slogan "Where Id was, there Ego shall be" *can* be read in the old sense of appropriation, and often it *is* still read in this sense. Opposed to this interpretation is Lacan's attempt at a systematic rereading or even misreading of this slogan (in the sense that the Ego is constituted precisely by displacing the Id or unconscious). On the other side, within the phenomenological movement, attached to a certain Cartesian legacy, are attempts at radicalizing the process of appropriation until it turns into a disappropriation of consciousness and at demonstrating that consciousness has its own blind spots (as is the case in the later Merleau-Ponty). Here we are moving from an embodiment of reason, to its broadening, and finally to its dispersion; that is, the way leads from Husserl through Merleau-Ponty to Foucault and Derrida.[2] This process of rethinking rationality can be tracked in both directions, starting either from Husserl or from Freud, and the lines of thinking will partly meet, partly miss each other, as in the case of Lacan and the later Merleau-Ponty.[3] In what follows I shall take the first direction, outlining the philosophical process of transformation, starting from phenomenology and glancing occasionally in the other direction. My primary focus is on the contrast between the *own* and the *alien*. I start with a brief conceptual survey. Then I outline the attempt to overcome the contrast either by appropriation or by disappropriation. Finally I try to get a footing in the intertwining of own and alien, seeking a solution beyond the alternatives of appropriation and disappropriation.

1. THE ALIEN AND THE HETEROGENEOUS

On the linguistic level we may distinguish between what is alien (*fremd*) and what is heterogeneous (*fremdartig*). In a similar way Alfred Schutz makes the distinction between what is "new" and what is "novel."[4] Wherever this distinction does not matter very much I will simply speak of "own" and "alien." The *alien*, contrasted with the *own*, concerns content and regions of experience. Alien is everything that is to be found beyond the boundaries of what we may call the "sphere of my ownness" (*Eigenheitssphäre*), to use Husserl's term. *Ownness* is to be understood broadly as belonging, familiarity, disposability, be it the ownness of one's own body, clothes, bed, domicile, friends, children, generation, home country, occupation, or whatever. Here the question of how to conceive the contrast between own and alien arises. Should it be conceived in the way of core and shell or in the way of front and back side? Whatever the case, if it should turn out to be indeed true that man is not master in his own house, then every property or ownness will be indelibly marked by the deficiency engendered by disownment and disappropriation.

The *heterogeneous*, in contrast to the homogeneous, is related to structures and orders of experience. In the case of language this corresponds to what is not unknown but incomprehensible. The heterogeneous that transgresses the boundaries of certain orders presupposes a certain style of normality. Here we may distinguish some central forms of heterogeneity. The heterogeneous may appear on the *same level* as in the case of highly developed forms of life or culture. But it may also appear on an *earlier level:* in the frame of individual history, as childhood opposed to the state of the adult; in the frame of collective history, as so-called primitivity opposed to the state of the civilized; and in the frame of natural history, as animality opposed to the state of the human being. Finally there are irregular states that show themselves as anomalous, heterological, and pathological phenomena, as in dreams, ecstasy, and delusion, and generally in the case of illness. Thus the gravitational field of heterogeneity is centered on three figures, the *child*, the *savage*, and the *insane* or the *fool*, and, moreover, in shadowy twilight, the anthropoid *animal*. These paradigmatic figures populate the unconscious and haunt man in his private and public lives in multiple ways.

Here the question of how the homogeneous and the heterogeneous are related to each other also arises. Is there a core of untouchable normality, or do homogeneous and heterogeneous spheres interpenetrate in such a way that we should speak with Rousseau of a child in the adult and a savage in the citizen, or with Freud of an ill or insane person in the healthy one, and with Darwin of an animal in man? Now, all that is alien and heterogeneous shades in a delicate way from the bewildering to the alluring and threatening, and this calls for measures and methods of damming up, of restricting and excluding; briefly: it calls for control. Appropriation and disappropriation appear in this context as forms of overreaction and counterreaction.

2. APPROPRIATION AS CONTROL OF THE ALIEN

The overcoming of the alien through appropriation is a characteristic of Western rationality insofar as it promotes rationalization in the form of "world domination"[5] and insofar as it creates a technic that already in Hobbes includes social technics and life technics.

Appropriation as transforming something into ownness presupposes two operations: first, a *separation* of own and alien, and second, an *atomization* of the physical and the social world. The separation appears in Descartes's definition of substance as "res quae nulla alia re indiget ad existendum," as something that needs nothing else for existing.[6] The atomization is to be found in Hume, who writes, "What consists of parts is distinguishable into them, and what is distinguishable is separable."[7]

The separation of own and alien is accompanied by a kind of *egocentrism. Self-consciousness* and *self-experience* are privileged. The alien is overcome and mastered by being measured against the own as double (alter ego), as variation, or as "appresence," as it is called, up to Husserl. The methods of empathy presuppose a Cartesian splitting into interiority and exteriority, and they are not free from "overtones of possessive individualism."[8]

The atomization of the physical and the social world is accompanied in turn by a kind of *logocentrism.* In this case the alien is overcome by *gathering everything to be understood into a logos.* The alien is segregated from the own by the constitution of a formal, preliminary space of thinking. Thus we read in the introduction to the *Critique of Pure Reason:* "Any knowledge is entitled pure, if it be not mixed with anything extraneous."[9]

Another possible way of accomplishing the same goal is the attempt to integrate own and alien into a total, all-encompassing space of thinking. Hegel's return from estrangement in terms of the "self-actualization of spirit" takes on the form of an "identity of identity and difference." Taken as a whole, logocentrism and egocentrism do not contradict each other; rather they relate to each other, insofar as Hegel's spiritual substance is centered on subjectivity and, conversely, the Cartesian subject is a thinking subject, a *cogito.*

The consequences of such a strategy of appropriation emerge clearly if we refer to the abovementioned central figures of heterogeneity. Thus Merleau-Ponty speaks in his lecture "The Child Seen by the Adult" of a triple *monopoly of reason,* more precisely: of a certain type of reason. The adult is right against the child, the civilized men against the so-called primitive, the healthy against the ill or insane—not to mention animals and plants, which have no rights whatsoever. In the case of children and primitives we are confronted with *premilinary forms* of reason; in the case of the ill or insane, with *defective forms* of reason.[10]

Egocentrism and logocentrism come together in a distinctive kind of *ethnocentrism*. Within the Western tradition this further form of centrism results not only in a defense of one's own form of life—which seems unobjectionable—but in the unlimited vindication of that form of life as the vanguard of universal reason. The defense by cross and sword, which is directed against Huns, Turks, Tartars, that is, against barbarians of all sorts, always serves a higher reason. Even the pillaging of African cult places, dramatically recorded by Michel Leiris in his book on Africa, serves the collecting rationality of our museums. Thus the "colonization of the life-world" is not restricted to bureaucratic and economic encroachments by magistrates and markets; it appears wherever "foreign land" is definitively appropriated, be it by way of civilization, of education, or of therapy, processes that are today facilitated by technically refined apparatuses.

3. DISAPPROPRIATION AS SELF-SURRENDER TO THE ALIEN

In the face of the arrogance of a restrictive rationality it may be tempting to renounce reason altogether. Universal appropriation then turns into a *dispossession* (as Georges Bataille, the rebel against Hegel, puts it), into a disappropriation in favor of the alien. This movement is of doubtful value insofar as it involves a mere *reversal* in which all defects are transformed into their mirror image.

Egocentrism is overcome by putting the alien and heterogeneous in place of the own and of the homogeneous. The child turns into the saving child, the savage into the good savage, illness into holy illness. The result is a cult of the exotic and esoteric. But a European Buddhist remains a European converted to Buddhism. Insofar as the alien is regarded and evaluated *only* in contrast to the own, ethnocentrism remains intact, even if it is only in the harmless form of *chinoiseries*.

Logocentrism is challenged in a similar way. The focus on a *logos* is broken by a *dissipation* into multiple *logoi*. The "excessive settledness" of reason[11] is remedied by a nomadism that roams freely in time and space; some call it postmodernity. Or, still more radically, others turn toward a delimitation that leads to a *dissolution* of any limits between own and alien.

If the foregoing strategies are best interpreted as overreactions against dubious forms of appropriation, then one still faces the problem of sketching better strategies. Rousseau, who in his life as well as in his work anticipated so many of today's problems, writes in his essay on the origin of language: "When one proposes to study men, one has to look close by, but in order to study *man* one has to learn to cast one's glance afar."[12] This detachment or *dépaysement* that Lévi-Strauss takes as the starting point of every serious ethnology[13] does not mean a fleeing from oneself but a detour through the alien that will never lead back to a pure own. I shall remain another forever. In this situation it is desirable to locate one's acting and thinking *on the borderline*.

4. INTERTWINING OF OWN AND ALIEN

Intertwining or enlacement (*entrelacs*), as the later Merleau-Ponty calls it, means neither fusion in the sense of nondistinction nor separation in the sense of sharp differentiation. Rather, it means a kind of standing out against a common field, a simultaneous congruence and noncongruence, as in the entangled bands of enlacement that we sometimes find on the capitals of the columns of Romanesque churches. Whoever tries to untangle the enlacement destroys the pattern. In this case a synthesis is no more to be expected than in the case of the duality of figure and ground. This can be shown by discussing three forms of otherness: the otherness of the other, the otherness of myself, and the otherness of an alien order. They all point to what Dallmayr calls "the unfamiliar within the familiar."[14]

a. Otherness of the Other

The otherness of the other has to do with what is treated as *intersubjectivity* by Husserl and what is condensed into *intercorporeality* by Merleau-Ponty. As mentioned before, appropriation and disappropriation presuppose a separation of own and alien, that is, a hiatus that has to be bridged if we do not want to lose ourselves in an oceanic feeling. We can try to bridge the hiatus in different ways. We can attempt to do it by *affective participation* in the sense of empathy, or by a *technique of communication* in which sender and receiver are linked by a common code, or by a *logic of communication* in which a reciprocity of perspectives or a reversibility of standpoints is offered as remedy.

What eludes these attempts from the beginning is the interplay of question and answer that creates a coordination in speaking and acting. Here we have to make an important distinction. The perpetuation of the separation of own and alien is all the more likely if the discourse remains *reproductive* and *applicative*, restricted to the reproduction and transmission of a preestablished sense. On this level the "sender" possesses mastery to a high degree over the "information" that the "receiver" accepts. In the extreme case we can speak of self-programming, just as previously one spoke of self-alienation. The separation of own and alien is lessened to the degree that the discourse is *productive* and helps to create new conditions of comprehension and to change standards instead of merely applying them. In the "formation of thoughts through communication," where one word gives the other, we must take account of a variable mix of initiatives and cooperation. Speaker and listener, author and reader can at this point no longer be taken as strictly separate instances. A speaking that, as Lacan characterizes it, signifies something *for somebody* before signifying *something*, and whose *saying* will never be absorbed by what is *said*, is situated in a field of speaking that belongs to nobody and everybody.[15] If we want to continue speaking of projection and introjection we should follow Lagache and Hesnard in stressing that both are originally inserted into one another. I find myself in the other and the other in myself by way of an interplay that Merleau-Ponty calls *chiasm* and which Bakhtin tries to conceive as the original plurivocity of a polylogue.

b. Otherness of Myself

If the own is formed in the interplay with the alien, then otherness invades the sphere of *intrasubjectivity* as well. There is then no original sphere of ownness that allows for an appropriation by myself or by the other. There is no speaker or actor who could parade himself (herself) as pure author of his (her) speeches or acts. There is no speaking or acting that does not appear also as a response. Speakers and actors can be identified only insofar as they are integrated into an existing order to the point of being mere functionaries of a fixed system. By contrast, an emerging and changing order results in a *slippage* of the ego; the ego can never completely find a place of its own and thus can never become completely itself, but remains always affected by a certain otherness.

The fissure that runs through the ego and the subject, undermining its integrity and totality, constitutes one of the most crucial points around which different theories of the subject currently revolve. A splitting and multiplication of the ego and a prereflective core of anonymity are already to be found in Husserl. The self-delay that affects every attempt at self-appropriation is likewise a component of Husserl's theory of the self-temporalization of the ego; the later Merleau-Ponty, Levinas, and Derrida have only radicalized this aspect in terms of an original otherness and an irrevocable absence within presence. We find the splitting into *I* and *Me*, into *je* and *moi*, in such different authors as James, Mead, Husserl, Sartre, Lagache, and Lacan.

From this series of attempted revisions I want to select a paradigmatic case in which the otherness of myself shows up in a striking way. I am thinking of Daniel Lagache's thesis of 1934, in *Les Hallucinations Verbales et la Parole* (reprinted in 1977).[16] That author seeks to explain the strange phenomenon of verbal hallucinations that consists in my hearing my own voice as if it were coming from the outside. Take Moosbrugger's reflections in Robert Musil's *Man without Qualities*, which are directed against the specialized *Klugköpfe:* "He himself treated these voices and visions no differently than monkeys. It amused him to watch and listen to their goings-on."[17] Lagache explains this phenomenon by suggesting that my voice is *never* completely my own voice, even in the normal case. The belief that underlies the hallucinations is possible only on the condition that the primary indifference of own and alien is never resolved into a sharply circumscribed difference. The "I say" or "I do" must imply an aspect of "one says or does" and finally an aspect of "it says" and "it happens."

Lacan's new reading of Freud's Id is anticipated by Lichtenberg: "One should say: *It thinks,* in the same way as one says: *It* is raining."[18] Nietzsche even says: "After all, one has gone too far with this 'it thinks'—even the 'it' contains an *interpretation* of the process and does not belong to the process itself."[19]

This finds its refracted echo in Italo Calvino: "I read, therefore *it* writes."[20] Lacan's putting together the question "who speaks?" and the topological question "Where does somebody speak?" opens up fields of speaking and acting that reach into anonymity and allow for different directions and degrees of both individuation and socialization.

Thus total appropriation by which the borderlines are fixed and total disappropriation by which they are effaced appear merely as extreme attempts at escaping the unsettling border play between own and alien.

c. Otherness of the Alien Order

This border play that takes place in the regions of intersubjectivity and intrasubjectivity follows in turn discursive patterns and norms that enable and limit our common speaking and acting. Inclusion and exclusion act together in the formation of spaces of speaking and acting. Otherness appears in this way as the otherness of an alien order, an *interdiscursivity.* The clash between own and alien order may be illustrated by a foreign language that I do not understand, or by the adult's language that a child does not understand (and vice versa). Otherness in this case must not be exaggerated into total strangeness. The understanding of a foreign language starts with experiencing the "fact of meaning" (as Jakobson observes).[21] The event of speaking involves something more basic than the content of what is said: I hear somebody speaking. This initial understanding of language that precedes the speaking of language does not occur blindly; rather, it relies on a symbolic of sound that is prior to the mastery of any semantic and syntactic rules and that cuts across different languages, their peculiarities notwithstanding. In this context one can refer to a linguistic experiment originating with Edward Sapir. The subjects of his experiment had to decide how the syllables *mal* and *mil* should be assigned to two tables, one large and the other small. The result was that 80 percent of the test persons decided to combine *mal* with the large, *mil* with the small table.[22] Without such an initial grasp and understanding of linguistic events it would remain a mystery why a child would ever seek access to the linguistic world of adults. Things are similar in the case of exchange between different orders of language and culture.

But this is not sufficient. The otherness of the alien order that is intimated, but not completely appropriated, by interdiscursivity must be sustained by an otherness within our own order, that is, by a certain kind of *transdiscursivity*. Without the possibility of transgressing existing orders, something that is put and kept in movement by a superabundance of what is unordered, the "subject" would be degraded to a pure subordinate who does not say anything but only repeats what is already said. This "man with *fixed* qualities" would leave nothing to be wished.

NOTES

This essay was translated from the original German by the author with the assistance of Fred Dallmayr and Stephen White.

1. Bernhard Waldenfels, *Ordnung im Zwielicht* (Frankfurt: Suhrkamp, 1987); also Fred Dallmayr, *Twilight of Subjectivity* (Amherst, Mass.: University of Massachusetts Press, 1981).

2. Bernhard Waldenfels, *In den Netzen der Lebenswelt* (Frankfurt: Suhrkamp 1985), chaps. 3, 6.

3. Bernhard Waldenfels, *Phänomenologie in Frankreich* (Frankfurt: Suhrkamp, 1983), chaps. VI:9, VII:3.

4. Alfred Schutz, *Reflections on the Problem of Relevance* (New Haven, Conn.: Yale University Press, 1970), pp. 70–71.

5. Max Weber, *From Max Weber: Essays in Sociology*, trans. H. H. Gerth and C. Wright Mills (New York: Oxford University Press, 1946), pp. 299, 327.

6. René Descartes, *The Principles of Philosophy* I, trans. V. R. Miller and R. P. Miller (Dordrecht: Reidel, 1984), p. 51.

7. David Hume, *A Treatise of Human Nature*, 2d ed., ed. L. A. Selby-Bigge and P. H. Nidditch (Oxford: Oxford University Press, 1978), p. 27.

8. See Fred Dallmayr, this volume, p. 44.

9. Immanuel Kant, *Critique of Pure Reason*, trans. Norman Kemp Smith (New York: St. Martin's Press, 1965), p. 58.

10. Maurice Merleau-Ponty, "L'Enfant vu par l'adulte," *Bulletin du Groupe d'études de psychologie de l'Université de Paris*, vol. 3 (1949–50). This journal appears today under the title *Bulletin de psychologie*.

11. André Leroi-Gourhan, *Geste et la parole* (Paris: A. Michel, 1964–65).

12. Jean-Jacques Rousseau, *Essay on the Origin of Language* in *The First and Second Discourses*, trans. Victor Gourévitch (New York: Harper & Row, 1986), p. 260.

13. Claude Lévi-Strauss, *Structural Anthropology* II, trans. Monique Layton (New York: Basic Books, 1976), p. 35ff.

14. Fred Dallmayr, this volume.

15. Jacques Lacan, *Écrits* (Paris: Éditions du Seil, 1966).

16. Daniel Lagache, *Oevres* I (1932–46) (Paris: Presses Universitaire de France, 1977).

17. Robert Musil, *The Man without Qualities* I (London: Secker & Warburg, 1955), pp. 283–84.

18. Georg Christoph Lichtenberg, *Lichtenbergs Aphorismen*, vol. 5 (1793–99) in *Deutsche Literatur-Denkmale des 18. und 19. Jahrhunderts*, no. 151 (Wiesbaden: Kraus Reprint, 1968), p. 128.

19. *Basic Writings of Nietzsche*, trans. Walter Kaufmann (New York: Modern Library, 1968), p. 214.

20. Italo Calvino, *If on a Winter's Night a Traveler*, trans. William Weaver (New York: Harcourt, Brace, Jovanovich, 1981), p. 176.

21. Roman Jakobson, *Child Language, Aphasia and Phonological Universals* (The Hague: Mouton & Co., 1968), p. 27ff.

22. Hans Hormann, *Psychologie der Sprache* (Berlin: Springer, 1970).

PART II

Loosening Rationality in the Social Sciences: Reasoning toward the Other

RATIONALITY BETWEEN MODERNITY AND POSTMODERNITY

Calvin O. Schrag

There are certain recurring themes that are orchestrated throughout Professor Dallmayr's published writings. It is not surprising that the topic of rationality is one of them. As a political philosopher, Professor Dallmayr has grasped clearly enough the importance of the role of reason in the sociopolitical life of humankind. His comprehension of the history of political thought is at once vast and profound, and he has few peers in his ability to detail the philosophical assumptions of classical and current modes of social analysis and reflection. However, this prodigious scholarly production, which spans a number of decades, is not a species of scholarship for its own sake. It resonates with an existential élan in quest of a rational social order. Yet, Professor Dallmayr is acutely aware of the difficulty of pinning down the justificatory claims of reason that might inform such a social order. Rationality appears to have become the most elusive of all the ingredients that make up contemporary social life. It is thus that disciplined reflection on the claims of reason for our present age becomes an urgent and unavoidable requirement. Professor Dallmayr has quickened our sensitivities to this requirement. Our current project comprises an effort at a *weiterdenken* with him on this all-important topic. Such a project of "thinking further" on matters of rationality is one of the most pressing challenges of our age.

81

Currently it has become popular to define the issue
against the backdrop of a span of tension created by the postmodern reaction to the constraints of rationality within modernity. This proposed overcoming of modernity exhibits a
spate of interrelated defining features, not least of which is
the jettisoning of subject-oriented reflection and its commitments to an epistemological-theoretic paradigm of knowledge.
The jettisoning of the rational, knowledge-bearing subject of
modernity is coupled with the celebration of paralogy, plurality, dissension, and an incredulity toward metanarratives.[1]
With this reaction to modernity the bankruptcy of the logos
of Western rationality appears to have reached the stage of
foreclosure. The logos, we are told, has withered away, and
reason has been divested of any rights for guardianship within
the polis of public concerns. So speak the prophets of postmodernity. Any claims for the unifying labors of reason are
rendered suspect, and we are advised to make do with the inescapable pluralization and relativization of our beliefs and
practices. Indeed the very question about the meaning of reason—as pretty much the "meaning" of anything else—is written off as an unfortunate habit of thought that one had best
learn to live without.

Now one cannot tell the story of modernity and postmodernity without giving some attention to the episode of premodernity, which has shaped the reactions of modernity and
postmodernity alike. Once upon a time there was a classical
Greek notion of rationality that spoke of theometaphysical
unities bonded by a transcendent logos that resided on the
hither side of mortal mental activity. According to this premodern view, it is not so much that reason is in the mind as
it is that the mind is in reason. The human mind itself is rational insofar as it participates in a cosmological structure of
rationality. Hans-Georg Gadamer provides a consummatory
statement on this classical notion of rationality when he
writes: "The rationality of being, this grand hypothesis of
Greek philosophy, is not first and foremost a property of human self-consciousness but of being itself." Human reason, according to this hypothesis, continues Gadamer, "is far more
appropriately thought of as part of this rationality instead of

as the self-consciousness that knows itself over against an external reality."[2]

The Greek concept of rationality was a dominating factor in medieval philosophy and continued to register its impact during the modern period. The effort of Hegel to amalgamate the Greek notion of reason with modern subject-oriented consciousness so as to achieve a new unity of substance and subject is a global construction that is now familiar to us all. Postmodernism has grasped the opportunity to accentuate the failures of this totalizing Hegelian metanarrative. Consequently in recent discussions the failures of this attempted unification of classical and modern concepts have received more attention than have its successes. The present task is not that of enumerating these failures and positive achievements. Rather, we make reference to the contribution of Hegel at this juncture simply to aid us in marking out the contours of the premodern, modern, and postmodern portraits of reason.

Modernity in its response to premodernity, either by way of a Hegelian *Aufhebung* or an Age of the Enlightenment reactive stance, is a plea for the rationality of the autonomous subject. Modernity turns on the principle of subjectivity, which grounds the human subject as at once rational and free, liberated from the fetters of tradition. The rationality of modernity resides in a centered subject, an imminent logos, functioning as an epistemological foundation from which all justification of knowledge claims proceeds. The classical period of modernity, from Descartes to Kant to Hegel to Husserl, saw a progressive deepening of the structures of subjectivity, guided by the ideal of apodicticity, geared to a comprehension of the world through the resources of a translucent cogito. In all this a rather profound confidence in the claims of human reason and the potentialities of human freedom became manifest. If one could only harness the resources of subject-oriented rationality the worlds of nature and society would be adequately represented and effectively controlled. Indeed, the subject-centered epistemological paradigm of modernity invited at every step a fraternization of the knowing and the willing subject, marking the modern age not only as the age of representational knowledge but also as

the age of technological control. Today it is no longer necessary to inform the reader about Heidegger's contribution toward an elucidation of this particular point.

To get a handle on our topic, addressing rationality between modernity and postmodernity, it is necessary to isolate
some of the main events that occurred in this space of "be-
tweenness." The tracking of the constellation of events that
produced postmodernity is beset with peculiar problems, issuing from the elusiveness of the phenomenon under investigation. More of a cultural attitude than a doctrinal platform and
more of a point of view than a systematic survey, postmodernism escapes any and all linear characterizations. The difficulties of definition are compounded by the interdisciplinary
ramifications of the phenomenon. There is postmodern art,
postmodern literature, postmodern politics, postmodern cultural studies, postmodern philosophy, postmodern this, and
postmodern that. In an effort to sharpen up some of the
fuzzy edges of the phenomenon, and particularly with regard
to its philosophical expression, we suggest five interrelated
marks of postmodernity: (1) the decentering of the subject as
an epistemological foundation, (2) a recognition of the social
sources of rationality, (3) the embeddedness of power and desire within the claims of reason, (4) the undecidability of
meaning and the inscrutability of reference, and (5) the
congealing of the dichotomy of transcendentalism versus
historicism.

The reaction against the epistemological paradigm of
modern philosophy is one of the more explicit features of the
postmodernist attitude. The Cartesian cogito, the Kantian
transcendental ego, Husserlian transcendental subjectivity, as
well as the empiricist concept of mind, have all been placed
under suspicion. The quest for epistemic certainty and the accompanying program of laying the foundations are seen by
the friends of postmodernity as a version of the quest for the
Holy Grail, as a dream for the impossible, fictions of a philosophical imagination run wild, projects that are undermined
in the moment that they are completed.

Coupled with the postmodernist deconstruction of the
epistemological paradigm of modern philosophy is a recogni-

tion of the social sources of rationality. Reason is disseminated in such a manner that it no longer issues from an isolated, translucent, epistemic consciousness. Instead, it is portrayed as a coefficient of variable sociopolitical forces and constellations. The consequence of all this is a radical pluralization of reason comported by a multiplicity of language games that play themselves out in a variety of social functions. This in turn sets the stage for an acknowledgment of the insinuation of power and desire in the various forms of rational deliberation and decision. The contributions of Foucault and Deleuze are of particular significance on this point. Foucault has made much of "regimes of knowledge" as forms of social practices that reflect, either consciously or unconsciously, certain power relations within the existing social order. Deleuze has given notice of the insinuation of desire in the motivations and projections of humankind as a complex of "desiring machines." Reason cannot remain innocent of power and desire. (The Nietzschean background of Foucault's interpretive analysis of power and the Freudian background of Deleuze's economy of desire are quickly discernible, and indeed made explicit, in their writings.)

It should come as no surprise that the rupture of the modern epistemological paradigm and an accentuation of the play of power and desire in the claims of reason would have some far-reaching consequences for the fates of "meaning" and "reference," the two linchpins of modern epistemological thought. From Kant to Frege to Husserl to Russell the task of philosophy was defined principally as that of coming to terms with these two well-honed philosophical issues. Indeed, to be a modern philosopher is to engage in an analysis of meaning and a determination of reference. With the displacement of the epistemological paradigm there is no longer a center from which such analysis of meaning and determination of reference can proceed. Against the backdrop of the pluralization of social practices that congeal into regimes of knowledge meaning escapes the constraints of decidability and reference remains inscrutable. The multiplicity and heterogenity of our language games effectively foreclose a space for stable meanings, in the guise of either intuited essences or invariant rules, and disperses the corresponding entities to which our assertoric claims refer. The signifiers of our grammar, according to the postmodernists, are too lame to lead us to the identification of the properly signified. Meaning and reference perpetually elude our efforts toward epistemic control.

Our fifth mark of postmodernity, somewhat more general than the preceding four, involves a peculiar pairing of opposites, congealed into transcendentalism on the one hand and historicism on the other. The mapping of the terrain of postmodernity displays a set of forced options. Either espouse transcendental unities or embrace the relativity and plurality of a radical historicism. Accept either commensurability or incommensurability, logos or antilogos, consensus or dissension, royal science or nomad science, the arborescent or the rhizomatic, unity or multiplicity, logology or paralogy—to name but a few of the proliferating sets of opposition. The persisting tendency of postmodernist thought is to accent the latter in each of these polarities, occasioning a *reactive* stance in celebration of a radical historicism in the wake of a jettisoning of the transcendental unities of modern thought.

It is these features of postmodernity that provide an energetic challenge to the proponents of rationality. If this challenge is taken at all seriously, then the map of reason will have to be recharted, if indeed some utility can still be found in speaking of the claims of reason at all. In the following discussion an effort will be made to take the postmodernist challenge seriously and to respond with a refiguration and redescription of the resources of rationality. Such a refiguration and redescription, it is hoped, will at once enrich our notion of rational social practices and avoid the nihilism and blatant relativism of the more militant antireason postmodernists. Our current effort, most broadly articulated, must be understood as an attempt to refigure the map of reason by steering a course between the Scylla of modernity and the Charybdis of postmodernity, avoiding what Gadamer has deftly named "the self-crucifying subjectivity of modernity,"[3] but at the same time navigating around the directionless pluralism of postmodernity.

We propose for consideration a refiguration of rationality as interpretive narration and praxial critique. Setting aside, at least for the time being, the modernist notion of rationality as a mental act (or a set of mental acts), let us consider rationality as a social practice, albeit of a special kind. It is a social practice that involves the telling of a story, laden with interpretation, containing resources and strategies for critique. In this notion of rationality there are three principal moments that overlap and intercalate: narrativity, interpretation, and critique. As such it contains features of postmodernity (and particularly "narrativity"), features of modernity (and particularly "critique"), and a middle or mediating term, "interpretation." Rationality is embodied in the telling of a story that provides a critical account of our interpretive understanding of self and world.

To talk of rationality as in some manner a vehicle for or instrument of criticism would seem to violate one of the principal tenets of postmodernity. Has not postmodernism displaced, once and for all, the project of criticism itself? Is not an appeal to the resources of critique but a facile return to the rationalism of modernity? Among the postmodernists Lyotard would appear to be the most adamant on this point. According to Lyotard critique remains language-bound and is thus unable to reach its object. More specifically, critique is bound to language as a vehicle for representation and remains stuck in the aporias that the representational theory of language produces. Beholden to language as representation, critique can only move about within a space of negativity as a power ploy to unseat its object of criticism. But it can never move beyond the critical relation itself, beyond the representational schemata in which linguistically constituted objects are negated through the annihilating power of language. Critique is thus unable to room out a space for a criticism of itself.[4]

How does one respond to this postmodernist displacement of the very space of critique? Is there indeed a forced option of *either* the critical reason of modernity *or* the interventionist strategy of postmodernity? We think not. The project of "critical philosophy," inaugurated by Kant and be-

queathed to his successors, including the more recent school
of "critical theory" (which admittedly has retrenched the Kantian critical principle in significant ways), is indeed open to
some of the charges that postmodernity has leveled against it.
Such is the case, however, not because of the employment of a
grammar of critique but rather because critique has been construed as a theoretical grounding-oriented project. The problem, we submit, is not with the critical resources of rationality
per se, but rather with an overly determined conceptual or
theoretical posturing of the telos of criticism. This theoretical
posturing became evident not only in Kant's *Critique of Pure
Reason* but in his *Critique of Pure Practical Reason* and his *Critique of Judgment* as well. All three critiques were engineered
from the perspective of transcendental interests, designed to
provide a grounding for our judgments within the three cultural spheres of science, morality, and art. We agree with the
postmodernists that this threefold theoretical scaffolding, and
the proffered judicative grounding in each, should be placed
under suspicion.

But the displacement of critique in the interests of purely
conceptual and theoretical grounding does not entail a displacement of critique in all manners conceivable. At the "end
of philosophy" as theoretical critique, we encounter a refiguration of rationality as *praxial* critique. Critique is resituated within the dynamics of our sociohistorical engagements.
Rather than a centripetal activity of an isolated epistemological, moral, or aesthetic subject, we understand critique as a
centrifugal deployment within a constellation of social practices. Critique becomes a communicative project, a praxis that
finds its resources in the dialogic transactions and institutional
forms that make up the fabric of our historical existence.
Critique is inseparable from the social practices of the various communities of investigators and interpreters as they attempt to understand and explain the various constellations of
sense in their personal and public life. Rationality as praxial
critique fills the void occasioned by the displacement of the
epistemological-theoretic paradigm of modernity.

The refiguration of rationality as praxial critique can be
aided by a recovery of the originative Greek notion of *krino*

(κρινω), which carries the related senses of separating, discerning, assessing, and choosing. *Krino* is the etymological root of both "critique" and "criterion," in advance of their epistemologization as protocols of theoretical cognition. *Krino* is a performance of *praxial* critique, a discernment and assessment of social practices and institutions as they play with and off each other. This praxial critique through discernment was still present in the Latin rendering of *krino* as *cerno*, the basis for the English *discern*. But in the philosophical grammar of modernity this praxis-oriented discernment, deliberation, and assessment was taken up into an epistemological quest for certainty, facilitating the slide of *cerno* into *certo*. Modern philosophy construed discernment as a quest for certainty that sought its criteria in clear and distinct ideas issuing from an insular *res cogitans*. Here critique and criterion fuse into an impossible epistemological requirement that demands unimpeachable foundations for certain knowledge.[5]

Critique, properly refigured as praxial critique, enjoys neither the modernist desire for foundations nor its hopes for certainty or apodicticity. It rests content to discern and assess the play of beliefs and practices against the background of changing and historically conditioned patterns of signification. In all this we can see the postmodernist notion of intervention as playing an important role. Social beliefs and practices are modified and reassessed through intervention, but this is not an intervention devoid of discernment or critique as a praxial accomplishment.[6]

Praxial critique as at once discernment and intervention unfolds within the telling of a story. It is thus that one must make explicit the interwovenness of critique and narrativity within the intertexture of rationality. In making this interwovenness explicit one is able to articulate, in a single move as it were, certain failures within modernity and postmodernity alike. Whereas modernity tended to gloss the role of narrativity in its preoccupation with subject-oriented critique, postmodernity tends to lose sight of the inescapable moment of criticism in its enchantment with the dynamics and form of narrativity. In refiguring the map of reason in such a manner as to highlight the complementarity of critique and narrativ-

ity we are in position to split the difference between modernity and postmodernity.[7] Admittedly, in such a move both the
modern concept of critique and the postmodern uses of narrative are resituated, but their singular contributions remain
intact.

The narratives that bind our communicative practices
are at once performances of discernment and articulation.
Through our story telling we articulate the sense of lived-
through historical experience as we attempt to achieve both a
measure of self-identity and a comprehension of our social
and natural world. Narratives are accomplishments of sense.
They illustrate the configurative meaning-structures of our
social practices. They are also vehicles of reference. They are
about something. Their sense-giving performance is fulfilled
through reference. Narratives articulate, disclose, make manifest, intimate, reveal and thus comport their own agency of
reference. There is a narrational referentiality, articulating
background conditions, contextual wholes, styles of life, and
modes of existence, which is older than the empirical, osten-
sive, and objectifying reference that became such an obsession
for the modernist mind.

The rationality within the workings of narrativity thus
proceeds via a peculiar articulation of sense and reference. It
is important to recognize, however, that this articulation of
sense and reference is not the result of an adequation or mediation of internalized mental acts and external reality, a correspondence of concept and fact, a coming together of subject
and object. Narrativity is not an after-the-fact accomplishment
of ordering and unification, an imposition of form on a pre-
narrative manifold of fact. Narrativity is an indigenous feature of life and world disclosure.[8] Storytelling is a way of
presencing sense and reference as moments within a configurative project of understanding. Narration articulates the
background practices and shared beliefs in which meanings
and facts first come to a stand. Only through our storytelling
are meanings and facts called into being. What the stories
mean and to what they refer do not antedate the narrative
discourse. Facts do not fall into the lap of the narrator. They
become facts only through a species of hermeneutical consti-

tution. A fact becomes a fact only within a disciplinary matrix established by a community of interpreters that provides the plot for the telling of a particular story. It is in this fashion that narrative rationality is able to surmount the modern epistemological dichotomies of meaning and fact, sense and reference.

As the workings of narrative rationality unfold on the hither side of the epistemologically based meaning/fact dichotomy, so also they overcome the self/other bifurcation. The stories that are told are told by a narrator. They issue from a speaking subject, and no matter at this juncture that this speaking subject is effectively decentered, no longer the sovereign legislator of meaning and the primal authority. No amount of decentering and deconstruction can displace the voice of the narrator, who achieves whatever self-identity can be achieved through his/her narrations. Narrativity is always a "narrative of self," exemplifying a species of autobiographical reflection. The self as *homo narrans* remains implicated in the practices of speaking and writing that it takes up time and again. The dismantling of the subject as epistemological point and foundation does not entail a dismantling of the subject in every sense you please.[9] Yet—and this is the crucial point at issue—this autobiographical narration of self, geared to the achievement of self-identity, is always woven into a network of stories involving a tradition of historical memories, shared language, and common social practices. It is thus that no narrator is an island entire of itself, cut off from the mainland of the tradition. Autobiographical narration severed from the stories in the tradition lapses into a twilight zone of abstraction, decontextualized from the space of beliefs and social practices that provides its originative habitat. The voice of narrative is thus a conjugated voice, at once the voice of the self and the voice of the other, an intersubjective and intercultural voice, articulating patterns of amalgamated self and social understanding. Again, the epistemological paradigm of rationality is burst asunder, not through a banishment of the self per se, but through a displacement of an isolated knowing subject that effectively cuts itself off from the social sources of rationality.[10]

In our refiguration of rationality within the space of praxis as an interweaving of critique, interpretation, and narration, the postures and requirements of reason undergo an unavoidable pluralization. There is no single requirement that answers to the question, What does it mean to be rational? The unity of knowledge paradigm, engineered from the side of either methodological or metaphysical protocols, was a passing modernist fancy. The postures and claims of rationality are multiple.

There is an existential posture of rationality, illustrated in the dynamics of reason in the guise of *application* and *coping*. Gadamer has made much of the moment of *applicatio* in his universal hermeneutics and Richard Rorty time and again instructs us on matters of coping as we attempt to make our way about in the plethora of conflicting beliefs and social practices. Gadamerian "application," however, should not be confused with the modernist notion of application as the utilization of a prevalidated theory, and Rortyian "coping" is never the instrumentation of rule-governed directives for our personal and social actualization. Application and coping are forms of praxis that keep us attuned to the encountered existential realities in our everyday lives.

Closely allied with the existential posture of rationality as application and coping is the pragmatic posture of rationality as an interest in consequences. The resources of our reason get us somewhere. They lead us from the present to anticipated future consequences. And in their critical function they provide us with a healthy skepticism about those philosophical doctrines and social institutions that have outworn their usefulness. Again, the praxial requirement runs deep. To be rational is to be able to discern and assess the practical consequences of a proposed belief or projected plan of action. The contribution of the classical American philosophical tradition, and specifically the thought of James and Dewey, becomes patently evident in all this. This contribution has been given a renewed expression in the proliferating varieties of "neopragmatism" across an interdisciplinary spectrum involving philosophy, literature, and the human sciences. This can all be properly seen as an effort to room out a space between modernity and postmodernity.

There is a third posture that our refigured notion of rationality assumes. This posture is itself a redescription of a traditional standard for guiding the claims of reason, inscribed in textbooks of philosophy as the coherence theory of truth. Unfortunately, the modernist construal of coherence in the interests of grounding a theory of truth invited an empty formalism in the guise of an abstract logical consistency that found its measure in the criterion of certainty supplied by putatively clear and distinct ideas. We propose a shift from this criteriological construal of coherence to coherence as a patterning of our changing belief-systems and configurations of social practices. The coherence posture in our refigured notion of reason thus enables us to discern how our beliefs and our practices hang together. For the most part these beliefs and practices hang together rather loosely, resisting closure or sedimentation into a unified worldview. This is the case because the contextual background of these beliefs and practices is temporalized by a continuing ingression of a past and a continuing advance into a future. The contextual background suffers temporal passage. This does not, however, displace the requirement for a discernment and articulation of patterns among the beliefs and practices themselves, as well as in the way that our beliefs and practices are contextualized within a wider sociohistorical dynamics. This constitutes a call for a notion of coherence situated somewhere between the formal unities of modernity and the rampant pluralities of postmodernity. Coherence as a praxial requirement is a strategy of totalizing that retains an open texture, thus avoiding at once the indefensible claims for completeness and totality and the self-refuting claims for an unmitigated pluralism.[11]

A recognition of the play of our beliefs and practices against the background of an explicit temporalization of the forms of life that we live through provides a fourth posture of our refigured rationality. We name this the inventive posture. This is a posture occasioned by the temporalized texturizing of the horizon of our beliefs and practices as at once a "back" ground and a "fore" ground, at once recollective and anticipative, at once tradition and project, perpetually moving from a past to a future. It is within this temporalization, binding all our narratives as progeny of memory and augury of hope, that the inventive posture finds its space, defining rationality as the accomplishment of new descriptions and new configurations of human behavior. It is at this juncture in particular that the broadening of rationality to include the performance creativity of poiesis becomes visible. We have in mind here the originative sense of poiesis as a "making" and an "inventing," the sense illustrated, for example, in Heidegger's notions of poetic thinking and poetic dwelling. What is at issue is the saying of that which has not yet been said and the doing of that which has not yet been done, the inauguration of new ways of perceiving the world and new forms of acting within it. This is rationality in the guise of creativity.

The recognition of the workings of invention and creativity in the operations of rationality places into question the utility of modernist models of language and human behavior alike. Language as an embodiment of inventive rationality bursts through the constraints of the semiotic model, in which language is construed as a system of rule-governed signs. The performatives of language operative within the inventive posture occasion the descent of semiotics into hermeneutics. The elemental phonemic, lexical, and syntactical units of semiotics follow the creative impetus of inventive discourse. They do not direct it. This, however, does not mean that the sign/signified matrix of linguistic analysis is to be jettisoned as such. What is required is a resituation of semiotic analysis within a broader context of the dynamics of language in use. A recognition of the creative use of language requires a recontextualization of the alleged context-free semiotic units. The functions of phonemes, lexemes, and grammatical rules must be integrated with the performance of language as an interpretive accomplishment.[12]

As the language of inventive rationality dismantles and resituates the semiotic model it also carries us beyond the construal of language as a series of speech acts. The contribution of speech act theory in refocusing the proper emphasis on *language in use* has indeed been considerable, and in this it has supplied its own telling critique of the semiotic model. Yet, for the most part speech act theory remains beholden to an empiricist epistemological paradigm that atomizes and se-

rializes all contents of experience. To view language as a series of speech acts, issuing from the intentionality of serialized
speaking subjects, somehow effecting a correlation of meaning and world, is still to accept a modernist epistemological
paradigm that at once glosses the social sources of rationality,
the role of the communicative telos of language, and the
weight of tradition. Admittedly, it is the speaking subject that
speaks and in his/her speech performance intends to say this
and not that. Yet, these speech acts with their expressed intentions are always spoken *from* a language and *within* a tradition. The narratives of the speaking subject always remain
embedded in the narratives of a wider sociohistorical tradition. An isolated speaking subject, searching for a correspondence of its intentions with states of affairs, is as much of an
abstraction as is the lonely epistemological subject of modernity, severed from an objective, external world.[13]

Not only does the exercise of inventive rationality dismantle the modernist models of language, of both the structuralist and empiricist varieties, it also conspires to jettison the
modernist models of behavior that attempt to explain human
motivation and action through an after-the-fact reconstruction of the past. The behavioral model seeks to render an account of human behavior simply in terms of the facticity of
the past. The field of fact to be investigated is that which has
already transpired. For the behaviorist, reality is that which
has been. Consequently the only motives that have explanatory force are "because-motives." The efficacy of "in-order-to"
motives, and indeed the inscription of the projective thrust of
human action and our social practices more generally, is not
taken into account.[14] It is precisely the inventive posture of
rationality that enables a recognition of the futural orientation of human behavior, which is that upon which all deter-
ministic explanations of human thought and action founder.

Our refiguration of rationality between modernity and
postmodernity led us in our first maneuver to a recognition of
an intertexturing of praxial critique, interpretation, and narrativity in the life of reason. We then attempted to articulate
the complementing postures of rationality vis-à-vis the fourfold requirements of existential application, pragmatic test-

ing, coherence, and invention. The "truth" of rationality, seen most generally as an event of disclosure through articulation, proceeds via a *discernment* (which itself is a refiguration of the modern pairing of "critique" and "criterion") of strategies for coping, of envisioned consequences, of the patterning of our beliefs and practices, and of new descriptions and new configurations of experience. We have named these four requirements the existential, pragmatic, coherence, and inventive postures, respectively.

Our concluding task is that of elucidating how our refigured notion of rationality might address somewhat more specifically the impasse of "*either* transcendentalism *or* historicism," as this impasse resulted from the collision of the modernist and postmodernist cultures. This impasse has forced us into the intolerable situation of opting for either a pure verticality or a pure horizontality. The former is the way of transcendentalism, in which the grounding and validation of all forms of thought and practice issue from an atemporal universal, an invariant essence, a priori and necessary conditions, or rule-bound regularities. The latter is the way of historicism, in which the variegated forms of thought and action are all granted an equal claim to thrive, divested of any claims to universality, and shorn of any obliging character. As a possible way out of this impasse we recommend the utility of a new metaphor: that of transversality. This new metaphor is designed to overcome the limitations and distortions of the metaphor of pure verticality on the one hand and the metaphor of pure horizontality on the other. Our refigured notion of rationality is thus seen to be operative in a new space, the space of transversality.

A common error of modernity and postmodernity alike is the confusion of the *transhistorical* with the *ahistorical*. Modern philosophy, insofar as it continued to accept the epistemological paradigm of transcendental grounding, fused the transhistorical with the ahistorical and sought to ground all knowledge in a priori, atemporal conditions. This comprised the effort of modernity to counter the twin threats of historicism and relativism. Postmodernism, in its displacement of the modern epistemological paradigm and in its pluralization and relativization of all narratives, jettisoned the search for atemporal conditions and foundations of knowledge and happily embraced the consequences of historicism. Modernity opts for a vertical grounding, whereby criteria for validation are supplied from the *other* side of history. Postmodernity celebrates the horizontal dispersion of local and incommensurable narratives that make their appearance on *this* side of history. In both cases the distinction between the transhistorical and ahistorical collapses and the stage is set for the sedimentation of a dichotomy that polarizes the collapsed transhistorical-ahistorical against the historical. We propose to dismantle this dichotomy and effect a detour around the impasse by marking out a movement of transversality that legitimates transhistorical critique and cross-cultural evaluation without the problematic appeals to transcendental, atemporal conditions.

Jean-Paul Sartre has already hinted at the utility of the metaphor of transversality in his celebrated critique of Husserl's appeal to the transcendental ego as the residium of the phenomenological-transcendental reduction. Arguing that the ego is not the transcendental, identical pole of our conscious acts but rather the result of a constituting act of consciousness, Sartre alleges that the very concept of a transcendental ego is flawed. It is at once superfluous (we do not need it to account for unity and individuality) and a hindrance (it is like an "opaque blade" that severs consciousness from itself). Sartre recommends that the problematic ego of transcendental philosophy be replaced with a notion of "consciousness which unifies itself, concretely, by a play of 'transversal' intentionalities which are concrete and real retentions of past consciousness."[15]

Sartre's reference to "a play of transversal intentionalities" is suggestive and promising. Unfortunately, however, given the boldly subjectivist framework of his existential philosophy (and particularly that of his earlier works), which continues to move out from a philosophy of consciousness, he was unable to grasp the explicit sociohistorical region in which transversality is at play. What is required is an acknowledgement of the play and performance of transversality as a play of social practices and institutional constellations whose intentionality antedates the constituting activity of an individuated consciousness.[16] Also by giving primacy to the present

in his existentialist view of time, Sartre was unable to fully
appreciate the role of the future, the not-yet, in the unification of consciousness. Thus, transversality remained for Sartre
principally a movement from the present to the past, and
then back to the present as retentionally qualified. There is
little space allowed for the protentional or futural thrust of
transversality in Sartre's scheme of things.

The related senses of extending and lying across while
altering and transforming or even overturning inform the
metaphorical uses of transversality in mathematics (transversality of a line as it intersects a system of lines), physiology
(the dense transversality of a band of fibers), anatomy (the lateral process of a vertebra), and physics (transversality of mass
as a ratio of accelerating forces). These related senses, we suggest, are also in play in the processes and forces of our sociohistorical experience. Our social practices are suspended over,
lie across, intersect, a plurality of historical epochs and current forms of life. We make note of these related senses in the
polysemy of a metaphorics of transversality, illustrated in
mathematics, science, and sociohistorical experience, not to
set the stage for a species of reductionism whereby the gathering of the senses in one disciplinary matrix becomes literal-
ized and is then made normative for all the rest. Rather we
are intent on highlighting the surplus of meaning in the pol-
ysemic play on the boundaries of the various disciplines.
There is no algorithim of transversality (as is attempted, for
example, in structuralism). The different senses escape closure within a mathematized matrix of binary connections and
invariant relations.

The transversality of our sociohistorical experience is related to concretized practices rather than abstracted relations.
Sometimes these practices link up with practices in other historical epochs and other sociological spaces in such a manner
that they line up with them laterally, intersecting at decisive
points in terms of simple continuation or further enrichment.
At other times they stand in opposition to them, occasioning a
rupture that leads to alteration and transformation or indeed
reversal and overturn. Postmodernity has made us sensitive to
the realities of rupture and dissension that invade our para-

digms of thought and our social practices. We certainly must remain cognizant of such rupture and dissension—for which our metaphor of transversality remains accountable. Yet, the recognition of rupture and dissension within the wider socio-historical fabric does not entail the dissolution of transversality into a mere horizontality of random pluralization in which each paradigm and each social practice remains isolated and self-sufficient, cut off from any transversal play of challenge and response through critical reflection and corrective action. Such is the myth of radical pluralization of postmodernity, which simply refashions the isolated epistemological subject of modernity into a serialization of equally isolated local narratives and cultural enclaves.

The bonding and the binding effected by the transversality of sociohistorical experience, always cognizant, to be sure, of the intrusion of rupture and dissension, is the remarkable achievement of the dynamics of communication in the life of interpreting and narrating social agents. Our notion of transversality carries with it a notion of truth, as did also Plato's notion of reminiscence. Professor Dallmayr has suggested a strategy for a possible deconstructive retrieval of the Platonic doctrine of anamnesis, a retrieval that at once appropriates a shared insight and jettisons the pure theoretical construal of cognition that traveled with the classical doctrine.

> I consider it preferable, following Plato's suggestion in the *Meno*, to approximate cognition more closely to the process of *recollection*. In contrast, however, to interpretations which equate the Platonic notion with a priori principles of reflection or with a return to an unspoiled rationality I am inclined to the reverse view: one which sees recollection as a probing of opacity or as an effort to decipher the signals of a precognitive or prereflective practice—a practice which is not synonymous with individual or collective designs and which seems less akin to reason than to imagination (or to the poetic wisdom discussed by Vico).[17]

In this very suggestive passage, Dallmayr's proposed turn to praxis is made explicit. It is of particular significance that in this turn praxis is not divested of rationality. Praxis affords its own insight and comprehension, and it does this through a recollection that is infused with an imagination and poetic wisdom that make it more creative and wiser than the recollection of theoretical recognition.

Our project of recharting the map of reason with the help of the metaphor of transversality, wherewith to overcome the historicism and relativism of postmodernity, can be defined as an effort toward *weiterdenken* with Dallmayr on the topic of truth as recollection. Our notion of rationality as praxial critique and interpretive narration blends with a notion of truth that incorporates recollection into transversality. However, given the explicitly sociohistorical context for our ruminations on rationality and truth, this truth always remains *truth as communicability*. Our metaphor of transversality does not chart a reminiscence of stable, atemporal, untrammeled essences; nor does it provide a foundation for a theoretical recognition of invariant rules that can be reproduced through a sheer act of intellection. The facile recovery of such stable essences or invariant rules by moving backward is blocked because the lines traversed by transversality also move forward, marking out new possibilities for discourse and action, inviting the invention of new forms of thought and life through the call of the future. It is within this span of tension between past and future that the play of sociohistorical transversality takes place, always against the background of the achievement of truth through communication. But this achieved truth remains the truth of finitude, never immune to the fractures of dissension and the negativities of distorted communication. The marvel is that as interpreting and narrating agents we are able to achieve communication *in spite of* the fractures, discontinuities, ruptures, and incommensurabilities to which our sociohistorical fabric is heir. Thus truth as communicability, proceeding via a hermeneutical interplay of recollection and projection, is at once a disclosure of similarity and difference, unity and multiplicity, the commensurable and the incommensurable. Historicism forgets similarity, unity, and commensurability; transcendentalism forgets difference, multiplicity, and incommensurability. And each forgets the other because both decontextualize the intentionality of communicative praxis.

Coupled with our notion of truth as communicability, emerging within the transversal play of modes of discourse and forms of life, is a new notion of universals. The universals that emerge from the crossing over, suspension between, alteration, and transformation of configurations of discourse and action neither exhibit a vertical anchorage nor are pulverized into a melange of discontinuous particulars. The nominalism of local narratives falls away with the disassemblage of the realism of vertical universals. They both disfigure the intentional fabric of our communicative practices. What communication achieves is what might appropriately be called "transversal universals," somewhat reminiscent of Merleau-Ponty's "lateral universals."[18] Transversal universals, as the achievements of communication, span the changing scene of historical forms of description and evaluation. Resident neither in *rerum natura* nor in an a priori structure of the human mind, transversal universals display an open texture, subject to revision through the innovation of new forms of communication. The achievement of universals is thus a perpetual achievement, a goal that must be accomplished time and again. As one eventually needs to recognize that the modern Western European notion of justice is not that of ancient Greece (because the configuration of the polis has undergone modification) so one also needs to recognize that modern and postmodern notions of justice are subject to revision. Universals are the progeny of historical experience, the result of the workings of a narrative rationality that can never outstrip its finitude. In all this we have to acknowledge an unavoidable relativity and perspectivity in the framing of our moral judgments and evaluative claims.

Yet, this evident relativity and perspectivity, as intrinsic ingredients of historical experience itself, do not reduce to a historicism and moral relativism. The relativity and perspectivity at issue here are those that work themselves out in the transversal play of communicative practices. The proposed universals never issue from an isolated subject nor an insular institution. They span the spectrum of historical time, emerging from a past and subject to revision in the future. Different local narratives inform the conceptual frameworks and systems of beliefs of different historical epochs. Narrative rationality attends to the background practices of these local narratives, from which conceptual constructs and systems of value emerge, in the hope of fashioning a dialogue with those removed from us in time and space. A dialogue with the ancient Greeks is still possible, in the process of which commonalities with respect to interests and concerns in our social practices could come to light. This could lead to an acknowledgment that the Greek notion of virtue may still have some applicability for our time, disclosing a sameness-in-difference, a consensus-with-dissension, patterns of commensurability-in-spite-of-incommensurability.

The result of such a dialogue or project of communication, with the Greeks or with whomever, is the achievement of transversal universals, bound not by a conceptual glue but by shared concerns, interests, and social practices that are incorporated into the stories that we tell. In the telling of our story, in which our local narratives are always situated transversally, lying across a spectrum of other stories already told and many yet to be told, we are able to avoid the Charybdis of modernism with its illusion of a transcendentally grounded apodictic certainty as well as the Scylla of postmodernism with its hurried embrace of historicism and relativism. And we are able to tell such a story because of the communicating, narrating, and interpreting creatures that we are.

NOTES

1. Jean-François Lyotard has appeared on the current scene as one of the more zealous spokespersons for the postmodernist manifesto. See his work *The Postmodern Condition: A Report on Knowledge*, trans. G. Bennington and B. Massumi (Minneapolis: University of Minnesota Press, 1984), and particularly his defining marks of postmodernity: "incredulity toward metanarratives," "sensitivity to differences," "ability to tolerate the incommensurable," and "the inventor's paralogy," pp. xxiv–xxv.

2. *Reason in the Age of Science*, trans. Frederick G. Lawrence (Cambridge, Mass.: MIT Press, 1981), p. 18.

3. Ibid., p. 15.

4. "The critical relation cannot criticize itself, it can only parody itself in the derision of autocritique. And in this impossibility, it shows that it is still an authoritarian dominating relation, that it is negativity as power. This power is that of language which annihilates what it speaks of. Criticism can only redouble the empty space where its discourse plunges its object, it is cloistered in this space of vacuity, it belongs to language and to representation, it can no longer think the object, the work and history, except as language," "Adorno as the Devil," *Telos*, no. 19, 1974, p. 135. Lyotard's postmodernist move beyond critique proceeds via an intervention that is not that of language but rather "libidinal investment." "What brings us out of capital and out of 'art' (and out of *Entkunstung*, its complement) is not criticism, which is language-bound [langagière], nihilistic, but a deployment of libidinal investment," ibid., p. 136. See also *Driftworks*, ed. Roger McKeon (New York: Semiotext(e), 1984), pp. 15–17.

5. For an illuminating tracking of the etymology of *criterion* from its Greek usage to the present, see David James Miller, "Immodest Interventions," *Phenomenological Inquiry*, vol. 11, 1987.

6. We read Hans Blumenberg's notion of "self-assertion," which he outlines in his project of philosophy as rhetoric, as pointing in the same direction as does our refigured postmodernist notion of intervention. Self-assertion is a species of praxial critique, oriented not toward the grounding-oriented notion of critique within modernity, but rather toward a rhetorical self-understanding of a human reality embedded in its social practices. See "An Anthropological Approach to the Contemporary Significance of Rhetoric," in *After Philosophy: End or Transformation?*, ed. Kenneth Baynes, James Bohman, and Thomas McCarthy (Cambridge, Mass.: MIT Press, 1987).

7. This strategy finds its analogue in Richard Rorty's splitting of the difference between Habermas and Lyotard in his provocative article "Habermas and Lyotard on Postmodernity," in *Habermas and Modernity*, ed. Richard J. Bernstein (Cambridge, Mass.: MIT Press, 1985).

8. David Carr has incisively addressed this point in his recent work *Time, Narrative, and History*, where he has shown with consummate skill that the narrative structure is a "configuration" that "inheres in experience itself," countering the view that "such structure is overlaid or imposed upon experience by a retrospective and 'literary' effort extrinsic to experience itself" (Bloomington, Ind.: Indiana University Press, 1986), p. 45.

9. For a consecutive and detailed discussion of the recovery of the subject in the wake of the displacement of the modern epistemological paradigm, see Calvin O. Schrag, *Communicative Praxis and the Space of Subjectivity* (Bloomington: Indiana University Press, 1986), and particularly chap. 6, "Hermeneutical Self-implicature," and chap. 7, "The Decentered Subject."

10. Alisdair MacIntyre has given particular attention to the integration of self-narrative with the tradition in his book *After Virtue* (Notre Dame, Ind.: University of Notre Dame Press, 1981). See particularly chap. 15, "The Virtues, the Unity of a Human Life and the Concept of a Tradition."

11. It should be noted that Max Weber wrestled, albeit not all that successfully, with the limitations of formal rationality in its service of a coherence theory of truth—and particularly as it applied to the sphere of economics. He distinguished formal rationality from substantive rationality. Formal rationality is "used to designate the extent of quantitative calculation or accounting which is technically possible and which is actually applied." Substantive rationality, on the other hand, "is the degree in which a given group of persons, no matter how it is delimited, is or could be adequately provided with goods by means of an economically oriented course of social action. This course of action will be interpreted in terms of a given set of ultimate values no matter what they may be." *The Theory of Social and Economic Organization*, trans. A. M. Henderson and Talcott Parsons (New York: Free Press, 1974), p. 184–85. Although the distinction between formal and substantive rationality clearly has a point to it, it gets in the way when Weber formulates his general principle of rationality. In the moment that the value component is introduced into his notion of substantive rationality, an equivocation begins to surface, because values as such are for Weber beyond the ken of rational criteria. They issue from a stance of decisionism and as such are at least nonrational, if not irrational. Weber was simply unable to surmount the strictures of the modernist conception of rationality.

12. Paul Ricoeur's discussion of the limitations of a semiotic approach to language in his response to the challenge of structuralist linguistics still remains one of the most illuminating treatments of the subject. Ricoeur defines his project as a two-stage operation in which one first grafts a semantics of the sentence onto the semiotics of the word, and then grafts a hermeneutics of the text onto a semantics of the sentence. Quite independent of whether one might experience some discomfort with Ricoeur's extended use of the met-

aphor of grafting in tracking the interwovenness of the requirements of semiotics, semantics, and hermeneutics, the fact remains
that he has identified with a penetrating clarity the limitations of
the semiotic model and has recognized the need for a recontextualization of language as event and process within a broader hermeneutical project. See particularly "The Problem of Double Meaning
as Hermeneutic Problem and as Semantic Problem," in *Conflict of
Interpretations*, ed. Don Ihde (Evanston, Ill.: Northwestern University
Press, 1974), pp. 62–78; "Structure, Word, Event," in *The Philosophy of Paul Ricoeur*, ed. Charles Reagan and David Stewart (Boston: Beacon Press, 1978), pp. 109–19; and *The Rule of Metaphor*,
trans. Robert Czerny (Toronto: University of Toronto Press, 1927),
p. 65–133.

13. In his book *Language and Politics* (Notre Dame, Ind.: University of Notre Dame Press, 1984) Professor Dallmayr has provided
a trenchant analysis and evaluation of both the positive contributions and the shortcomings of speech act theory, particularly as it
relates to the role of language in political philosophy. See especially
chap. 4, "Ordinary Language and Existentialism: Verbal Praxis,"
pp. 86–114.

14. For an illustration of the use of the distinction between
"because-motives" and "in-order-to-motives" in addressing the limitations of the classical behaviorist model of scientific explanation see
Alfred Schutz, *The Phenomenology of the Social World*, trans. George
Walsh and Frederick Lehnert (Evanston, Ill.: Northwestern University Press, 1967), pp. 86–96.

15. *The Transcendence of the Ego: An Existentialist Theory of Consciousness*, trans. Forest Williams and Robert Kirkpatrick (New York:
Noonday Press, 1957), p. 39.

16. Gilles Deleuze has adumbrated such a nonsubjectivist space
of transversality with his notion of transversality as a communication
across the "viewpoints of a landscape." This results from his reconstruction of Proustian reminiscence as a creation rather than a
simple reproduction. This reminiscence comported by transversality
creates not from a vantage point above but rather through a lateral
productive retrieval. This is not the Platonic reminiscence of a lost
essence, given in advance; it is the creation of a new viewpoint that
only appears afterward. See particularly chap. 8, "Antilogos, or the
Literary Machine," in *Proust and Signs*, trans. Richard Howard (New
York: George Braziller, 1972). Felix Guattari has made the social dimension of transversality even more explicit with his notion of
"transversality in the group" as it is operative in the institutional

setting of a psychiatric ward. "Transversality is a dimension that tries to overcome both the impasse of pure verticality and that of mere horizontality; it tends to be achieved when there is a maximum communication among the different levels and, above all, in different meanings," *Molecular Revolution: Psychiatry and Politics*, trans. Rosemary Sheed (Harmondsworth, England: Penguin Books, 1984), p. 18. Guattari's interest in the notion of transversality stems from his effort to detail the integrative functioning of the different constellations of power and decision making within the institutional setting of psychiatric therapy—administrators, doctors, nurses, assistants, patients, families of patients, and so on. The degree of transversality achieved depends upon the effectiveness of a dialogue across the institutional lines of force and social roles, fostering a recognition of the otherness of each of the subgroups, leading to a "dialectical enrichment" (p. 22). Transversality thus at once heightens self-understanding within each subgroup and occasions a recognition of the need to make adjustments because of the presence of other subgroups.

17. *Twilight of Subjectivity: Contributions to a Post-Individualist Theory* (Amherst: University of Massachusetts Press, 1981), p. 251.

18. Merleau-Ponty has submitted the distinction between "lateral" and "overarching" universals. The latter are the products of an objectifying reflection that seeks to bind the varieties of human experience from above—from the vantage point of a godlike survey. Lateral universals, on the other hand, are acquired through ethnological explorations in which differing points of view (those of the native and the civilized man, for example) are described, analyzed, compared, and tested in the interests of "constituting a more comprehensive experience which becomes in principle accessible to men of a different time and country," *Signs*, trans. R. C. McCleary (Evanston, Ill.: Northwestern University Press, 1964), p. 120.

WINCH AND SCHUTZ ON THE REGULATIVE IDEA OF A CRITICAL SOCIAL SCIENCE

JOHN O'NEILL

Some time ago Peter Winch rescued interpretive sociology from the clutches of scientism by arguing that its fundamental subject matter, as well as its method of investigation, need not wait upon the findings of empirical science.[1] This is because understanding is not a matter of looking for generalizations that can be applied to human action from the outside, as it were, in the same way that a physicist is free to apply the concept of gravity to the behavior of falling objects. The concepts that explain human behavior have rather an "internal relation" to the conduct they account for and are essentially constitutive of the conduct that falls under them. But this means that, once sociologists see the mistake in their scientistic pursuits, they really have nothing to do since the task of clarifying the rules that are constitutive of human action is properly philosophical work: "It is not a question of what empirical research may show to be the case, but of what philosophical analysis reveals about *what it makes sense to say*. I want to show that the notion of a human society involves a scheme of concepts which is logically incompatible with the kinds of explanation offered in the natural sciences."[2] Winch, then, exacts rather a high price for his manumission of sociology hitherto enslaved by science. At the same time, he himself seems to realize that sociologists do not quit the field that easily.

Much of Winch's argument can only be understood as providing precepts for a more responsible—and by no means subjectivist—conduct of interpretative sociology. Thus, in addition to the claim that understanding language and understanding society are virtually the same process; Winch argues that for this very reason the practice of sociology is subject to a "double hermeneutic."[3] In other words, sociology is doubly responsible both to the interpretative practices it encounters among its subjects of study and to the standards of rational explanation that prevail in the community of sociologists:

> reflective understanding must necessarily presuppose, if it is to count as genuine understanding at all, the participant's unreflective understanding. And this in itself makes it misleading to compare it with the natural scientist's understanding of his scientific data. Similarly, although the reflective student of society, or of a particular mode of life, may find it necessary to use concepts which are not taken from the forms of activity which he is investigating, but which are taken rather from the context of his own investigation, still these technical concepts of his will imply a previous understanding of those other concepts which belong to the activities under investigation.[4]

I believe that we can read Winch's appeal to what Schutz would call the *postulate of adequacy* as an attempt to ground interpretative sociology by making it responsible both to the requirements of professional practice and to the privilege of lay opinion in democratic societies. I also believe the same can be argued with respect to Schutz, and thereby some reply made to the criticisms that interpretative sociology is idealist and conservative in a way that blocks the development of *critical* social science.[5]

Several commentators feel that nothing can be raised from the ashes of Winch's argument since Gellner[6] last dealt with it. I should begin by showing why I still think there is something to build on. Gellner engages in a reductio ad absurdum of the argument that language and society are intrinsically tied realities. He finds in it nothing but a *collectivist anthropomorphism*[7] engaged in a regressive defense of the cherished illusion that the world cannot be meaningless: "These thinkers are not concerned or able to demonstrate that the human world is a *moral* tale, with justice and truth vindicated and some noble purpose attained: but they are concerned to show that it is, at least, a *human* tale. They wish to defend *the anthropomorphic image of man* himself."[8]

In Gellner's view, Winch's argument on the social nature of language and the linguistic nature of society represents the latest form of the idealist separation of man and nature. It is intended to cut off our understanding of social behavior from causal explanation of a naturalist kind. The implications of claiming that concepts are socially governed practices are best seen, according to Gellner, if we reverse the proposition: it can then be seen to amount to the claim that all social practices are meaningful. But that is clearly not so, given the manifest practices of deceit, interpersonal conflict, and organized attempts to overthrow ruling but unjust social practices. While disclaiming this reversal of the sense of Winch's argument as nothing but an expository device—and one hardly intelligible at that!—everything in fact turns upon it for Gellner's own case:

> If "meaning = use", then "use = meaning". Of course, no one actually formulated the first equation *as* a formal equation (which would give us the premise for the second, reverse order reading), and in any case, it is not very clear what the thing means when formulated in reverse order. Nothing in the present argument hinges on this: I use this merely as a kind of expository device, to bring out the underlying pattern of Winch's argument.[9]

Thus, by means of an entirely gratuitous imputation, Gellner is able to hang Winch for indifference to all the troublesome predicaments in the lives of persons and societies, pushing him into a sublime relativism. All this, because it is supposed to be implicit in Winch's view that forms of life cannot be criticized from an *external* (by which Gellner means a causal) point of view that would furnish a standard for judgments about what is real and rational and what is not.

Now, it may well be asked why a *critical* standpoint need be *external* to the reality it pronounces upon. There seems to be a surreptitious reliance upon the notion of the natural scientist's external standpoint vis-à-vis nature (a somewhat old-fashioned view, in view of more recent social studies of science.)[10] Moreover, what does it mean to say the scientist is unbiased toward nature, as though this were in any way like the lack of moral bias? The whole point is that nature's indifference to scientific formulation puts moral questions out of court. But the social world is not similarly indifferent to social science formulations of it since its members have an ethical as well as cognitive investment in their own versions of their world. This does not mean, however, that there are no socially instituted practices of criticism and evaluation internal to social institutions. Indeed, so far from being *external* to its institutions, criticism is deeply institutionalized in Western society.[11] Such criticism is not restricted to social science analysis, nor to Popperian critical rationality. It pervades our ethical, religious, legal, and political institutions. It may be that within these institutions we *dramatize* right and wrong, good and evil, left and right, conservative and radical as though we had some radically external viewpoint upon ourselves. Among such practices are Gellner's own rhetorical arts. But a society that changes its religious, political, and economic institutions over time does not do so because it is always looking outside itself toward some external standard of reality. A society changes in view of its own grammar of change and improvement:

> To be emphasized are not the actual members of any "stock" of descriptions; but the *grammar* which they express. It is through this that we understand their structure and sense, their mutual relations, and the sense of new ways of talking and acting that may be introduced. These new ways of talking and acting may very well at the same time involve modifications in the grammar, but we can only speak thus if the new grammar is (to its users) intelligibly related to the old.[12]

A society changes by redeploying its own moral and material resources. How this happens is formulated by its historians and social scientists, who may well find certain institutional arrangements more fundamental than others in the narrative they recount. But it is far from obvious that human history is the study of a reality behind the affairs men take themselves to be engaged in, albeit without complete control. Historical study is rather like Max Weber's study of the relationship between capitalist economic behavior and certain Protestant beliefs. Thus, as Louch points out in a grudging defense of Winch, Weber's study is misconceived as a project of discovering statistical relations between capitalism and Protestantism, and yet it is not simply an exercise in a priori conceptual analysis.[13] Weber to the contrary, his own explanatory practice was neither statistical nor empathetic *verstehen*: It was reasoned inquiry into the moral consequences of holding certain religious beliefs, such as the doctrines of predestination and the calling, which could then be used to justify the cycle of saving and investment in profit-making industries. So conceived, history and sociology are ethical studies. They seek to show the logical relations—Weber spoke of affinities (*Wahlverwandschaften*)—between important practices in a society that are explained by showing how certain principles at work in it could justify the particular practice that comes under study:

> If this is the way the historian and sociologist go about their business, their explanations do not require further evidence in the way that an account of physical movement is acceptable only if it extends to or embraces further cases. The way in which the background relates to the actions within which they are performed is not causal or statistical. Nor does it have the kind of opacity which requires the invention of theoretical "models" to render the relation between them intelligible. *The explanation is instead moral; i.e., it presents features of the background as justifying or providing grounds for the action.*[14]

In respect to Winch's claim that inasmuch as sociological understanding involves conceptual analysis it is more like philosophy than empirical science, Louch makes the following observations.[15] Winch's argument is strongest where sociological understanding involves ad hoc reference to settled institutions, conventions, rules, and habits. But it does not tell us how the sociologist or anthropologist goes about acquiring knowledge of institutions and practices that are removed from everyone's knowledge and not clearly formulated even among members whose lives and occupations may be patterned by them. Moreover, institutions and conventions, although superficially the same, change over time and from society to society. Winch's method of conceptual analysis does not help with empirical studies of historical and comparative variations in conventions. Indeed, it seems as though in stressing the contextual features of explanation and understanding, Winch has lent to Wittgenstein's insistence upon their function an aprioristic rather than strictly empirical injunction to look and see how they work in practice. Weber could not presume upon capitalist institutions for the background sense of Calvin's *Institutes* and Franklin's autobiography. The issue is how well it can be argued that these texts exhibit ways of ethical reasoning that might be used to justify or legitimate a mode of practical reasoning about the primacy of profit in economic affairs. The cogency of Weber's argument is not rendered by trying, as he himself did in his methodological writings, to cast it in the form of a causal-probabilistic design. Nevertheless, it was necessary for Weber to do a great deal of historical research into the nature of markets, money, rent, and property in order to grasp the nature of the institutional developments in the rise of capitalism. This enabled him to discern the points at which capitalism both required and fostered certain ethical justifications that later on it could do without. Thus Weber was well aware that profit making was an activity engaged in throughout the ancient and medieval world. What he set himself to explain was how profit making came to be justified on ethical grounds. The comparative perspective, once narrowed in terms of specific Protestant doctrines such as those of predestination and the calling, allowed him to identify a nonsacramental redemptive activity— saving and investing—that eased Protestant anxiety at the same time that it oiled the wheels of capitalist industry. We see, then, that Weber's argument had to meet certain restraints furnished by the materials of inquiry and that the plausibility of his famous theorem on the Protestant ethic and the spirit of capitalism lies very much with its very own economy of argument.

We might say, then, that a society is a set of internal moral relations, never wholly coherent, yet such that any direction of change it assumes cannot impinge upon it from wholly external sources. Thus, although there was a huge shift from feudalism to industrial capitalism, which was morally offensive to many, it was a shift mediated by changes in the religious consciousness of Western Christianity. The specific nuances of this development are available to us only through historical and sociological study. Gellner, however, reifies social change into a conflict between guardians and martyrs, in which the guardians fight hopelessly and blindly against wave after wave of deviants without whom the European tradition is unthinkable. Winch, then, is on the side of the Pope and the Inquisition. Gellner stands, if not with the angels, at least with the prophets and martyrs. They come from two different camps. But *there is nothing to explain their encounter* unless we withdraw Gellner's assumption that different societies, or stages of the same society, can be isolated by some comparative standpoint entirely external to them. But the sources of social change are found *within* societies. In other words, the critical practices of any society are not external to it, except for the romantic and alienated postures of its artists and scientists. This becomes all the more obvious once Gellner himself moves in on Winch for the kill. Then we find that what condemns Winch is that it is he who, after all, seems to have challenged the evident external standard of the *cognitive inequality of cultures*, a challenge that Gellner views only as an affectation of the study, having no relation to real life:

> The philosophical significance of the scientific industrial "form of life", whose rapid global diffusion is the main event of our time, is that for all practical purposes it does provide us with a solution of the problem of relativism—though a highly unsymmetrical one. (It is for this reason that no symmetrical solution can be entertained.) The cognitive and technical superiority of one form of life is so manifest, and so loaded with implications for the satisfaction of human wants and needs—and, for better or worse, for power—that it simply cannot be questioned.[16]

Winch, if we believe Gellner, is blind to reality and fails to comprehend the real working methods whereby social scientists lead men out of the closed society.[17] There is no word in Gellner about how it is that in fact so many critical theorists have turned to the Wittgensteinian analysis of language as an institution that might furnish a more radical grasp of the problems of power and repression in modern society.[18] In doing so, they have all treated Winch with more care than Gellner. And it is this aspect that we must try to understand. For I think there is a critical basis to Winch's view of the relation between language and society that can be developed to answer such critics as Gellner, whether or not in a version that Winch would necessarily adopt. Even the latter reservation might be withdrawn once we have elaborated Winch's position in terms of some Schutzian arguments.

From the very start, sociologists have wondered whether they had a method of their own. In their worst moments, they are inclined to wonder even whether they have a distinctive subject matter. The wolves at the door assure them that they do not have any worries not taken care of by history or economics. These cries make sociologists more nervous and even more determined to find their own way. But the severest temptations come from those who, like Peter Winch, help sociology to fight off the wolves of science by showing that human conduct cannot be represented in any other language (physicalistic, sociological, or whatever) than persons ordinarily use to convey the sense and purpose of their activities. The price of such defence is that sociology is subsumed by philosophy, once we see that the analysis of linguistic meaning is a philosophical and not a scientific undertaking. At first sight, Winch is an ally since he liberates philosophy from its self-imposed task as a scientific underlaborer, clearing the way to knowledge by stripping language of its idols, and reducing it to patterns of efficient communication, free of the knots of ordinary language. But this is a conception of philosophy that depends upon a false view of the relation between language and the world. It may well be that there is a contingent relation between the language of science (it is really a notation system) and the processes of nature. At least, it is quite possible to imagine nature outside scientific representations, though perhaps not apart from religious, magical, and poetic conventions. Scientists themselves are fond of speaking of the power of science to refer to its findings as in some sense independent of their expression.[19] They have spoken this way, however, not because it represents their actual practice but because it defends their interests against religion and the arts, which they sometimes consider sheer word play. Inasmuch as the social sciences have been concerned to fight for ideological autonomy, they too have tried to reduce the language of the social sciences to a notational system for the definition and explanation of social processes that are conceived as an extralinguistic material of investigation. Now that sociologists begin to weary of scientism, Winch is there to explain to them that they have to recover the autonomy of language and with it the competence of social actors. Once they see that there really are no scientific windmills to tilt at, they can sit at home with the good sense of philosophy's Sancho Panza.

Winch's story has been told often enough. It amounts to this: what we call "the world" has no existence for us apart from the language that provides the conceptual machinery whereby we articulate the world, its objects, persons, interests, values, and evils. Indeed, as Schutz argues, we actually deal with several "worlds." This is evident, once we stop to think of the worlds of our friends, relatives, and children; the world of the sick and dying; the world of fashion; the worlds of the particular sciences, physics, biology, economy, literature; the worlds of religion, magic, alchemy, and so on.[20] We know that we cannot gain access to these worlds without acquiring their language, just as a child senses he will never grow up unless he learns to talk like those around him. Of course, we persist in talking about "the world" and "language," as though we all spoke a common language with reference to a single external reality. In practice, however, we know that the world is "my world" and its extent limited by my command of language. We don't know what we can't talk about, although we may talk about things we don't understand very well, whether from reading newspapers, listening to lectures, watching television, or traveling abroad. We inhabit small worlds on the basis of a fine command of language that is nevertheless far below the requirements of scientific and literary discourse. No one agonizes about this in the ordinary course of affairs, although we may well admire and encourage anyone concerned to increase his knowledge and command of the language of particular sciences: "Remember that the language-game of everyday life underlies the various language games of science. And while each concrete scientific discipline and each sub-speciality has its own grammar, there is some overlap among these extraordinary (technical) languages and also an overlap with the language-game of everyday life."[21]

This is not to say that we are not sometimes limited in our enterprises because we lack the requisite conceptual discriminations. On such occasions, we may stand in need of science. Or there may be other occasions when we sense we are in trouble because the expressions we use are contrary to our intentions or exceed the limits of our language. This is frequently the case between children and their parents. The child's question "If God made everything, who made God?" usually produces a parental grunt, eked out with a grudging recognition of the logical fervor of children. But it is hardly likely to result in linguistic therapy to reduce the child's illegitimate totality claims. This is work for philosophers and is perhaps satisfying to them alone.

What is not the case is that our use of "ordinary" language in the conduct of our affairs that obliges us to be intelligible to others and responsible toward them for our actions—in other words, to risk the negative sanctions of being found incomprehensible or irresponsible—is totally inadequate for these very purposes. On the contrary, ordinary language is designed for nothing else and is therefore not to be regarded as a weak form of scientific language. The latter may well be suited to the pursuit of specific cognitive interests but is not adequate to the articulation of our everyday affairs: "When I talk about language (words, sentences, etc.) I must speak the language of everyday. Is this language somehow too coarse and material for what we want to say? *Then how is another one to be constructed?*—And how strange that we should be able to say anything at all with the one we have!"[22]

As Schutz observed, the questions that are real and important in everyday life do not require any philosophical or scientific address.[23] They are given to us as the framework of the linguistic community in which we grow up. They are not issues that, as it were, lie behind language. Rather, they arise only for persons who are sociolinguistically competent. Such persons seek to convince others of their participation in communal tasks as a moral accomplishment that confirms their own identity while affirming the collective way of things. In short, there are no private ethics, any more than there are private languages. This does not mean, however, that a community may not differentiate public and private spheres, as well as articulate a language of rights and obligations respective to each domain. What it does mean, despite Rousseau, is that no man has a language of the heart that is prior to the social contract. On the contrary, as Durkheim saw better than Rousseau, we need a complex division of social labor in order to create a society with the moral density that permits the quest for personality and authenticity for some, if not for everyone.

Winch builds upon Wittgenstein's notion of rules that claims that language is a constitutively social achievement and not the work of private persons. It is necessary to be very clear about what this involves. It means that we never deal with human conduct as though it were something with an inside all of its own that has to be deciphered in any way that an ingenious social scientist can devise in order to bring it to a public level of understanding. An action, an emotion, an idea, a promise, or an insult counts as nothing unless it has a social setting of which the agent is cognizant and toward which he is oriented, as though toward a rule of expression. This does not mean that an action or emotion may not be misunderstood. Indeed, it is only in terms of the notion of a rule that it makes sense to speak of a misunderstanding, or a misfiring; but that is not the same thing as an act whose idiosyncrasy condemns it to meaninglessness:

> Imagine someone using a line as a rule in the following way:
> he holds a pair of compasses, and carries one of its points

along the line that is the "rule", while the other one draws the
line that follows the rule. And while he moves along the ruling
line he alters the opening of the compasses, apparently with
great precision, looking at the rule the whole time as if it determined what he did. And watching him we see no kind of
regularity in this opening and shutting of the compasses. We
cannot learn his way of following the line from it. Here perhaps one really would say: "The original seems to *intimate* to
him which way he is to go. But it is not a rule."[24]

What Wittgenstein or Winch might have added is that
anyone who was found to be playing with the notion of the
rule in this way would risk his or her claim to moral serious-
ness. If not discovered after all to be joking, and then willing
to concede the discovery, he or she might then face charges of
stupidity and thereby enter the path of moral degradation
that is the price of toying with collective representations. We
see, then, that the idea of human behavior's standing in need
of sociological clarification because it is otherwise inherently
confused at the base level is just a myth of social science and
its search for a dumb material of representation. In the social
world conduct that fails to be inherently meaningful, even if
misguided or awkward in some fashion, falls outside the pale
of society. But this is ignored by social agents to their cost. It
may sound banal to recall the story of the boy who cried
"wolf" too often. It is hardly so to children or to members of
minority groups whose experience of language convinces
them of its sanctioned use. It could only be overlooked by
someone bewitched by the scientific use of language in which
such identity concerns are supposedly absent.

Wittgenstein's conception of language consists in the discovery of the irreducibility of the connection between language and society. Language is a social institution, and it is
the accomplishment of individuals oriented ethically as well as
cognitively to its rules of useage. It is part of this position that
society does not wait upon the discoveries of science for its
intelligibility. The constitutively spoken nature of social life
means that its massive and ordinary intelligibility consists of
the very same practices that comprise its members' sociolin-

guistic competence. This saves sociology from scientism. For Winch, however, it justifies the dismissal of sociology altogether in favor of the philosophy of ordinary language as the proper instrument of social intelligence. Here, then, we have a potential double bind that I think Schutz can resolve for us. On the one hand, it is necessary to defend the autonomy of lay social theorizing via-à-vis the pretensions of scientistic sociology. The latter requires that its "materials" be free of any prior interpretation other than the formulation provided by sociological concepts. In this struggle critical sociology is happy to make alliance with the ordinary language philosophy of action, especially in its Wittgensteinian emphasis upon the social contexture of language. However, once it appears, to Giddens for example, that critical sociology thereby risks an "idealist" alliance with the self-sufficiency of lay versions of society and personality, the professional power of sociological language vis-à-vis ordinary language will be invoked: "Winch does not wish to argue that the sociological observer, in his attempts at explaining social conduct, must confine his vocabulary to that used by lay actors themselves. But apart from a number of passing comments, no indication is given of the relationship which exists between lay and technical concepts, nor, indeed, is it very clear why the latter should be called for at all."[25]

Winch takes it that the most general task of sociology is to examine the very notion of a "form of life," that is, the definite modes of meaningful action that prevail under specific forms of human association. However, rather than develop this line in accordance with a formal sociology such as that of Simmel or Goffman,[26] Winch chooses to rest upon Wittgenstein's formulation "what has to be accepted, the given, is—so one could say—forms of life."[27] He uses this formulation in order to make the claim that the heart of sociology is philosophical business and that it is entirely misplaced elsewhere. Of course, it is necessary for Winch to show that Wittgenstein's analysis of language can be extended to treat other forms of social interaction. So he chooses to deal with Max Weber's conception of specifically human action defined in terms of conduct to which an agent assigns a subjective sense that in the light of his circumstances appears as the "reason" for his behavior. A man is sometimes mistaken about his reasons for acting, both in the sense that what he takes to be the outcome of his action, say, bringing about industrial peace by voting for the Labour party, and that his motives for voting Labour, which may be less than purposive in the first sense, perhaps express merely sentimental ties to his father's values. But such cases, in the first instance, only make sense provided that there are occasions when a man's actions *do* have the sense he gives to them, and, in the second case, where it is possible for him to understand what it means for an observer to say that he voted from habit, sentimental ties, or even unconscious aggression toward his father:

> If you are led by psychoanalysis to say that really you thought so and so or that really your motive was so and so, this is not a matter of discovery, but of persuasion. In a different way you could have been persuaded of something different. Of course, if psycho-analysis cures your stammer, it cures it, and that is an achievement. One thinks of certain results of psycho-analysis as a discovery Freud made, as apart from something persuaded to you by a psychoanalyst, and I wish to say this is not the case.[28]

An action may be counted meaningful in a technical language other than that of the agent, provided the agent can understand the observer's use of such concepts. Thus, it is not possible to understand the therapeutic goals of psychoanalysis unless the patient is accorded the ability to understand the concepts of Freudian analysis, although he would never use them in first-order expressions of motive. It is this requirement of social science explanation that lacks any counterpart in natural science. Schutz speaks of this principle as the *postulate of adequacy* and makes it a requirement of the proper conduct of interpretative sociology:

> Each term in a scientific model of human action must be constructed in such a way that a human act performed within the life-world by an individual actor in the way indicated by the typical construct would be understandable for the actor himself

as well as for his fellow-men in terms of commonsense interpretation of everyday life. Compliance with this postulate war-
rants the consistency of the constructs of the social scientist
with the constructs of commonsense experience of the social
reality.[29]

This, of course, is a postulate that the protagonists of scientistic sociology would be unwilling to observe. They would see
in it nothing but a hindrance to the formation of scientific
theories that cannot possibly be tied to common sense in this
way. They might well be confirmed in this belief, in view of
Winch's use of the postulate of adequacy to deny to sociology
any other status than a philosophical enterprise. Indeed, I am
arguing that Winch, by overlooking his relations to Schutz,
misses the fully critical implication of his own arguments.

Consider once again Winch's voting example. Suppose
we say a man voted Labour as an act of unconscious aggression toward his father. Is such aggression a reason or a motive
for acting in this way? Winch would say it is not a reason in
the sense of a *cause* for action inferred by the agent from what
he knows about the relations between voting, his father's expectations of him, and the like.[30] He says that it might well be
a motive, however, in the sense that to vote contrary to his
father's expectations was something the agent wanted without
either knowing exactly why or being able to give any justificatory reasons. Winch believes that when we find an action condemnable we are more likely to look for its motives than its
justifying reasons. In the present example, it would be odd for
the agent to justify his disappointing voting behavior as the
result of "unconscious" aggression, though one can imagine
his seeing his anger against his father as something making
sense of many seemingly odd acts of his done previously, but
without any such confrontation as in the voting case. Now
Winch wants to say that an action done from condemnable
motives, although not being reasonable in the sense of justifi-
able, may nonetheless be *intelligible* in terms of modes of behavior familiar in our society. Thus, in view of the way fathers
can abuse the authority given to them, and insofar as their
sons are often lacking in resources for self-expression and are

tempted to blame this upon their niggardly fathers, a son
might well vote Labour in the hope of threatening his father
with some redistribution of power between them. Anyone living under such institutions would find this intelligible. In my
view, they might even find it *reasonable* in the sense of justifi-
able because they believe that paternalism is intolerable and
should be removed. It then depends upon which side of the
convention one stands as to how one characterizes the son's
aggression. Given the status quo, it is a condemnable "motive"
that will be regarded as irrational, if not unconscious, by
those in authority. In this context, the submissive agent will be
encouraged to speak of his own motives as "unconscious."
However, once there is a general challenge to paternal authority, it becomes liberating to recognize the sources of one's anger, and therapeutic to vent it upon an appropriate figure
rather than to be consumed by it. In short, *there are changeable
ratios in the grammar of reason, motive, and cause that depend upon
the degree of reflexivity in individuals and the openness of their institutions to such critical appraisals.* In the voting example, because
of the interpretation of everyday language by at least vulgar
Freudian concepts, most people would find it intelligible to
connect political behavior with the oedipal relations between
father and son, at least insofar as questions of general resources are concerned, whether or not they would consider
access to mother to be the cause of causes. Where serious differences over the logic of political institutions or the property
system might occur would be in differential evaluations regarding strategies of reform. Given that family life and the
property system are intimately related, what is the best way to
achieve an analytical understanding of these relationships,
and what in practice, is the best place to attempt changes?

We should set aside this rather overburdened case for
now. Suffice it to say that the critical discussion suggested by it
becomes wholly fictitious unless we devise discursive scenarios
for an exchange between the relevant parties to the case,
where each is considered competent to address his own motives and reasons, and each is aware of the interplay between
individual and institutional resources, including the problem
of asymmetry, oppression, and unequal power. In short, it

would be necessary to pursue the discussion in the framework of what Habermas has called an *ideal speech situation*.[31] Only in that way can we grasp the dialogic preconditions of critical reflexivity either as therapy or as institutional reform.

This is not the direction taken by Winch. He is concerned to limit the scientistic ambitions of sociology but not, on balance, to discourage the possibility of a critical interpretative sociology. Toward this end, Winch makes a double appeal to the *postulate of adequacy*, though he does not use this expression or in any way connect his argument with Schutz's formulation. Winch nevertheless imposes the adequacy rule upon the social scientist in relation both to the community of study and to his relations to his own professional community: "So to understand the activities of an individual investigator we must take account of two sets of relations: first, his relation to the phenomena which he investigates; second, his relation to his fellow scientists."[32] The regularities that a social scientist claims to find in the world can only be understood relative to given institutional contexts that provide the framework within which human beings act in such a way that it is in turn possible for the social scientist to speak at all plausibly of investigating the regularities of human behavior.[33] The social scientist, however, misinterprets these regularities as naturalistic events when in fact they are nothing but the sedimentations of the reasoned conduct of persons in society. But more. The social scientist's own conduct in making judgments about the sense and uniformity of human conduct is itself subject to similar interpretative rules. The scientific behavior of the sociologist can only be understood in relation to the maxims of scientific procedure that prevail in his own professional community. Indeed, it is the consensus prevailing in the community of scientists that enables the investigator to engage meaningfully in the work of first-order observation. However, we cannot speak without a regress when referring to the scientist's grasp of his own community's procedures for sense making as itself based upon observation:

> The phenomena being investigated present themselves to the scientist as an *object* of study; he observes them and notices cer-

tain facts about them. But to say of a man that he does this presupposes that he already has a mode of communication in the use of which rules are already being observed. For to notice something is to identify relevant characteristics, which means that the notices must have some *concept* of such characteristics; this is possible only if he is able to use some symbol according to a rule which makes it refer to those characteristics. So we come back to his relation to his fellow scientists, in which context alone he can be spoken of as following such a rule.[34]

What follows from this, although it is Schutz rather than Winch who saw it, is that the rationality assumption applied by sociologists to bring order into their observation of human nature ought to be regarded as a rule of procedure for the production of knowledge satisfying the standards prevailing for the production of the sociological corpus.[35] Rationality is therefore not a uniquely first-order construct of human behavior that the sociologist simply abstracts from his observations of persons in society. But Winch, unlike Schutz and Garfinkel, turns away from the study of the social sciences regarded as courses of practical reason.[36] This is because Winch believes that the double requirement of sociological explanation, namely, that, in addition to being referred to sense-making procedures in the scientific community, it must also be referred to the rules of sense making in the community that is his field of study—and to which there is no self-interpreting counterpart in the objects of natural science investigation—puts an end to sociology. It certainly places a particular *hermeneutic obligation* upon sociology and, to the degree that it is honored, makes it impossible to proceed with a scientistic version of sociology. At the same time, Winch anticipates that this obligation will in fact be shrugged off by social scientists, if the price of its observance is to reduce their practice to the kind of unreflective understanding that characterizes laypersons caught up in custom and in ultimate ignorance of the social forces shaping their lives. Winch must then rescue his own philosophical expropriation of social phenomena from the charge that it merely endorses commonsense address of persons and society and abjures anything like the reflexive task of the social sciences. So he insists that all he is saying is that, although the social sciences must use technical concepts not to be found in lay language (and here he seems to concede the continued existence of the social sciences), the use of these concepts, unlike that of those of the natural sciences, implies a previous understanding of the lay concepts that are constitutive of the phenomena of social investigation. Thus, although businessmen do not use such a technical concept as "liquidity preference," it has explanatory value only because it is logically tied to the notions businessmen use in the conduct of their affairs. Winch is not, incidentally, claiming that the economist's use of technical concepts presupposes anything like an empathic understanding of business affairs. What he means to say, I think, is that there is nothing in principle that prevents the businessman from giving a first-order account of his operations intelligible to the economists who, in turn, ought in principle to be able to communicate the sense of such concepts as liquidity preference to his business clientele. Indeed, such translations[37] occur all the time in consultancy, journalism, and conferences. I think we can best understand the sense of Winch's relativism, which has so exercised his rationalist critics, if we take it as part of his recognition of the ethics of social science investigation made necessary by its expanding practice that shows no signs of abating as the result of philosophical exorcism of any kind.

Winch is opposed to the ironies of the social sciences, their so-called estrangement-effect. Their practice is to ignore the competing ways of life in human society and to subject their different standards of self-interpretation to the overriding social science assumption of *utilitarian rationality*. Winch discusses the rationality assumption in connection with Pareto's distinction between logical and nonlogical action:

> "A logical action then is one that fulfills the following conditions: (a) it is thought of by the agent as having a result and is performed by him for the purpose of achieving that result; (b) it actually does tend to have the result which the agent envisages; (c) the agent has (what Pareto would regard as) good

(i.e., 'logico-experimental') grounds for his belief; (d) the end
sought must be one that is empirically identifiable."[38]

The presumption of scientific explanation—its imperialistic
rationalism—requires that magic be treated as poor science or
that martyrs be considered hedonists in the next life if not
this one. Indeed, everyone can furnish his or her own pet example of the kind of irony today's public is supposed to swal-
low, setting aside its own good sense in favor of the accounts
of crime, perversion, and idleness favored by social scientists
as keepers of the standards of social rationality.

    Winch objects to the social scientist's practice of *decontex-
tualizing* lay reasoning in order to make human behavior nothing but a sequence of strange uninterpreted events whose
sense is then reattributed to them insofar as they approximate
the rationality model of action favored by the social scientist.
Thus we might experiment, as comedians do, with an account
of men's running after a piece of pigskin filled with air, risk-
ing great injury to themselves in order to produce alterna-
tions of joy and misery in a crowd of bystanders who are
otherwise engaged in eating and drinking to cool themselves
in summer or warm themselves in winter. Such accounts by
systematically exploiting the removal of the rules of the game
that give these events the sense of a game of football may be
useful as an exercise in comparative sociology, as well as in the
practice of comedians or dramatists. Indeed, such *incongruity
procedures* are a powerful instrument for displaying the massive trust that persons have in the unchallenged course of
their lives. Precisely because of our ordinarily unthematic
grasp of social practices, there is a considerable danger in the
use of such dramaturgical concepts as that of "role" when em-
ployed by sociologists to suggest that social realities require of
us none of the sincerity we ordinarily invest in them.[39] In this
respect, Winch's position represents a strong moral defense of
the prima facie reasonableness of everyday practices: "The
only legitimate use of such a *Verfremdungseffekt* is to *draw attention* to the familiar and obvious, not to show that it is *dispens-
able* from our understanding."[40]

Winch perhaps goes too far in separating understanding and causal explanation. In practice, the two may be seen to be *complementary* aspects of human knowledge, excluding but presupposing one another.[41] We might think of the process of the quasi objectification of behavior through the use of statistical data and psychoanalytic and sociological concepts as a methodological device—a temporary estrangement of interpretative meaning—that is then reintegrated with the subject's understanding once the social scientist provides his or her final analysis. This is clearer in the practice of psychoanalysis than in sociology, where so much investigation is never reported to those affected by the studies. All the same, what the sociologist neglects to do in this direction, he is obliged to do on behalf of those who commission his studies. Here we have a political asymmetry, and Schutz's postulate of adequacy, or Apel's complementary thesis, serves to point this out. By the same token, we allow for the expansion of commonsense understanding through the accumulation of objectified scientific data, avoiding the false impression that interpretative understanding is always self-sufficient. Winch overstresses the internal relation between language and experience in order to defend lay understanding from external scientific explanation. In practice, commonsense understanding is capable of critical comparison, reflection upon facts, and removal of obvious contradictions. And the scientific community is not worlds ahead of it in this regard. Winch's objection to the exploitation of the *Verfremdungseffekt* is not simply an endorsement of unenlightened common sense. It is not a question of praising common sense rather than science. It is instead the insistence that commonsense knowledge of persons and society is a structure of ethical competence that could not conceivably be replaced by social science programs.[42] Winch defends this position, as I understand him, in his doctrine of the internality of social relations, although he risks giving it an idealist formulation, upon which Gellner siezed: "If social relations between men exist only in and through their ideas, then, since the relations between ideas are internal relations, social relations must be a species of internal relations too."[43]

We cannot separate language and social relations. For example the difficulty we sense in answering today whether we are "real" citizens arises because we sense that modern political relations are governed by instrumental considerations, subject to welfare repairs, that hardly meet the criteria for the old notion of citizenship. The term survives but we sense its hollowness, without being able to abandon the values it connotes. It is not that we think that our fellow men are only "pretending" to be citizens. We are expressing a common plight: those who wish to be citizens in modern society have particular trouble to realize the depths of that experience. The concept of citizenship, then, both generates and is generated by the particular conduct it describes-prescribes. Those who understand themselves to be citizens will in a variety of circumstances expect of one another certain acts that in turn are taken as evidence and confirmation of their citizenship. Thus it is possible to look at the particulars of behavior as descriptive evidence for the relations between citizens and to appeal to the concept of citizenship to accept or reject actions proffered as instances of it. This is not to deny that there is no behavior independent of the concept. It is rather to say that what behavior *counts* as citizenship rests upon the criteria of what is appropriate to citizens in a given society. What looks like an instance of war may simply be a skirmish, a patrol error, a reprisal, depending upon how governments choose to interpret it. Thus, in practice we observe complex arguments, exchange of missions, cease-fires, peace talks, all involved in finding whether or not countries are at war. Anyone who remembers his or her youth will remember similarly complex negotiations over whether so-and-so was really his or her friend and, of course, even greater discriminations to decide whether he or she was in love.

No one would think of calling in a social scientist, or a philosopher, to decide the issue of war or love. And this, as Winch would say, is because to make these discoveries is not like discovering that the law of gravity obtains with respect to the fall of objects within the earth's sphere. Furthermore, these examples may serve to show just how false it is to underestimate the complexity and reflexiveness that enter into lay reasoning. There may in fact be a desirable reversal of the status of commonsense and scientific reasoning. In a democracy, we take it that such decisions as whether to go to war may be reached with technical advice duly weighed, but not decisive. There seems to be little reason why this should not be the same for social scientists advising governments. Indeed, it is essential to the preservation of parliamentary democracy. Likewise, in our personal lives we would regard it as pathetic to find a man or a woman consulting a psychoanalyst in order to reach the decision to fall in love or to have children and raise a family. This does not mean to say that family psychologists may not have advice to offer on the problems of marital and parental relations. It is rather that we only resort to this advice when our own competence falters and that we should only contract to the therapeutic relation with the intent to restore our ordinary competence in everyday living. If social scientists have advice to offer us, it is because the social sciences are themselves practices that are part of the very culture they seek to analyze. It is this relationship that makes it practical and sensible for members to make use of them—not some other grammar of society.[44]

There is after all no intrinsic hostility between common sense and scientific knowledge once we understand these to be historical acquisitions, always relative to one another. Unfortunately, social phenomenologists have emphasized the static, if not conservative, aspects of what Schutz called "the stock of knowledge."[45] But Schutz himself has warned against this static bias:

> A word of caution seems to be needed here. The concept of finite provinces of meaning: world of art, of science, of work, of everyday life does not involve any static connotation as though we had to select one of these provinces as our home to live in, to start from or to return to. That is by no means the case. Within a single day, even within a single hour our consciousness may run through most different tensions and adopt most different attentional attitudes to life. There is, furthermore, the problem of "enclaves", that is, of regions belonging to one province of meaning enclosed by another. . . . To give an

example of this disregarded group of problems: any projecting
within the world of working is itself . . . a fantasizing, and involves in addition a kind of theoretical contemplation, although not necessarily that of the scientific attitude.[46]

Inasmuch as science and common sense build upon one another, common sense can only be ignorant in its mockery of
scientific failure, just as science would be blind to ignore common sense as an essential resource in its own working practices. There are, of course, social scientists who do not share
any of these worries. They presume upon the subject/object
model of investigation in which other subjects, persons like
them, are reduced to objects of study, interview, and tabula-
tion. Furthermore, the palpable sense of laypersons' activities
in their own minds is made to appear strange, confused, and
in essential need of reformulation according to scientific standards of adequate sense and rational efficiency. That the social scientist is himself partner to these very standards of
commonsense rationality and procedure that he judges to be
nothing but poor science is either overlooked or else recognized in the role-split between the scientist's own civic and
professional attitudes. This split is often referred to as the
value neutrality of the scientist. It represents his or her com-
mittment to lines of scientific argument regardless of where
they lead him and his fellow citizens, whose moral beliefs,
families, pace of work, urban environment, and the like, are
subjected to the privileged pronouncements and interventions
of the social sciences. Today it is clear that citizens, consumers,
workers and students, as well as ethnic minority groups and
the women's movement, do not easily accept the implicit silence imposed upon them by those who claim to have the
blueprint for their lives. Those who are the guardians of the
official institutions that have been subject to citizens' questions, demonstrations, and civil disobedience are likely to see
in these events evidence only of the need for securing order
through even more rational social planning and legislation.
But what is really at stake in these political confrontations is
the breakdown of the privileged say-so of the applied social
sciences, whose dependence upon the physical science para-

digm prevents them from making any accommodation to the lively, self-interpreting presence of persons whose moral competence with their own affairs is injured by the passivity required of them by social science intervention. It is to such a critical common sense and its appropriate subordination of the practice of the social sciences within democratic institutions that we think Winch's idea of a social science makes a defensible contribution once we expand upon it in terms of Schutz's postulate of adequacy as rule for delimiting the privilege of social science discourse. We may then reformulate Winch and Schutz in terms of the following regulative principles for the production of a democratic knowledge-society:

1. Recognize the moral/rational competence of individuals.
2. Recognize that institutions are not on an entirely different rational/moral level from individuals.
3. Find a language of translation between institutional discourse and individual discourse.
4. Find a language of translation between scientific discourse and commonsense discourse.
5. Treat the institutionalization of the two languages of translation (3 and 4) as fundamental to the practice of democratic institutions.
6. Treat the rule of translation as a cross-cultural imperative in order to minimize the cultural imperialism of Western institutions and scientific discourse.

What Schutz's postulate of adequacy emphasizes is the fictionality of scientific reasoning and its ultimate dependence upon the commonsense communicative competence of the community of scientists in general and the larger lay society in which they live and work. Although Schutz's phenomenological descriptions may suggest a static division between scientific and commonsense knowledge, he in fact insisted upon the need to create mediating institutions between them, for each is "impossible" without the other. That is to say, in Western industrial democracies we are bound—in terms of our own "form of life"—to cross-fertilize common sense and science in every domain of experience. In this our science and our morality are inseparable. Yet we know that we increasingly suffer from the subordination of common sense and morals to expert knowledge and scientific neutrality. We do so at great peril to democratic institutions. It is precisely at this juncture that it is valuable to link Winch and Schutz to arrive at a set of regulative principles and practices that would confirm our will to democracy, which is currently the weak link in liberal and socialist societies. It must be recalled that Schutz saw each of us as simultaneously (1) the man or woman on the street, (2) the expert, (3) the well-informed citizen.[47] Thus each of us possesses a good deal of knowledge that is a collective legacy and not particularly the result of any inquiry of our own. We owe such knowledge to our family, school, community, newspaper, radio, television, books, and theatre, as well as to life's smaller conversations and experiences. Yet each of us possesses some specifically occupational or scientific knowledge in virtue of which we claim competences and rights on our own behalf while making similar concessions with respect to other's claims to expertise. At this level, we separate ourselves from commonsense street knowledge in order to amplify the total knowlege of society through specialization. Then, again, as well-informed citizens we seek to reembody in ourselves the best knowledge we can acquire in the general conduct of our affairs. But if this is to happen we need mediating institutions such as public education, honest journalism, and parliamentary democracy through which we may join in a common civic effort to enhance our humanity.

NOTES

1. Peter Winch, *The Idea of a Social Science, and Its Relation to Philosophy* (London: Routledge and Kegan Paul, 1958). A convenient collection of papers around Winch's argument and a bibliography are available in *Understanding and Social Inquiry*, ed. Fred R. Dallmayr and Thomas H. McCarthy (Notre Dame, Ind.: University of Notre Dame Press, 1977), pt. 3. "The Wittgensteinian Reformulation." See also Alasdair MacIntyre, "The Idea of a Social Science," in his *Against the Self-Images of the Age: Essays on Ideology and Philosophy* (Notre Dame, Ind.: University of Notre Dame Press, 1978), pp. 211–29.

2. Winch, *Idea of a Social Science*, p. 72.

3. Anthony Giddens, *New Rules of Sociological Method* (London: Hutchinson University Library, 1976), p. 79. See also John O'Neill, "Mutual Knowledge," in *Changing Social Science: Critical Theory and Other Critical Perspectives*, ed. D. R. Sabia and G. Wallulis (Albany: State University of New York Press, 1983), pp. 53–70.

4. Winch, *Idea of a Social Science*, p. 89.

5. John O'Neill, "The Mutuality of Accounts: An Essay on Trust," in *Theoretical Perspectives in Sociology*, ed. Scott G. McNall (New York: St. Martin's Press, 1979), pp. 369–80.

6. Ernest Gellner, "The New Idealism—Cause and Meaning in the Social Sciences," in *Positivism and Sociology*, ed. Anthony Giddens (London: Heinemann, 1974), pp. 129–56. For a defense of radical anthropomorphism as a necessary communicative practice, see John O'Neill, *Five Bodies: The Human Shape of Modern Society* (Ithaca, N.Y.: Cornell University Press, 1985).

7. Despite his appeal to physical and medical models, Freud seems also to have believed that psychoanalytic understanding depends upon the agent's linguistic competence. He puts it as follows: "Our understanding reaches as far as our anthropomorphism." *Minutes of the Vienna Psychoanalytic Society*, ed. H. Nunberg and E. Federn, vol. 1, 1906–1908 (New York: International Universities Press, 1962), p. 136.

8. Gellner, "New Idealism," p. 131.

9. Ibid., pp. 133–34.

10. John O'Neill, "Marxism and the Two Sciences," *Philosophy of the Social Sciences* 11, no. 3 (Autumn 1981), pp. 1–30.

11. For an account of how moral change arises within social systems, see P. F. Strawson, "Social Morality and Individual Ideal," *Freedom and Resentment, and Other Essays* (London: Methuen, 1974), pp. 26–44.

12. Peter Winch, "Understanding a Primitive Society," in *Understanding and Social Inquiry*, ed. Dallmayr and McCarthy, p. 174.

13. A. R. Louch, "The Very Idea of a Social Science," *Inquiry* 6 (1963), pp. 273–85.

14. Ibid., p. 276. My emphasis. Louch then says that the relationship between moral facts, although *logical* and thus seeming to support Winch, is nevertheless only discoverable *empirically*, or else history and sociology evade their obligation to provide descriptions and comparisons that provide intelligible grounds for explaining conduct by appeal to conventions or justifying practices prevailing in a given society.

15. A. R. Louch, *Explanation and Human Action* (Berkeley and Los Angeles: University of California Press, 1966), pp. 164–65; also "The Very Idea of a Social Science," pp. 273–86.

16. Gellner, "New Idealism," p. 155.

17. I have expressed my position on the question of the comparative inequality of cognitive cultures in my introductory essay, "Scientism, Historicism and the Problem of Rationality," in *Modes of Individualism and Collectivism*, ed. John O'Neill (London: Heinemann, 1973).

18. See Albrecht Wellmer, "Communication and Emancipation: Reflections on the Linguistic Turn in Critical Theory," in *On Critical Theory*, ed. John O'Neill (New York: Seabury Press, 1976), pp. 231–63; John O'Neill, "Decolonization and the Ideal Speech Community: Some Issues in the Theory and Practice of Communicative Competence," in *Critical Theory and Public Life*, ed. John Forester (Cambridge, Mass.: MIT Press, 1986), pp. 57–76.

19. John O'Neill, "Some Issues in the Realist Use of Science," in *Realizing Social Science Knowledge*, ed. B. Holzner, K. Knorr, and H. Strasser (Vienna: Physica-Verlag, 1983), pp. 64–70.

20. O'Neill, *Five Bodies*.

21. Derek L. Phillips, *Wittgenstein and Scientific Knowledge: A Sociological Perspective* (Totawa, N.J.: Rowman and Littlefield, 1977), p. 109.

22. Wittgenstein, *Philosophical Investigations* (Oxford: Basil Blackwell Publishers, 1953), I: 120.

23. Alfred Schutz, "The Problem of Rationality in the Social World," *Collected Papers* II: *Studies in Social Theory* (The Hague: Martinus Nijhoff, 1964), pp. 64–90.

24. Wittgenstein, *Philosophical Investigations*, I: 237.

25. Giddens, *New Rules*, p. 49.

26. See John O'Neill, "On Simmel's Sociological Apriorities," *Phenomenological Sociology, Issues and Applications*, ed. George Psathas (New York: John Wiley and Sons, 1973), pp. 91–106.

27. Wittgenstein, *Philosophical Investigations*, II: xi, 226e.

28. Ludwig Wittgenstein, *Lectures and Conversations* (Berkeley and Los Angeles: University of California Press, 1972), p. 27.

29. Alfred Schutz, "Common-Sense and Scientific Interpretation of Human Action," *Collected Papers*, vol. 1 (The Hague: Martinus Nijhoff, 1967), p. 44.

30. The analysis of the relation between reason, cause, and motive is not settled, and I do not pretend to contribute to it. However, I do not think that the ordinary senses of reason and cause need to be separated. See Donald Davidson, "Actions, Reasons, and

Causes," *Journal of Philosophy* 60, no. 23 (November 7, 1963), pp. 685–700. I also think that the self-interpretative or teleological nature of ordinary discourse makes it unnecessary to separate desire, sensation, and intention. See Charles Taylor, "Explaining Action," *Inquiry* 13 (1970), pp. 54–89.

31. Jürgen Habermas, "Toward a Theory of Communicative Competence," in *Recent Sociology, no. 2, Patterns of Communicative Behavior*, ed. Hans Peter Dreitzel (New York: Macmillan, 1970), pp. 115–48. See also John O'Neill, "Decolonization and the Ideal Speech Community."

32. Winch, *Idea of a Social Science*, p. 84; see also note 4 above.

33. See H. T. Wilson, *Tradition and Innovation: The Idea of Civilization as Culture and Its Significance* (London: Routledge and Kegan Paul, 1984), for a remarkable reading of Wittgenstein and Weber on our form of life and its conception of scientific rationality and technical progress.

34. Winch, *Idea of a Social Science*, p. 85.

35. Harold Garfinkel, *Studies in Ethnomethodology* (Englewood Cliffs, N.J.: Prentice-Hall, 1967); Aaron Cicourel, *Method and Measurement in Sociology* (New York: Free Press, 1964).

36. John O'Neill, "From Phenomenology to Ethnomethodology: Some Radical 'Misreadings'," in *Current Perspectives in Sociological Theory*, vol. 1, ed. S. G. McNall and G. N. Howe (Boston: JAI Press, 1980), pp. 7–20.

37. Stephen P. Turner, *Sociological Explanation as Translation* (London: Cambridge University Press, 1980), nicely defends Winch to a considerable degree along these lines.

38. Winch, *Idea of a Social Science*, pp. 97–98.

39. For an appraisal of the emancipatory and destructive options in the dramaturgical approach to persons and society, see John O'Neill, "Self Prescription and Social Machiavellianism," *Sociology as a Skin Trade: Essays Towards a Reflexive Sociology* (New York: Harper & Row, 1972), pp. 11–19. This essay treats the works of Erving Goffman and Peter Berger.

40. Winch, *Idea of a Social Science*, p. 119.

41. Karl-Otto Apel, *Analytic Philosophy of Language and the Geisteswissenschaften* (Dordrecht: D. Reidel, 1967), p. 23.

42. This is argued at length in John O'Neill, *Making Sense Together: An Introduction to Wild Sociology* (New York: Harper & Row, 1974). See also, Alvin W. Gouldner, "Sociology and Everyday Life," in *The Idea of Social Structure: Papers in Honor of Robert K. Merton* ed. Lewis A. Coser (New York: Harcourt Brace Jovanovich, 1975), pp. 417–32.

43. Winch, *Idea of a Social Science*, p. 123.

44. John O'Neill, "Sociological Nemesis: Parsons and Foucault on the Therapeutic Disciplines," in *Sociological Theory in Transition*, ed. Mark L. Wardell and Stephen P. Turne (Boston: Unwin Hyman, 1986), pp. 21–35.

45. Peter L. Berger and Thomas Luckmann, *The Social Construction of Reality: A Treatise in the Sociology of Knowledge* (New York: Doubleday, 1967), chap. 2.

46. Schutz, "On Multiple Realities," *Collected Papers* I, p. 253.

47. Alfred Schutz, "The Well-Informed Citizen: An Essay on the Social Distribution of Knowledge," *Collected Papers* II, pp. 120–34.

PART III

Tripping Rationality: Strategies for Seeing What Is Too Close by Looking from Afar

WEIGHING ANCHOR: POSTMODERN JOURNEYS FROM THE LIFE-WORLD

MICHAEL J. SHAPIRO

INTRODUCTION: THE TERMS OF THE DEBATE

For some time, the debates over the politics of postmodernism have tended to be debates over the way to treat representation. The more conservative postmodernists, reacting against radical modernist styles, have preached a return to "representation," which they understand as a close connection between what "is" and the style of expressing it. The more radical forms of postmodernism, such as poststructuralist postmodernism, advocate a different view. Eschewing a truth-falsity axis for treating representations, they focus on the domains of power and authority with which various modes of representation are complicit.[1]

This latter focus, which is central to the contributions of the more radical forms of postmodernism to political insight, cannot be easily domesticated within traditional epistemological conceits. Even the more recent epistemological positions developed by critical theorists, who have abandoned correspondence theories of truth in favor of more dialectical or conversational models, fail to come to terms with the political impetus of this kind of postmodernism. For example, in a critique of Lyotard's influential treatise on postmodernism, Seyla Benhabib charges that he conflates power and validity (the kind of charge that has been characteristic of critical theorists' reactions to the poststructuralist version of postmodernism in general).[2]

This is not the place to treat what I regard as the many misconceptions in Benhabib's treatment of Lyotard's arguments. What is central to her reading is her attack on Lyotard's position that language moves are power moves. Here she displays a tendency to assume that discourse is primarily a face-to-face, conversational exchange of intentionally controlled meanings (for example, she refers to the effects a speaker "wants to generate").[3] Because of her focus on language as conversational communication, she infers that Lyotard is equating the persuasive effects of a statement (what Austin calls the perlocutionary level of meaning) with the illocutionary or meaning force of the statement (the speech act or what is done in saying something).[4]

But Lyotard recognizes, as indeed Austin did, that what gives a statement its force is not merely its psychological correlates but the institutional context in which it is uttered. Like other postmodernist thinkers, Lyotard recognizes that statements are situated in structured interpersonal relations. Power and authority regulate their circulation and contextualize their meaning and value. At present, therefore, their use value cannot be separated from the power configurations that characterize modernity. Moreover, because meanings exceed what speakers may want to do with statements, persuasion is as much a function of who is speaking and under what circumstances as it is of whatever personally motivated markers may exist in the statement. To erect the conversational genre as the context in which to apprehend the postmodernist treatment of discourse is to create a dehistoricized and decontextualized frame that cannot adequately encode the politics of postmodernist analyses. To appreciate the politics of postmodernism, one must become alert to the depth politics of linguistic forms rather than simply heeding their intentional or strategic usage.

THE POLITICS OF LINGUISTIC FORMS

There is a tension between participation in a collectivity and analysis of it, between the linguistic competence one

needs to join in intelligible conversations and the linguistic resources one needs to create discursive practices productive of
political insight. In everyday life this tension tends to be suppressed because the achieving or exercising of a competence
in the dominant social forms of intelligibility is the major social problematic. In the case of children or others in marginal
positions (such as recent immigrants) the phenomenology of
everyday life is organized around showing one's eligibility for
full participation within the institutionalized forms of intelligibility. The objects and events that dominate their mental lives are produced within the motivated conceptual space
of seeking full membership. However, even those with full-
fledged social credentials often remain in a membership-
oriented praxis because negotiating one's way through a
complicated public space requires an energetic exercise of acquired interpretive and conversational skills.

To the extent that a culture is well articulated, that mutual expectations are readily discernible, and insofar as people's situations and tasks are represented unambiguously, the
tensions associated with resistant, insurrectional, or merely
questioning modes of interpretation remain suppressed. And
there are few day-to-day occasions in which the tensions are
revealed, for most linguistic genres, whether presentational or
interactive in form, are merely communication-oriented; they
emphasize joint task achievement rather than rendering problematic the society's systems of meaning and value.

In this context, those less socially accommodative genres,
among which are the poetic and aesthetic, are especially note-
worthy. For example, in the case of a play, it is the very form
of its relationship to discourse that produces a distance between whatever communicative functions are involved and the
interpretations that are engendered. Because those attending
a play are at once audience and spectator, they are able to
perceive that the ownership of actions is problematic. This is
because, as Jameson has pointed out, there are at least two
domains of the production of facticity, that which is voiced
and that which is seen.[5] With two different voices, the verbal
and visual, one gains insight into the constructed nature of
events. Unlike participation in a conversation, in which mean-

ings are achieved and shared rather than observed from a distance and contrasted with practices, significance in the play becomes an issue as verbalizations and actions are distanced from those who commit them.

The play thus affords the audience a distancing or analytic capability that is difficult to achieve in those other linguistic forms in which one is less able to perceive how discourse is situated. Nevertheless, despite its limitations, conversational imagery predominates in many interpretive and critical genres of social analysis. This is worthy of scrutiny, especially in connection with debates over the politics of postmodernism, in which questions of the epistemological status of conversations hold center stage.

THE PROBLEM OF CONVERSATION

In the midst of a discussion about poststructualism, Michel Foucault's interviewer from the journal *Telos* evoked the concept of postmodernity. In response Foucault remarked, "What are we calling post-modernity? I'm not up to date."[6] To grasp the ironic turn of Foucault's remark we must recognize its different levels. At one level, it is a remark about him. He seems to be saying that because he is not au courant, he is not prepared to discuss the issue. Indeed, seizing on only this simple level, his interviewer produces a long soliloquy on the concept of postmodernity. At another level, however, the remark is not an observation about personal knowledge but a more general, epistemological point. Foucault is saying that "we," those of us situated in this historical period, cannot understand our age if we remain within contemporary conversations. Foucault's playful response is therefore more than merely dismissive. It becomes significant and theoretically provocative when considered in the context of the different genres in which Foucault expressed himself in his last years. On the one hand, there were his writings, historical analyses that both situate and defamiliarize, or make remarkable, contemporary conversations. On the other, there were his public conversations, the increasingly frequent interviews on his work and its relationship to contemporary intellectual and political positions. Foucault's remark has the effect of announcing that there is an ironical dimension to such interviews, for his work is, among other things, a concerted effort to distance us from contemporary conversations; its logic cannot be elaborated easily in a conversational mode, which necessarily treats the present situation as a shared and unproblematic background, which facilitates conversation, rather than as part of the problem for investigation.

Foucault's unusual perspective on the conversation is addressed obliquely in several of his well known historical works, but it achieves optimal lucidity in a brief and rarely noted essay on the origin of contemporary preoccupations with "criminal danger."[7] There his initial object of analysis is a 1975 conversation in a Paris criminal court, the interrogation of a defendant accused of several rapes and attempted rapes. When questioned by the presiding judge—"Have you tried to reflect upon your case?" "Why at twenty-two do such violent urges overtake you?" "Why would you do it again?" and so on—the accused remains silent, and his silence impedes a judicial process, which in the modern period registers its interest in "the criminal" by asking the accused to elaborate his or her self-understanding. Summarizing the import of the judge's question as "Who are you?" Foucault points out that this kind of question, which is perfectly intelligible and appropriate in modern tribunals, "would have a strange ring to it 150 years ago."[8]

Prior to the nineteenth century, criminal law paid attention only to the offense and the penalty, whereas the new criminology peers through the crime, which has become "but a shadow hovering about the criminal, a shadow which must be drawn aside in order to reveal the only thing which is now of importance, the criminal."[9] In showing, with this exemplary conversation, that legal justice today is focused more on criminals than on crimes, Foucault is distancing us from the conversation in order to show that what we have come to regard as perfectly normal and intelligible is the result of some significant historical changes. He then proceeds to take us back to the early nineteenth century to elaborate some stages in "the psychiatrization of criminal danger," which created and legitimated "discussions between doctors and jurists." It is shown that this new field of knowledge of criminals was correlated with other developments, for example, "the intensive development of the police networks, which led to a new mapping and closer surveillance of urban space and also to a much more systematized and efficient prosecution of minor delinquency."[10]

Without considering various aspects of the political context of crime, which Foucault's analysis helps to disclose, we see, at a minimum, that his analysis situates the courtroom conversation in a highly politicized field of power relations and, further, that such a field is not easily recoverable within the confines of contemporary conversations. If we become involved in the conversation, we are drawn into the issue bothering the court during this 1975 case: whether it would be appropriate to invoke the death penalty without a more elaborate understanding of the accused. But Foucault's approach to conversations counsels resistance to being drawn into the problematic governing communicative interaction. Instead it makes remarkable the conversation as a whole, allowing us thereby to perceive the emerging power and authority configurations that the identities of the conversation partners represent. It becomes evident that insofar as one remains within the conversation in the courtroom, one must accept the policy terrain already implicated in the intersection of psychiatric and penal discourses and thus ponder the properties of the "issue" of capital punishment. Encouraged, under the direction of Foucault's brief genealogy of criminal danger, to resituate the conversation within the more policitized space of modernity's novel approach to crime and the correlation of that approach with emerging structures of power and authority, one encounters a range of political insights unavailable within the confines of contemporary conversations.

THE HERMENEUTIC ANCHOR

Foucault's way of resituating this conversation and modern poststructuralist resistance to society's communicative coherences in general does not deny the positive role that figuring understanding as conversation plays in representing the process of accommodation among parties seeking to move toward concerted agendas. But it does politicize the issue of understanding. To explore what is politically at stake between hermeneutic and the more radical postmodernist modes of writing and inquiry, we can consider the different forms of delusion toward which they are addressed.

The difference between philosophical hermeneutics and postmodernist approaches to knowledge and inquiry can be assayed in connection with problems of distance and intelligibility, and the distance concept is the most telling, for hermeneutics is dedicated to overcoming it, whereas such postmodernist positions as Foucauldian genealogy are dedicated to creating it. In figuring the process of understanding as a kind of conversation, hermeneutics presumes that the hope of reaching understanding (conversational agreement) closes the distance between individual conversation partners and the common ground they share. The Nietzsche-inspired genealogical and deconstructive modes of analysis open gaps by disclosing two kinds of delusion that the process of conversation uncritically accepts. The first has been presented by Derrida in his continuous attacks on "phonocentrism": the thought encouraged by seeing ourselves as involved in conversations that are wholly present to us. As he put it in one of his earliest works: "The subject can hear or speak to himself and be affected by the signifier he produces without passing through an external detour, the world, the sphere of what is not 'his own'."[11]

Much of Derrida's subsequent philosophical work is dedicated to demonstrating the delusion of the ownership of the meaning of one's utterances. Meaning, according to Derrida, is controlled instead by a prescribed structure of signification, which precedes individual speakers or writers. For example, Derrida shows that whereas the linguist Emile Benveniste thought he was inquiring into the question of whether thought and language can be regarded as distinct, he unwittingly accepted an inherited philosophical vocabulary (including the notion of the "category"), which already holds them to be distinct.[12]

The second delusion is one that naturalizes the spatialization of the society within which speakers converse. Foucauldian genealogy defamiliarizes such modern spaces as the prison with two different kinds of stylistic gestures. The first is a historicizing move in which he shows how prisons were invented as part of a series of strategic knowledge practices committed to a surveillant form of normalizing power, and the second is a form of linguistic impertinence in which he consolidates his historicizing move, further imperiling the seeming naturalness of the present by recoding it. For example, to emphasize the present as a stage in the process of increased surveillance, he expands the notion of incarceration to include such "services" as social work, education, caring, and curing as part of a "carceral apparatus."[13]

These observations are not meant to deprive the hermeneutic tradition of its one distancing effect, a distancing from the traditional conception of knowledge. It should be recalled that a founding gesture of the hermeneutic tradition, as it is represented by Gadamer, is an attempt to distance us from a history of social thinking based on epistemology.[14] A major dimension of Gadamer's contribution to social theory is a dramatic shift from the problem of knowledge, on which explanatory social science is predicated, to the problem of understanding, which supports interpretive analyses. Whereas the epistemological tradition constructs knowledge as a problem of method for allowing subjects to attain truth about the natural or social world of objects and relations, Gadamer's focus is on the situating of subjects in a background of practices—scientific, artistic, legal, and so on—that express fundamental aspects of human identities and can only be discerned through reflection. Such reflection is engendered through events, through concrete attempts to become familiar with what is initially unfamiliar. These episodes of understanding have the effect of enriching people's conversations about themselves as much as they create broader spheres of mutual intelligibility.

What this approach has implied for the practice of inquiry is represented in, among other works, the ethnographic analyses of Clifford Geertz. The Gadamerian problem of un-

derstanding as well as the grammar of Gadamer's philosophical hermeneutics hover in the background of Geertz's plunges
into exotic terrains, and despite Geertz's occasional use of the
typical vocabularies of more empiricist traditions (hypotheses,
concepts, theories, and so on); Gadamer's more reflective orientation supplies most of the consequences Geertz adduces
from his studies. Indeed, even Geertz's writing style is aimed
at creating intelligibility where understandings are partial or
inadequate. His approach is quintessentially hermeneutic, as
is shown, for example, in his attempt to overcome what he
regards as a delusion in our political understanding of both
nineteenth-century Bali and his own culture from which he
writes. Providing a telling contrast with the political delusion
toward which Foucault's genealogical analyses are aimed, he
presents the nineteenth-century Balinese state as a system of
governance directed "toward the public dramatization of the
ruling obsession of the Balinese culture: social inequality and
status pride."[15] State functions such as treaty making and water irrigation become intelligible when he shows how they
conform to the Balinese pattern of ritual obligation.

   In such analyses, Geertz sees himself as one helping to
overcome a fundamental delusion of mainstream Marxist and
capitalist forms of political analysis: the delusion stemming
from the fact that we are too "impressed with command." Because we focus on direct relations of power "we see little
else."[16] Bali makes visible, by virtue of its display orientation,
what our conceptual orientation makes invisible: "What our
concept of public power obscures, that of the Balinese exposes; and vice versa."[17] The delusion Geertz overcomes is
therefore a poverty of meaning, which, he thinks, stems from
a failure to pay attention to culture, for Geertz believes that
"a country's politics reflects the design of its culture."[18]

   Foucault's analyses are addressed to a similar delusion,
our inability to see the functioning of power as a result of our
impoverished construal of the political domain. The prevailing construction of the political discourse, the ways of putting
controversy over power and authority into language, are mo-
nopolized by a narrow notion of the "political," for the idea of
power operating in the West has been tied for centuries to the

sovereignty discourse. To the extent that the history of political discourse has concerned itself with the limits of sovereign power and the other face of sovereign power, the exercise of individual rights, what have remained silent are other forms of power.[19] Just as one is misled by writing a history of sexuality as the history of prohibited speech, one is misled by treating the history of the political as the history of the limitation of sovereign power. Emphasizing how the creation of a particular discourse is an imposition of a form of order, Foucault refers to the way an entrenched discursive practice, in this case, the one involved in constituting the "political," creates an economy that has the effect of silencing alternative (discursive) economies, other ways of constituting political problems.

> In a society such as ours, but basically in any society, there are manifold relations of power which permeate, characterize and constitute the social body, and these relations of power cannot themselves be established, consolidated nor implemented without the production, accumulation, circulation, and functioning of a discourse. There can be no possible exercise of power without a certain economy of discourses of truth which operates through and on the basis of this association.[20]

Within the confines of the political discourse, which emphasizes sovereignty and rights, what has been silent are the controls and potential challenges and refusals immanent in the creation of the human subject as we "know" it. This is the human subject scripted not only by recognized disciplinary agencies such as medicine, social work, education, and the recognized carceral institution, the prison, but also by knowledge disciplines themselves—political science, sociology, psychology, biology, and so forth. The creation of identities by knowledge agents is, according to Foucault, disciplinary in a sense similar to the discipline emanating from what are recognized as social control agents. Knowledge agents, the human sciences in particular, act as relays for power by both monopolizing the discourse controlling what can be said and by whom and by helping to script the kind of identity or self-understanding that is docile in the face of demands from controlling social, political, and administrative institutions. In the absence of alternative discursive possibilities for constituting the self, one cannot oppose power because, to the extent that power is only thought within the confines of the narrow sovereignty/rights political discourse, it is represented as something else, as, for example, caring, curing, educating, evaluating, motivating, and resolving disputes. Without interrogating the power implications of discourses that produce the modern subject, one cannot question power because power is continually reinscribed, even within forms of knowledge that seek not only to disclose it but, ironically, to disavow it or at least escape its worst excesses.

Thus although Foucault, like Geertz, refigures—with such rhetorical gestures as identifying education and social work as carceral functions—the domain of the political, his approach departs radically from the interpretive methods of Geertz and others of the hermeneutic persuasion. Foucault is not seeking a frame of analysis that shows how the behavior of various actors can be recovered if we know their cultures or background fields of meaning and use a more informed view of culture. To interpret, according to Foucault, is to accept the "rarity" of sets of statements unreflectingly; it is to seek to find their underlying meaning rather than to undertake a more politicized inquiry into the discursive economies they represent. Accordingly, Foucault has sought not to improve extant political conversations by making them more comprehensive, but to distance us from the various linguistic practices that give us objects, subjects, *and* the more general valuing practices within which they function, the discursive economies of meaning and value in given historical periods.

Although Foucault does not deny a place for the kind of hermeneutics practiced by ethnographers such as Geertz, he warns that the history of the subject "is" the history of interpretations. Rejecting an expressivist theory of language, Foucault is not involved in "interpretation" (in the sense of recovery of the subjectivity expressed in meaning systems). Interpretations are Foucault's data, not his mode of inquiry. Therefore, the delusions (political and otherwise) with which Foucault is dealing are not misunderstandings. Rather he is highlighting what amounts to a metalevel delusion within which particular delusions are wrought. This is the delusion of understanding itself, the idea that there is a truth or unmediated level of meaning to be discovered, a resting place for the mind in a field of concepts that opens reality to us. Accordingly, Foucault separates himself from the traditional conception of ideology inasmuch as he is not criticizing something masking the truth but showing how the very production of "knowledge" and "truth" is linked to systems of power.[21]

One way of underscoring the contrast would be to note that the Geertzian unmasking is one that aims at gaps in our conversations about society in general and the political dimension of social process in particular. These gaps are overcome when we achieve the approproate figuration (what Heidegger called "the capable word"). Our conversations about what is exotic thus begin to coalesce with our conversations about ourselves, and, as a result, we are enabled in the sense of being able to have better, less deluded conversations about ourselves. Foucault's delusion is the delusion that provokes conversations in the first place. *Any* discourse constitutes a delusion inasmuch as it administers dimensions of silence as soon as it begins; it establishes practices that force out other possible practices.

It is more appropriate, moreover, to use the metaphorics of scripting rather than conversation to characterize Foucault's notion of discourse. The prevailing discourses are not parts of one's conscious awareness. Perspectives are prescripted in the sense that meanings, subjects, and objects are sedimented in the dominant and thus most readily available discursive practices. When we reference an object in an available discourse, we reproduce it unreflectively. And, because we (our available identities) are scripted into these same discourses, we end up telling various "truths" about ourselves, be they medical, psychiatric, or political truths. Ultimately, for Foucault, the only way for an individual to avoid subjugation is by disavowing power, by refusing to be the self that power has scripted for that individual. What this involves is not improving conversations but the construction of counterdiscourses, modes of writing that oppose the terms of power and authority circulated and recirculated in prevailing modes of discourse.

However, despite all of the antihermeneutic gestures in the Foucaultian approach, there are what I call *hermeneutic anchors* in Foucault's analyses. Foucault is an incessant politicizer; he thus wants to insinuate his analyses into conversations about politics and power. This much is clear from the very fact that Foucault is intelligible; although his analyses depart in many ways from ordinary discursive modes and thus create discomfort with the prevailing fields of analysis, they communicate; they engage at least part of the ways of thinking and speaking already in circulation. He has stated quite explicitly that we in the modern age fail to incorporate the workings of power into our predominant political discourse because we neglect the normalizing power of disciplinary agencies and systems of "knowledge." We fail to encode in our political talk the way that modernity has witnessed a structure of domination elaborated through the various mechanisms of power. These mechanisms are not to be understood as things operating from a distance in the control of the willed forces of individuals. Power is incorporated into our identities such that power functions through what is "known" about us.

This, then, is Foucault's main *hermeneutic anchor*. He commits his analyses to our ongoing discussion of politics and power. In arguing that the terms of the discussion have been disabling, he lines himself up with others, such as Geertz, who are also trying to improve our political conversation. Foucault's hermeneutic anchor is tossed out explicitly in several places, but one general characterization he has offered should suffice for purposes of this discussion: "The question I asked myself was this: how is it that the human subject took itself as an object of possible knowledge? Through what forms of rationality and historical conditions? And finally at what price? This is my question: at what price can subjects speak the truth about themselves?"[22]

This statement is primarily a description of the genealogical mode of analysis, and Foucault's treatment of knowledge as a power-related practice draws us out of our customary discursive distinctions. But when we reach the "at-what-price" portion, we are into the hermeneutic dimension of Foucault's project. We have been encouraged to recalculate the economies of the exercise of power within this altered way of representing the locus of power. Thus, genealogy reveals the process by which humans invest the world with value, but as soon as we assume that we are already *in* a kind of world, we begin to ask value questions *about* it, and this kind of question *about* value is a hermeneutically, not a genealogically, inspired kind of question. Within the hermeneutics of value questions, Foucault is asking about the political costs of a disciplinary society in which that discipline, which is a form of power, is disguised within depoliticizing forms of discourse. He is inviting us to weigh the costs of this modern, masked form of power that represents itself as something else. The bulk of his analysis is taken up with a figuration, the politics of the body, that alerts us to a delusion encouraged by a more pacifying form of imagery, but then the conversation about the price we have been paying is offered. What does it cost to be dominated and subjugated in the names of healing, curing, nuturing, and educating?

Once we appreciate the way the different modes of analysis, the hermeneutic and radical forms of postmodernism, position themselves in relation to problems of intelligibility, we are better able to locate the politics of postmodernity. Certainly there is a readily available "politics" in every society, the politics that exists in what are recognized as political conversations and is part of the reigning system of intelligibility. And any mode of social analysis tries to connect the intelligibility of these aspects of politics to a more distanced view, to connect, as it were, the life-world to a less hectic conceptual world of analysis. The politics of the life-world contains recognized forms of partisanship, cleavages that can threaten social solidarity but are, for the most part, constitutive of that solidarity.

With this as background, we can locate a hermeneutically oriented politics as a politics of reconciliation. Richard Rorty, for example, tends to endorse the hermeneutic view, using the conversation as his justification for moving away from the epistemological tradition. And Rorty wants an engaged hermeneutics, one that helps to resolve extant forms of partisanship, one that makes a connection with "the daily problems of one's community, that enhances communication and harmonious solidarity."[23] Accordingly, he chides Foucault for maintaining his distance from existing forms of partisanship, referring to him as a stoic: "It takes no more than a squint of the inner eye to read Foucault as a stoic, a dispassionate observer of the present social order, rather than a concerned critic."[24] And he goes on to complain of Foucault's "dryness," which he sees produced by a "lack of identification with any social context, any communication." Rorty also complains that Foucault affects to write "from a point of view light-years away from the problems of contemporary society."[25] Finally, he states that there is no "we" to be found in Foucault's writings, nor in those of many of his French contemporaries.[26]

THE VIEW FROM OFFSHORE

There are several misapprehensions in Rorty's plaints against Foucault, each of which joins with issues others (such as Habermas and Lyotard) have raised in debates over the politics of postmodernism. To begin with, Rorty is insensitive to the politics of radical postmodernism's grammar. He is indeed on to something when he looks unsuccessfully for a familiar "we" in the writings of Foucault and "in those of his French contemporaries," for what radical postmodernists are doing is questioning the familiar theoretical constructions of the life-world that fail to situate actors in contentious terrains of meaning. Like Habermas, Rorty sees the life-world as a set of conversations about contemporary problems, and, also like Habermas, Rorty cannot see the relevance to social criticism of thinking that challenges the grounds of those conversations rather than entering them within the terms of the contemporary debates.[27]

Whereas Rorty (and Habermas) emphasize one aspect of language, communication, and one aspect of a social formation, the shared background of practices that support conversations, Foucault and others emphasize the discursive economies of language, its effects in constituting privileged actors and locations for the exercise of control over meaning and value. And rather than seeing the life-world as a relatively uncontentious sphere within which "problems" are approached, they view it as a potentially contentious domain of *problematization*. The grammar here is significant, for Foucault shows how a particular range of recognized social problems, those that have achieved recognition within dominant modes of policy discourse, is only one set or kind of problem among a vast variety of possibilities. It is one thing, for example, to ask what is the appropriate policy to respond to "crime" and "sexual deviance" and another to show how contemporary modes for problematizing crime and sexual deviance are peculiar when seen in a particular kind of historical context.

The life-world, in which Rorty and Habermas valorize communicative competence and solidarity, is quite different in Foucault's construction of it. It is a pattern of volubilities and silences, of problems about which some communicate and nonproblems, alternative possible modes of problematization. Moreover, what constitutes competence—knowledge, expertise, eligibility—is a product of the way a given social formation in a given age carves up its spaces. To return to the example introduced earlier, psychiatric discourse has juridically relevant meaning *now*; it helps to constitute knowledge of "criminals" in the present age because of the way in which modernity problematizes crime. It is therefore politically vacuous to speak about an intersubjectivity as the ground of communication without situating subjects in the distribution of spaces—professional, delinquent, administrative, marginal, and so on—that direct the meaning, value, and authority of their utterances.

In light of this we can consider the problem of the "we." We, in radical postmodernist terms, are not all the same. The meaning of an utterance is not controlled by the intentions of the speaker. Rorty, in his emphasis on conversations among nonsituated speakers, appears to adopt, with Habermas, a grammar of subjectivity in which subjects intentionally produce meanings. Despite his attempts to transcend a subject-centered version of reason by resort to the idea of communicative action, which presupposes an intersubjective meaning context, Habermas's grammar remains relentlessly subjectivist. Even his recent call for a "paradigm of mutual understanding" is constructed with an intentionalist rendering of the subject-meaning relationship.[28] But Austin's speech act theory, heavily relied on by Habermas, does not lend itself to an intentionalist, communication-oriented gloss. Although Habermas speaks of communicating actors who "pursue illocutionary aims,"[29] what gives an utterance an illocutionary emphasis is not the intention of the speaker but (as pointed out previously) the context of the utterance. An utterance, for Austin, becomes illocutionary as a result of the rule-governed context in which it is made. Although Austin never got around to historicizing those "rules" and problematizing or making contentious those contexts, his approach to language does not license an intentionalist grammar of subjectivity. The grammar that emerges in the analyses of postmodernists is radicalized to construe subjectivity as a historically specific practice, as something epiphenomenal to meanings, not a function of the intentional actions of subjects.

There is indeed a "we" in Foucault's approach, which assumes that meanings make subjects, but it is not a unitary, univocal we but a fragile series of produced we's that are resident in the institutionalized forms of utterance, and hovering in the background are alternative possible we's. The politics of Foucauldian grammar thus rests on a Nietzschean way of posing questions about subjectivity; the question is never "who" but "which one," which of the multitude of possible selves is being brought into recognition by a particular institutionalized form of intelligibility and the practices it encompasses.

Rorty is also on to something when he notes that Foucault is operating from "a point of view light-years away from the problems of contemporary society."[30] Distance is indeed what Foucault's analyses achieve. In allowing us to see the present as remarkable, as a peculiar set of practices for problematizing some things and naturalizing others, for allowing some things into discourse and silencing others, Foucault's distancing recodes the present. It turns current "truths" into power-related practices by situating them in relation to alternative past practices and tracing the correlated economies of their emergence.[31]

This is not, moreover, the dispassionate observation of a stoic but a textual practice oriented by a commitment to freedom, a freedom that is not the traditional, liberal individualist model of minimizing the domain of controlled public space but the freedom that allows one to see the possibility of change. Foucault argues, "by following the lines of fragility in the present—in managing to grasp why and how that-which-is might no longer be that-which-is," it is possible to "open up the space of freedom understood as a space of concrete freedom, i.e., of possible transformation."[32]

In short, Foucault's analyses politicize what passes for the uncontentious; they take us outside the politics resident in contemporary conversations in a frame that makes them peculiar. In so doing his writing does not consort with the distribution of conversations locked within the all-too-familiar present set of recognized problems: "The problem is not so much that of defining a political "position" (which is to choose from a preexisting set of possibilities) but to imagine and to bring into being new schemas of politicization."[33]

CONCLUSION: WEIGHING ANCHOR

Recognizing the conversational basis of hermeneutical forms of analysis, Fred Dallmayr notes, "for hermeneutics, inquiry is routine conversation."[34] After explicating the details of hermeneutics, thus going a long way toward demonstrating the "linguisticality" of understanding, Dallmayr laments the strangeness of the "poetic idiom" to political life.

> While pragmatic language and discursive argumentation occupy an acknowledged place in public proceedings, the poetic idiom seems to be a stranger to political life. Yet, its strangeness does not render this idiom negligible or marginal—as long as politics is not reduced to the simple reenactment of established routines.[35]

By following Dallmayr's suggestion, one can find an escape route from the political space constituted in conversations. Thus here I will pursue a postmodernist strategy, a form of literary strategy that demythologizes the foundational codes through which the political boundaries and recognized controversies are reproduced. Recall that I began with some remarks on the politics of genre, which were designed primarily to put pressure on the conversation, especially to point to the limitations in regard to political insight that stem from one's inability to gain distance when confined within the discursive terrains that make intelligible conversations possible. I suggested that Foucault operates from a position offshore, that he has anchored in a strategic position that gives him distance but at the same time a strategic view of modernity's present. It is now time to weigh anchor and sail to another distancing location, to Robinson Crusoe's island, which will allow for an exemplary demythologizing that will articulate with the political impetus of radical, postmodernist writing. My focus here is on Michel Tournier's version of the Crusoe myth, a version that makes Friday one who subverts rather than aiding and abetting Robinson Crusoe's rationalization of the island terrain within the understandings afforded by political economy.

At its origin, myth is designed to legitimate an order by either rationalizing the origin of its construction or providing a view that naturalizes it. Subsequent retellings or commentaries also tend to have a legitimating function, for they are retellings complicit with the various discursive procedures through which prevailing structures of power and authority are implemented.[36] However, some "work on myth" is demythologizing, pressuring institutionalized sources of authority and value rather than encouraging allegiance to them. Such is Tournier's, which seems to operate within the postmodernist assumption that political economy has mythological rather than foundational legitimacy.[37]

Recent analysis of the issue of the mythologizing impetus of Defoe's original treatment is convincing. Rather than creating distance from the dominant conversations of his age, Defoe was valorizing them. His Robinson Crusoe is at a distance only geographically, for he reproduces and rationalizes the political and economic practices of his age. Indeed, despite the popular assumption that the original Robinson Crusoe was designed to celebrate a concept of a nature free of the busy commercial behavior of England, Defoe identified the domain of commerce *as* natural. As he put it, "Nothing follows the course of Nature more than trade. There Causes and Consequences follow as directly as day and night."[38] And there is little doubt as to what model of trade Defoe's story is meant to exemplify. As Ian Watt points out:

> Defoe's hero—unlike most of us—has been endowed with the basic necessities for the successful exercise of free enterprise. He is not actually a primitive or a proletarian or even a professional man, but a capitalist. He owns freehold, an estate which is rich but unimproved. It is not a desert island in the geographical sense—it is merely barren of owners or competitors.[39]

As is well known, many subsequent commentaries on Robinson Crusoe enlist the story as material for the historical conversation about alternative models of political economy. The classical political economists simply explicate their systems through Crusoe, whereas, of course, Marx uses him in his critique of these political economists to attack the mystifications involved in their theorizing of the commodity. For Marx, Robinson Crusoe was an exemplar of clarity, the meeting of a man and his labor capacity with a nature filled with abundance. The result is the unambiguous transformation of nature into need-satisfying goods, "useful objects for himself alone."[40]

But, as Jean Baudrillard has pointed out, Marx had not achieved the distance from the discourse of political economy he thought he had, for insofar as he assumed that there can be a transparency in "man's relation to the instruments and products of his labor," he accepts that part of "bourgeois thought" that fails to register the politics of representation.[41] As he has argued more thoroughly elsewhere, in his remarks about Marx on Crusoe, Baudrillard claims that Marx's treatment of Robinson Crusoe is parasitic on the discourse of po-

litical economy that he scorns.[42] Marx continues to write
within a discourse that represents the production and exchange of value within a society wholly within the terrain of
the economic. It is a discourse that, in Baudrillard's terms,
continues "the apotheosis of the economic."[43] Marx, like the
political economists whose commentaries on Crusoe are his
object, thus accepts the two major determinants of their argumentation: (1) the idea that one's relation to value is transpar-
ent or unmediated by representational practices and (2) the
quarantining of social value within the imagery of economic,
productive relations.

By contrast, the radical forms of postmodernist writing
are highly attuned to representational practices. Showing this
level of attention, Tournier gives us a Robinson Crusoe story
that achieves a significant distance from the perspectives on
political economy that have marked the capitalist and Marxist
discourses that, in Baudrillard's terms, "were born together, in
the historic phase that saw the systematization of both political economy and the ideology that sanctions it."[44] What
Tournier's novel *Vendredi ou les Limbes du Pacifique* does is offer
a parody that shows the limitations and self-defeating difficulties of a view in which political economy is the only way to
represent value.

The subtitle of Tournier's novelistic parody is important
because "the limbo of the Pacific" expression locates Robinson
Crusoe's island both spatially and temporarily in a place remote from Crusoe's home, the English society of the eighteenth century. Although there are a number of significant
implications inherent in Tournier's changes in the frame—for
example, moving the story from the seventeenth to the eighteenth century—what is most significant here is the way that
the limbo in which the island is placed allows Tournier to sub-
vert the Robinson Crusoe myth.[45]

The beginning problematic in the novel is Robinson Crusoe's solitude, but rather than reinforcing the myth of the natural autonomy of the individual, Tournier's Crusoe becomes
disoriented by his solitude once he fails in his initial attempt
to build a boat to escape the island. Deprived for a while of a
social context, Crusoe degenerates into an animallike crea-

ture, finally hitting bottom when he wallows in a mud hole. Then deploring his state of degeneration from the familiar human condition, Crusoe attempts redemption through administrative organization. He begins ordering and administering his island, having decided that his choices consist of returning to the mire or reproducing, as governor and architect, a wholly "humanized estate."[46]

In the process of constructing this estate, Crusoe lives out a mythical human historical narrative, starting as a hunter-gatherer and proceeding to the role of cultivator and herdman, not because this sequence is demanded by the necessity for food and shelter but seemingly out of a symbolic necessity. Insofar as he constructs what constitutes humanity on the basis of the political economy of eighteenth-century England, he is led to reproduce the up-to-date conditions of production and the narrative of human progress that legitimates those conditions in order to affirm his humanity and achieved modernity. Tournier's Crusoe is thus laboriously involved not simply in surviving in a remote place, but in naturalizing the political economy of his homeland, thereby bringing home what is spatially and temporally remote. He even goes so far as to "humanize" plant life, taking as a sexual partner a "quillac-tree," which has been blown over by the wind and whose bark is "smooth and warm, even downy" and which has "two branches thrusting out of the grass" that appear to him to be "huge, black, parted thighs."[47] Among other things, Crusoe's conjugal relations with the island represent another aspect of his attempt to reproduce a familiar self. He makes of the island a feminized other in order to regain his purchase on himself as a "man."[48]

It becomes evident that the man-woman relations that Crusoe establishes are just as entangled with notions of proprietorship on the island as they were in eighteenth-century England. His "vegetable way," as he expresses his self-conscious ambivalence about his relationship to the plant, is not confined to the sexual act itself. He takes a proprietory attitude to "his tree," referring later to sprouting plants nearby as "his children," and subsequently administering a severe beating to Friday when he catches him "making love" to "his tree."[49]

This is but one of Friday's many transgressions of the island administration. His arrival and subsequent playful disregard for Crusoe's administered spaces provide Tournier with the parodic material he needs and Crusoe with the reductio ad absurdum he needs to think his way out of the confining political and economic codes with which he has constructed his understanding of humanity and his administration of the island. After Friday's arrival, Crusoe reproduces the conditions of a capitalist system, using the money he saved from the wreckage of his ship to make Friday a wage earner. But although Friday seems to accept his status in Crusoe's strictly administered island, complete with a money system and a penal code, ultimately he subverts the system, destroying almost every aspect of Crusoe's rationally administered island, at the same time creating another kind of island, one dedicated to play rather than the duties of administrator and wage earner.

It takes some time for Robinson Crusoe to discover this other island. In the transition from stern island administrator to Friday's student, he evinces strong ambivalence before finally succumbing to "Friday's devotion and calm logic," allowing him to rid himself of his administrator's consciousness.

> there were times when the Governor, the General, and the Pastor gained the upper hand in Robinson, His mind dwelt on the ravages caused by Friday in the meticulous ordering of the island, the ruined crops, the wasted stores and scattered herds; the vermin that multiplied and prospered, the tools that were broken or mislaid. All this might have been endurable had it not been for the *spirit* manifested by Friday, the tricks and devices, the diabolical or impish notions that entered his head, setting up a confusion by which Robinson himself was infected.[50]

When eventually Crusoe's bafflement and ambivalence are replaced with recognition, what he is able to discern through Friday's subversion is that his administered island is but one among other possible islands. Friday has existed on such an other island all along, dedicated not to a system of rational exchange (which in any case makes little sense on the island with no market) but to an order based on play. Accordingly, he takes objects that have a high exchange value in eighteenth century England and uses them to decorate plants and then enlist them in his elaborate rituals of imagination. Once, with Friday's help, Robinson Crusoe discovers this other island and is thereby able to denaturalize his home, England, that is, he is able to see that political economy is but one possible model for representing value, he has extricated himself from the confines of his old domestic conversation. And, very much in the style of the intellectual orientation of radical postmodernist thinkers, Robinson Crusoe elects to remain at a distance. When a ship arrives and he is offered passage home, he decides to stay offshore, living in a world that had, before his tutelage under Friday, existed in the shadows of England's mythic discourse on political economy. For "us" (those involved in theorizing the language of analysis) it is not a question of choosing a permanent venue, either on- or offshore; it is a question of seeking distant terrains that are exotic to the extent that every homecoming (every subsequent conversation) takes on its meaning and value in a broader context of possibilities.

NOTES

I am grateful to Jane Bennett, William Connolly, Thomas Dumm, Kathy Ferguson, and Stephen White for their critical reactions to the first version.

1. For a discussion of the difference between radical and conservative forms of postmodernist thinking, see Hal Foster, "(Post) Modern Polemics," *New German Critique*, no. 33 (Fall 1984), pp. 67–78.

2. See Jean-François Lyotard, *The Postmodern Condition*, trans. Geoff Bennington and Brian Massumi (Minneapolis: University of Minnesota Press, 1984); and Seyla Benhabib, "Epistemologies of Postmodernism," *New German Critique*, no. 33 (Fall 1984), p. 114.

3. Benhabib, "Epistemologies of Postmodernism," p. 115.

4. The relevant work is John Austin, *How to Do Things with Words* (Cambridge, Mass.: Harvard University Press, 1962).

5. Fredric Jameson, *Sartre: The Origins of a Style* (New York: Columbia University Press, 1984). p. 27.

6. Gerard Raulet, "Structuralism and Post-Structuralism: An Interview with Michel Foucault," trans. Jeremy Harding, *Telos*, no. 55 (Spring 1983), p. 206.

7. Michel Foucault, "About the Concept of the Dangerous Individual in 19th-Century Psychiatry," *International Journal of Law and Psychiatry* 1 (1978), pp. 1–18.

8. Ibid., p. 1.

9. Ibid., p. 2.

10. Ibid., p. 12.

11. Jacques Derrida, *Speech and Phenomena*, trans. David Allison (Evanston, Ill.: Northwestern University Press, 1973), p. 78.

12. Jacques Derrida, "The Supplement of Copula: Philosophy before Linguistics," in *Textual Strategies*, ed. Josue Harari (Ithaca, N.Y.: Cornell University Press, 1979), pp. 82–120.

13. Michel Foucault, *Discipline and Punish: The Birth of the Prison*, trans. Alan Sheridan (New York: Pantheon, 1977).

14. Hans-Georg Gadamer, *Truth and Method* (New York: Seabury Press, 1975).

15. Clifford Geertz, *Negara* (Princeton, N.J.: Princeton University Press, 1980), p. 122. This part of the discussion is a slight revision of what I have done in Michael J. Shapiro, *The Politics of Representation: Writing Practices in Biography, Photography and Policy Analysis* (Madison, Wis.: University of Wisconsin Press, 1988), chap. 1.

16. Geertz, *Negara*, p. 13.

17. Ibid., p. 14.

18. Clifford Geertz, "The Politics of Meaning," *The Interpretation of Culture* (New York: Basic Books, 1973), p. 311.

19. Michel Foucault, "Two Lectures," in *Power/Knowledge*, ed. Colin Gordon, trans. Colin Gordon, Leo Marshall, John Mepham, Kate Soper (New York: Pantheon, 1980), pp. 78–108.

20. Ibid., p. 93.

21. Ibid., p. 102.

22. Raulet, "Structuralism and Post-Structuralism," p. 202.

23. Richard Rorty, "Habermas and Lyotard on Postmodernity," in *Habermas and Modernity*, ed. Richard J. Bernstein (Cambridge, Mass.: MIT Press, 1985), p. 174.

24. Ibid., p. 172.

25. Ibid., p. 171.

26. Ibid., p. 172.

27. For Habermas's attack on Foucault's failure to provide a critical position see Jürgen Habermas, "The Genealogical Writing of History: On Some Aporias in Foucault's Theory of Power," trans. Gregory Ostrander, *Canadian Journal of Social and Political Theory* 10, no. 1–2 (1986), pp. 1–9.

28. See Jürgen Habermas, *The Philosophical Discourse of Modernity*, trans. Frederick Lawrence (Cambridge, Mass.: MIT Press, 1987), chap. 11.

29. Jürgen Habermas, *The Theory of Communicative Competence*, vol. I: *Reason and the Rationalization of Society*, trans. Thomas McCarthy (Boston: Beacon Press, 1984), p. 295.

30. Rorty, "Habermas and Lyotard on Postmodernity," p. 171.

31. For a similar rejoinder to Rorty's argument see Jonathan Arac "Introduction," *Postmodernism and Politics*, ed. Jonathan Arac (Minneapolis: University of Minnesota Press, 1986), p. xviii.

32. Raulet, "Structuralism and Post-Structuralism," p. 206.

33. Foucault, "The History of Sexuality," in *Power/Knowledge*, ed. Gordon, p. 190.

34. Fred Dallmayr, *Polis and Praxis* (Cambridge, Mass.: MIT Press, 1984), p. 193.

35. Ibid., p. 198.

36. See Michel Foucault's discussion of the commentary in "The Order of Discourse," *Language and Politics* ed. Michael Shapiro (New York: New York University Press, 1984), pp. 114–16.

37. See Michel Tournier, *Vendredi ou les Limbes du Pacifique* (Paris: Gallimard, 1967). All quotations are from the English edition: *Friday or the Other Island*, trans. Norman Denny (Harmondsworth, England: Penguin, 1974). My discussion of Tournier's novel benefits from an excellent reading by Anthony Purdy, "From Defoe's 'Crusoe' to Tournier's 'Vendredi': The Metamorphosis of a Myth," *Canadian Review of Comparative Literature* (June 1984), pp. 216–35.

38. Ian Watt, "Robinson Crusoe as Myth," in *Robinson Crusoe: An Authoritative Text, Backgrounds, and Sources of Criticism*, ed. Michael Shinagel (New York: W. W. Norton, 1975), p. 315.

39. Ibid., p. 322.

40. Karl Marx, *Capital*, vol. I, trans. Eden and Cedar Paul (New York: International Publishers, 1929), p. 52.

41. Jean Baudrillard, "Beyond Use Value," in *For a Critique of the Political Economy of the Sign*, trans. Charles Levin (St. Louis: Telos Press, 1981), p. 140.

42. Baudrillard's extended critique of Marx is in his *The Mirror of Production*, trans. Mark Poster (St. Louis: Telos Press, 1975).

43. Baudrillard, "Beyond Use Value," p. 141.

44. Ibid.

45. Tournier moves the Robinson Crusoe story from the seventeenth to the eighteenth century. The change in time frame does not enter my reading but is analyzed in depth in Purdy, "From Defoe's 'Crusoe' to Tournier's 'Vendredi,' " pp. 223–25. Among other things, the new date allows Tournier to imply a Ben Franklin parody in Crusoe's determined accumulative ethic.

46. Tournier, *Friday or the Other Island*, p. 96.

47. Ibid., p. 99.

48. For an extensive treatment of the feminization of the island theme, see Alice A. Jardine, *Gynesis* (Ithaca, N.Y.: Cornell University Press, 1985), pp. 218–23.

49. Ibid., p. 143.

50. Ibid., p. 141.

FREEDOM AND CONTINGENCY

WILLIAM E. CONNOLLY

1. FREEDOM AND MORTALITY

We secularists, it seems, know where we are going. We are on the road to nowhere: no illusions about eternal life, no need to pass a new battery of tests to qualify for immortality; no worries about infinite boredom haunting the afterlife of a disembodied soul. Perhaps we compensate by clinging to an ethic of health and longevity. Perhaps some of us have even transfigured the promise of personal salvation into a doctrine of collective progress. Still, these secular dreams and consolations seem innocent enough.

Appearances deceive here, though. For a pattern of secular insistence about the relation life must bear to death spawns illusions about the circumstances of contemporary life. Contemporary social theory contains within it a set of secular reassurances that compensate for those lost by the death of God.

To think critically about these compensations is to think about some commonalities that bind many opposing theories of contemporary life into a frame held together by that which is unthought by many of the participants. And it is, perhaps, to identify troubles and dangers on the horizon that are obscured by the terms of contestation within this frame. I will call these background assumptions the unconscious phenomenology of life and death in late modernity. My strategy will be, first, to summarize this phenomenology as if it were explicitly articulated by social theorists today: second, to lend greater credibility to the thesis that it contributes to the unconscious of contemporary thought by outlining an alternative reading of the late-modern condition that disturbs parameters of contestation within this frame; and, third, to probe more carefully the boundaries of this frame and the unthought that governs thinking shuffling around within it. The idea and experience of freedom, as it is interpreted at each of these sites, will provide the organizing instrument of this endeavor.

The unconscious phenomenology of life and death is significant, partly because it contains insights inside its constructions, partly because it screens out important shifts in the contemporary experience of freedom and unfreedom. Its contours might be relatively familiar, since it draws into its melody strains from thinkers such as the early Heidegger, Sartre, Merleau-Ponty, and Hegel. The following summary, however, drains it of nuance, variation, and complexity so that it can be reduced to a cultural stereotype.

Recognition that life is short encourages the self to contribute to the crystallization of its own individuality. Since, as Heidegger says, no one, however rich or powerful, can pay or order another to substitute for him in this performance, foreknowledge of death encourages everyone to establish priorities in life, to consolidate the loose array of possibilities floating around and within one into the density of a particular personality with specific propensities, purposes, and principles. Nudged by the prospect of death to ponder life, the individual may struggle to establish distance between himself and the common stock; the common good does not, after all, own me completely if its continuation is punctuated by my death. Since it is my death, I am more ready to assert that it must, to some degree at least, be my life. Pondering these issues, one may become more insistent about his or her importance in the order of things, even about one's intrinsic significance despite the order of things. Those ways of life that strive to absorb the self completely into the body of the community would not have to devise such demanding rituals of commonality if the prospect of death did not stir up, among other things, powerful drives to individuality.

The relation of individuality to foreknowledge of death creates an ambiguous context for the exercise of freedom. If I lived forever, I could be a philosopher, a professional basketball coach, a concert pianist, a transvestite, and a corporate lawyer. Here, where there was time for every possibility, the language of freedom would become too slippery. For freedom involves choice in a setting where it is impossible to pursue every valued option concurrently or serially; it presupposes a contrast with unfreedom that could not be maintained in a world functioning without the constraints of time. A free mortal forecloses alternative possibilities when it chooses to do or become x; and every act of freedom is therefore bound up with those possibilities it must forgo.

The actualization of a life is ambiguous because the process of becoming an individual with specific skills, memories, propensities, prospects, and liabilities rules out whole sets of options previously hovering in front of one. Hence anxiety, self-doubt, or even rage against the human condition often accompanies the actual exercise of freedom. Some try to defer choices indefinitely to avoid the experience of foreclosure. Others try to do a little of everything and accomplish little of anything. Time weighs heavily upon many agents of freedom because, more generally, foreknowledge of death enters into every decision that seems to define one in some fundamental way. The very structure of freedom and individuality is pervaded by the relation they bear to the self's implicit anticipation of its own end.

But foreknowledge of death also connects the individuated self to a larger world that enables and disables it. One dimension of this relation is conveyed by Hobbes. The fear of early, violent death becomes a tool deployable by the sovereign to regulate otherwise unruly, restless, variable, and unreliable individuals. Hobbes even piles on top of the individual's inclination to avoid death the obligation to do so, so that suicide becomes a sin against the law of nature and its God. He fears that the pull of individuality will overwhelm the dictates of an order strong enough to protect individuals from the constant threat of violent and arbitrary death *unless* the fear of death itself is converted into a weapon in the service of civil order. Thus the same foreknowledge of death that encourages the self to assert its individuality also becomes an instrumentality enabling power holders to restrict and domesticate the self.

Fear is not the only means by which the prospect of death can connect the individual to the larger world in which it is situated. Gratitude (or something akin to it) plays a role too. When we confront the ambiguity of freedom we also realize that an open society, housing diverse ways of living, enables us to cope with this ambiguity. A fortunate individual, acknowledging the distinctive possibilities this world opens to him and to those he loves, recognizing that he might have been thrown into a hellhole of one sort or another, allows a diffuse feeling of identification and gratitude to infuse daily transactions.

If one ponders child rearing, work, tax payment, writing, political action, tax cheating, and associatonal membership in the context of one's own finitude, eventually it becomes clear that one's life efforts do not redound only to one's own detriment or benefit; each, after life, bestows a legacy upon those remaining. You can't take it with you, nor can you consume every product or effect you have engendered before the onset of death. Thus in ways the pure individualist inadequately acknowledges, the very individuality of death connects one in life to others and to a future that continues without one after death. If preliminary connectedness to a larger way of life is operative, one now implicates oneself through specific, daily performances in the destiny of the society to which one belongs. One's current contributions connect oneself to a future that stretches beyond oneself. Maybe those you raised will remember you with pride; maybe a future generation will remember and respect the effort and sacrifices of the one in which you live. Connectedness to a future that stretches beyond my life and our lives provides me with pride in the present and consoles me somehow about the time my life ends. We desire this consolation, and its pursuit enters into readings of the future we now participate in preparing.

2. FREEDOM AND DEPENDENT UNCERTAINTY

This abbreviated phenomenology of freedom and death illuminates ambiguities in the self's relation to order and to its own individuality. Individualists tend to accentuate some of these elements, communitarians to emphasize others. The contemporary debate between them can be located in this space of contestation over the appropriate terms of accentuation. But the disputants also share assumptions forming the common pool from which these alternative pails of theory are drawn. For this phenomenology presupposes a rather stable and serene context of self-identity, social practice, state and interstate relations, and temporal projection.

The links it forges between life and foreknowledge of death, individuality and connectedness, choice and foreclosure, collective life in the present and individual projections of the common future, and individual life in the present and collective projections of the future prospects for individuals presume, first, a rather close alignment between the identity the self seeks to realize and socially available possibilities of self-formation, and, second, a shared sense of confidence in the world we are building, a confidence that the present and the future are linked through effort and anticipation on one side and memory and appreciation on the other. If these connections, sentiments, and projections became severely attenuated, the serene phenomenology of freedom and finitude would also become anachronistic. To retain it would be to cling insistently to a picture of the world belied by individual and collective experience.

I think something like this is occurring today. The secular drive to domesticate the prospect of death without immortality functions today as a filter to theorization. This compensatory code of secular reassurance screens out disciplines and dangers residing in contemporary experience. It contributes in its own way to dangers it seeks to contain.[1]

There are three characteristics of contemporary life that disturb and unsettle this phenomenology. There is, first, an intensification of the experience of owing one's life and destiny to world-historical, national, and local-bureaucratic forces.

There is, second, a decline in the confidence many constituencies have in the probable future to which they find themselves contributing in daily life. There is, third, an even more ominous set of future possibilities that weigh heavily upon life in the present. Each of these developments is distinctive enough, either in its newness, its intensification, or the extent to which it is inscribed in lived experience, to be treated as a defining dimension of contemporary life. The time is distinctive enough to give it a name. I call it late-modernity.

The first experience (of owing too much of one's life to world-historical forces) is so close and pervasive its political significance tends to escape explicit attention. It consists of an exacerbation of elements necessary and desirable in smaller proportions. Young people, facing the exigencies of a career or a job without one, feel it dramatically; so do older people, preparing for retirement.

The identity available to the late-modern self remains bound up with historically received standards of self-responsibility, self-discipline, and freedom. The individual is not merely responsible for particular actions, but, to varying and shifting degrees, for the character she develops, the stability of his mental life, the career she nurtures, the quality of his love life, the way their children turn out, the income level "earned," the social recognition attained, and so on. Background notions and institutions of love (where each chooses the other free of traditional constraints), self-responsibility (where one is held accountable for what one does and becomes), equal opportunity (where an individual's career and income flow from one's own ability, effort, and luck), individual freedom (where the consequences of one's actions are linked at least loosely to intentions which go into them), and citizenship (where each plays a part in shaping rules and laws governing all)—each of these practices is enabled and confined by relations it bears to the others.

But although these standards of identity and responsibility remain intact, the institutions in which they are situated have become more highly and pervasively organized. One must now program one's life meticulously to meet a more detailed array of institutional standards of normality and entitlement. Failing to measure up to one (or more) of these capacities, one runs a high risk of entrapment in one of the reciprocal categories of otherness attached to it: one becomes defined through a reciprocal category of delinquency, irresponsibility, dependency, criminality, instability, abnormality, retardation, unemployability, incapacity, obsolescence, credit risk, security risk, perversity, evil, illness, or contagion. And these latter categories of abnormality license bureaucratic correction, discipline, regulation, exclusion, conquest, help, conversion, incentives or punishment of those to whom they are applied.

In late-modernity old standards of freedom and responsibility impose a new set of hard choices. One can either treat one's life as a project, negotiating a path through a finely grained network of institutionally imposed disciplines and requirements, or struggle against those disciplines by refusing to treat one's life as a project. To follow the first route is to be indebted to the institutions in which one is enclosed: one's office space, self-esteem, income, merit, mobility, power, family, and personal identity now depend on microconformity to pervasive norms that come with the territory. And this is so whether those standards are established democratically or imposed from above. To select or be selected by the second path, on the other hand, is to be shuffled out of the good life available and to increase one's susceptibility to one of the categorizations that license institutional discipline from another direction. The choice, as they say, is yours.

When the self experiences itself to be penetrated too densely by disciplinary powers and standards, even the benefits it receives indebt it too much. One begins to experience uncertainty, contingency, and fragility residing in the status, power, and opportunities bestowed upon one. For anything given might also be taken away. A stock market can crash; a technical education can become obsolete; a liberal education can become irrelevant; a normal standard of family life can become abnormal; a pattern of mobility can become closed; a standard of merit can be reconstituted; the principles of self-respect can be modified; a mode of humor can be redefined as sickness; a previous pattern of affection can be redefined as illicit. Every newly institutionalized reward for attaining a current standard also creates new possibilities for deviant conduct and creates new possibilities for future revisions or extensions of old standards. And the very intensification and temporal extension of the typical life project decrease the probability that future standards of success will mesh with those projected by youthful pursuers. The late-modern definition of life as a project first demands intensive self-organization and then produces dependent uncertainty: dependence upon a more refined set of institutional standards and disciplines, uncertainty about the temporal stability of established rules of dependence.

Dependent uncertainty fosters a character type whose explicit consent to the ways of its life is laced with generalized resentment. The reactive attitudes of gratitude and resentment are linked to each other already in personal life, as Nietzsche knew. If you are grateful to me for my help you know that I know you were recently in a position of need or vulnerability. You can easily become resentful over actual or imagined misuses I might make of this knowledge.

A similar logic applies in social life. Those who experience themselves to be penetrated too thoroughly by disciplinary powers and standards resent even benefits they receive. Here, though, the object of resentment becomes less easy to fix; indefinite gratitude toward a way of life slides imperceptibly into floating resentment against its requirements and contingencies. Those burdened by this new weight are unlikely to bear new responsibilities lightly; they are also likely to evade old ones not tightly bound to their job description.

Generalized resentment (as I shall call it) finds expression in a diverse set of practices today, ranging from drug use through litigiousness, "mindless" violence, teenage suicide, and high divorce rates to tax evasion and work according to rule. But its most revealing and politically active sign resides in the hostility among those in positions of official independence to the complaints of those in officially recognized conditions of dependence such as Third World countries, convicted criminals, mental patients, welfare claimants, affirmative action candidates, coddled athletes, minorities, teenagers, illegal aliens, privileged college students—hostility, that is, to every constituency appearing to putative beneficiaries of prevailing institutional standards to whine about their treatment within officially defined arrangements of tutelage, punishment, assistance, dependence, or special privilege. What gives these "others" the right to complain when many struggling to measure up to the demands of life as a project already face as much self-discipline, dependency, and uncertainty as they can handle?

The second and third shifts in the context of contemporary life sharpen characteristics already elucidated. When people devalue the legacy the present bestows upon the future they divest selectively from common life in the present. This personal economy of divestment, achieving variable weight within any self at each point in the life cycle and each definable constituency at every point in the order, lodges itself in gender relations, child rearing, job performance, character of political coalitions, strategies of investment, and tax payment. In each domain the claims of self and immediacy gain leverage over those of connectedness and the future. And as economists of psychic investment are fond of iterating and reiterating, once divestment establishes itself in a few constituencies it becomes more irrational for others to withstand its temptations themselves.

What are these anxieties about the future? It seems probable that affluent states of late-modernity will be unable to protect their privileged position in the future without extending disciplinary control domestically and fomenting recurrent hostilities abroad. More pervasively, late-modernity is a time when the world-wide web of systemic interdependencies has become more tightly drawn while no political entity or alliance can attain the level of efficacy needed to master this system and its effects. This fundamental asymmetry between the appropriate level of political reflection (the world of late-modernity itself) and the actual capacity for collective action (the state and various regional alliances of states) cannot be transcended by any discernible means. Nonstate terrorism, the internationalization of capital, acid rain, the greenhouse effects, drug traffic, illegal aliens, the global character of strategic planning, extensive resource dependencies across state boundaries, and the accelerated pace of disease transmission across continents can serve as signs of this contraction of space and time in the late-modern world. Together, they signify the widening gap between the power of the most powerful states and the power they would require to be self-governing and self-determining.

This condition renders anachronistic and dangerous, I think, classic-modern conceptions of the state as a self-subsistent entity that enters into "foreign relations" or—within the frame of the democratic ideal—as an entity whose level of democratic accountability approximates the level of efficacy needed to control its destiny. No state can be inclusive enough to master the environment that conditions it, but the ideal of the modern, democratic state as the consummate agency of collective freedom is predicated on the assumption of this capacity. As long as this gap is treated simply as a deficiency to be rectified, the drive of late-modern states to close it will constitute a danger to global survival.

The size of this gap between world systematicity and state efficacy helps to explain the extension of discipline in late-modern states. The late-modern state is becoming a medium through which world systemic pressures are transmitted to its most vulnerable constituencies as imperatives of domestic discipline.

This prognostication of the future is widely felt if not publicly articulated. It finds covert expression in the intensification of a national chauvinism designed to close the gap between actual state power and the demand for self-determination. It finds further expression in the common pretense among candidates contending for national office that persisting deficits in state efficacy must flow only from defects in the leadership of the opposing party. But its most ominous expression is the general hesitancy to thematize politically a set of global contingencies located outside the effective reach of any individual state or regional constellation of states.

The belief in the possibility of collective freedom as mastery is secured today through a political conspiracy of silence

concerning the globalization of contingency. Thus: the greenhouse effect may sink large chunks of inhabitable land and
reduce the inhabitability of temperate zones; crises in supplies
of oil, safe water, good soil, or oxygen may flow from the effort to industrialize the entire world; state and nonstate terrorism may escalate into a condition of continuous insecurity
unconfined by state boundaries; and the impotency of a late-
modern state or nonstate fragment may produce a nuclear
exchange that destroys civilization or removes human life
from the face of the earth.

The defining mark of late-modernity is the globalization
of contingency. But to draw up a list of global contingencies
(that is, of uncertainties, possibilities, unplanned effects, dangers resistant to established modes of mastery) is today to re-
cite a series of banal truisms. These are more like idle words
than political enunciations because they are only precariously
linked to a public discourse that might state them as issues
susceptible to compromise or solution within the state-
centered frame of political debate and action. This banaliza-
tion of discourse about contingency is a sign of the gap
between global contingency and the efficacy of the state in
late-modernity; it also suggests an intimate relation between
the modern drive to mastery and the late-modern globalization of contingency.

Each possible scenario of future waste or destruction is
linked ironically to priorities definitive of the modern epoch,
especially to the drive to organize the state, the economy, and
the self so that the world itself can be mastered. These scenarios of possible reversal expose how the end of eliminating contingency recedes as the means to do so become more refined
and perfected. The effective mastery of microcontingencies
and the globalization of contingency advance together, while
the organization of political discourse celebrates the first effect and conceals the second.

In late-modernity, the personal experience of contingency and the fragility of things become more vivid and compelling while political reflection into the issues posed by this
condition is shuffled to the margins of state-centered discourse. Established disciplines and rules are experienced more
often as arbitrary restraints insecurely linked to the future that

justifies them. Resentment becomes more generalized and acute; it more actively seeks available targets of vilification. Politics becomes less attuned to the future and more locked into claims of the present, less attentive to the claims of the suffering, more willing to discipline those whose suffering cannot be ignored. The late-modern condition compromises the individual's bond of affection to the common life, disciplines individuality, disconnects present decisions from care about the future they engender, and disrupts stable contexts in which the ambiguous exercise of freedom occurs.

What is the experience of freedom like in this condition? Perhaps Milan Kundera, writing in a more extreme and particular setting, can clarify certain elements in this one. Kundera thinks specifically about Czechoslovakia after 1968, where collective memories are expunged from official records, where the reputations of courageous patriots are systematically ruined, where traditional rules and ethical guides become irrelevant to new circumstances, and where the state incorporates everyday gossip into a system of police surveillance. He teaches more generally, though, about disturbance introduced into the phenomenology of freedom when ruptures are opened between intention and result, personal identities sought and those validated by the order, the self and its tie to the common life, the present and the future it prepares. If an act of resistance and courage in photographing Russian invaders later becomes a source of information to authorities rounding up dissidents, what does that teach retrospectively about the unstable context of individual freedom? If an entire epoch finds itself facing new and dangerous contingencies after spending centuries trying to master contingency, what does that teach about the structure of collective freedom?

Kundera thinks about the paradox of freedom in a condition marked by structural binds and personal contingency.

> Human life occurs only once, and the reason we cannot determine which of our decisions are good and which bad is that in a given situation we can make only one decision; we are not granted a second, third, or fourth life in which to compare individual decisions. . . . History is similar to individual lives in this respect.[2]

Kundera revises Nietzsche's teaching of eternal recurrence. In this new condition the freedom depicted by the serene phenomenology could only be established through Nietzschean recurrence with a distinctive twist. If each lived life over many times, recalling in each new cycle what followed previous decisions and knowing that the only new agency to be introduced into the recurring setting would be one's own newly informed decision, the freedom of each individual and state would increase with each cycle of recurrence. Radical contingency, as we might call a condition in which the mastery of microcontingencies accentuates global contingency, could be contained by using the past to prophesy future results of current alternatives. But individuals and state actually go around only once: "living only one life, we can neither compare it with our previous lives nor perfect it in our lives to come."[3]

When the background presupposed by the serene phenomenology of freedom and mortality is destabilized each of its elements becomes disrupted. The experience of freedom is drained from the exercise of choice; the experience of choice is drained from the requirement to convert life into a project; the assurance of temporal stability is drained from the time covered by a life project. People often do what they want, but their uncertain, disciplined, and dependent condition unravels freedom in doing so. The anticipation of death, which was to foster individuality and connectedness, is prized loose from a context in which these consolations are assured.

The paradoxical element in the practice of freedom now becomes intensified: I can often do what I want or what I think will promote my long-term advantage, but my implication in an organized system of available life projects means that one or another institution might itself fall under pressure to transform the standards I have striven to meet; we can act together in a state to domesticate local contingencies, but the cumulative effect of such actions by a variety of states generates global contingencies resistant to mastery; late-modernity replaces acceptance of blind fate with mastery of contingency, but it creates global contingencies that haunt it with a new fatefulness.

Just as the serene phenomenology of life and death idealized the world in which it located the ambiguous practice of freedom, this revised phenomenology purifies an emergent world by adopting alternative principles of selection. It is an exaggeration, designed to crystallize elements simultaneously concealed by the first account and elevated to global significance by the late-modern condition.

3. FREEDOM AND NECESSARY CONTINGENCY

Contemporary politics should seek to mitigate generalized resentment and respond to historical contingency. But what understanding should inform this response? Many political theorists today seek to resuscitate individualism or, among those who find that response repugnant, to establish an equally familiar ideal of community. The first position promises to reduce state pressure on the individual by enabling self-reliance, thereby relieving the politics of resentment; the second promises to restore the experience of connectedness to a larger community, thereby dissolving resentment in a solution of common identifications. But each of these alternatives is also a complement to the other. The first concentrates disciplinary pressure in the privately incorporated economy; the second lodges it in an anticipated community that establishes legitimate norms and ends for all. Together they license a lot of discipline. But perhaps the contemporary crystallization of dependent uncertainty, generalized resentment, and global contingency provides an occasion to rethink the terms of this all too familiar debate. Perhaps it enables us to look with a new eye into the mobile idea of freedom.

As a prelude to this reflection we might note the multifaceted character of the term *contingency* itself. By contrast to that which is necessary and universal, it means that which is changeable and particular; by contrast to that which is certain and constant, it means that which is uncertain and variable; by contrast to that which is self-subsistent and causal, it means that which is dependent and effect; by contrast to that which is expected and regular, it means that which is an unexpected event and an irregularity; and by contrast to that which is safe and responsive to human agency, it means that which is dangerous, unruly, and obdurate in its danger.

Most contemporary theories of politics strive to reduce the threat of contingency in two ways. First, they select one or two dimensions in this family of loosely associated elements and treat them as the defining character of contingency. Second, they implicitly adopt a social ontology that allows them to domesticate the selected element while defusing the threat of those ignored. These alternative theoretical strategies for the domestication of contingency and the corollary glorification of freedom mirror a set of alternative political strategies competing for hegemony in late-modernity.

Heidegger, in "The Age of the World Picture,"[4] suggests that the competing ideals of individualism and collectivism, as well as those of negative and positive freedom, arise together in the same time. They share, amid their visible opposition, a contestable picture of freedom. The debate Heidegger alludes to has by now evolved into at least three positions, each with several alternative formulations struggling for hegemony within it. Call them the individualist, collectivist, and communitarian pictures of freedom.

The first two parties concur on a central thesis. Individualists and collectivists agree that we can master a world that is indifferent to us, that we can convert it into a deposit of resources amenable to our use. Mastery is the route to freedom. The individualist thinks that civil society is the road to world mastery, that freedom for the individual involves control over personal destiny, and that control over personal destiny is perfected to the extent that the impersonal structure of civil society succeeds in subjecting nature to human purposes. The collectivist agrees that freedom involves mastery over nature and insists that its highest locus of expression is in the collectivity (a state, a people, a class) that establishes a settled plan to achieve it. The individual is a member in a collectivity, and we achieve freedom together through collective mastery.

A third doctrine opposes these two quests for mastery. It sees more than indifference in nature; it discerns a bent or direction in the world to which the self and the community must strive to become attuned.[5] The self becomes more free by becoming more attuned to the deepest purposes inscribed in its community, and the community becomes more free by becoming more attuned to the bent of nature in the self and the world. Freedom is attunement to essence; it is fulfillment and realization. Advocates of this picture then debate among themselves how many concessions to individual diversity should be given in the realized community.

With respect to the idea of freedom these three positions can be located in the same frame. A matrix in which the categories across the horizontal axis are mastery and attunement and those on the vertical axis are the individual and the collectivity creates space for four theories of freedom.[6] The permutations can now expand indefinitely as compromises are forged by theorists of mastery who create a little room for attunement, theorists of individuality who give more credibility to the state as a site of collective freedom, theorists of community who concede a little more to the dictates of mastery, and so forth. But these contending theories share a certain affinity.

The first basic doctrine, linking freedom to mastery, and the second, tying it to attunement to a higher purpose, share a pattern of insistence: each demands, through a set of presuppositions about self and nature providing the measure against which all other assumptions and standards are to be assessed, that the order of things be susceptible in principle either to human mastery or to a harmonization that approaches the highest human essence. The world, at least in the last instance, must be FOR US in one way or the other. It—including external nature and the human material from which unified selves are constructed—must either be formed for us or plastic enough to be mastered by us.

Ontological narcissism—as we might label views that demand dispensations from within the world to replace those provided by personal, willful, and powerful God located above it—allows each of the contending parties to domesticate the protean idea of contingency: each of these orientations invokes ontological assumptions that domesticate contingency as the unexpected, the dangerous event, the obdurate condition that resists effective intervention, the inevitable outcome accidental only in its timing, the resistance to detailed design lodged in the human animal and nature. And each masks the conversion of a world of microcontingencies into a world of global contingency by its insistence that the world itself must be predisposed to us in one way or the other.

It is not easy to think outside the frame of these debates, and I do not claim to be ready to do so in any finished or refined way. But it may be important today to try to push against these boundaries. For within the terms of this debate the appreciation of incorrigible or necessary contingency is stifled in thinking about freedom. Freedom becomes equated with mastery or attunement because the world is treated (at least implicitly) as if it must be susceptible to one aspiration or the other: IT owes that much to US. When this bond of insistence is discerned between contending parties, we may also be in a position to locate the impulse to serenity inside the phenomenology of life and death summarized earlier. Perhaps a secret plea for secular consolation binds together contestants in this debate. If God is dead (or at the very least severely wounded), then the world itself must be for us in one way or the other: it *must* either be susceptible to our mastery or predisposed to our quest to become attuned to a higher essence. And perhaps that plea, inscribed pervasively in the twin projects of mastery and realization, simultaneously exacerbates dangers and disciplines residing in late-modernity and screens out interpretations that might dramatize them more cogently.

The contemporary experience of disruption in individuality and connectedness might encourage some to challenge the frame in which these debates are set. The contemporary condition, brought initially into focus by the engagement between Nietzsche and Heidegger over the sources and implications of modern nihilism, and crystallized by contemporary thinkers such as Michel Foucault and Milan Kundera while pondering that debate, encourages a rethinking of the modern demand that the world be for us in either or both of these ways. Each of these latter thinkers, at least at his best, resists consoling assumptions about the plasticity or providence of the world. Each thinks about freedom while confronting incorrigible discrepancies, resistances, and disjunctions between the world and the most magnificent human designs. Each, demanding less from the world, suggests connections between these modern strategies of freedom and the emergence of dependent uncertainty, generalized resentment, and enlargement of global contingency.

Suppose internal and external nature contains, because it was neither designed by a god nor neatly susceptible to organization by human design, elements of stubborn opacity to human knowledge, recalcitrance to human projects, resistance to every model of normal individuality and harmonious community. Suppose these elements of strife and dissonance enter into life, creating disturbances in the designs we inevitably impose upon it: each worthy design of the normal self, the common good, and justice, while realizing something good, encounters resistances that inhibit its transparency, coherence, and responsiveness and impede its harmonization with the other elements of social life to which it is bound by ties of interdependence. Each design engenders new contingencies while subduing old ones. The more perfectionist the demand imposed by any design, the more discipline must be applied to the selves called upon to achieve it.

With these suppositions, a revised idea of freedom becomes discernible, at least in rough outline, an idea appreciating whatever in the self and the world that is opaque to knowledge and resistant to organization while affirming the necessity and desirability of social designs in human life, an idea folding respect for discordance and contingency into its picture of freedom even while insisting that freedom cannot be reduced to a wholesale struggle against every and any social form given to the self or the world in which it resides.

Such a perspective might support a three-pronged effort to relieve discipline and to curb generalized resentment: first, by tracing the deepest well of resentment to the modern quest to eliminate contingency from a world not susceptible to its elimination: second, by attending to that in the self and its world that is defeated or subjugated by contemporary standards of normality and the common good: third, by relaxing modern dreams to bring everything under control or into attunement.

Freedom, Heidegger suggests, "is that which conceals in a way that opens to light . . . lets the veil appear as what veils."[7] I interpret the phrase "let the veil appear as what veils" to stand in opposition to modern enframing, in which everything is drawn into a pattern of knowledge and stands in reserve for organized use. It does not mean that we lift the veil created by enframing to expose Being as it is in itself; it does not mean that we find a higher direction in Being that tells us to stop dominating nature so as to do something else commanded by a higher being or principle. It means that enframing veils veiling, failing to appreciate the incorrigible discrepancy between the world it reveals and that concealed by its mode of revealing. Every revealing conceals. And a veil must always be in a world neither designed to correspond to our capacities for cognition nor composed of plastic material predisposed to human organization and mastery. It is a call, then, to appreciate difference between modern ideals and the world it draws upon to realize them without purporting to elevate that difference itself to a higher standard or meta-knowledge.

One stands in a more free relation to one's own ideals when one affirms that the world can never be exhausted by a single perspective or a constellation of contending perspectives. The world is always richer than the systems through which we comprehend and organize it. The veil of ontological necessity is thus lifted from the experience of social or economic or psychological necessity. Necessity becomes particularized while contingency becomes universalized; contingency becomes invested with necessity because every particularity must create and encounter it.

My Heidegger (there are several Heideggers) calls upon us to relax the dual drive to mastery and integration by giving more presumptive rights to elements in the self and the world that deviate from them. This room becomes more conceivable as we acknowledge that projects that would squeeze contingency out of the world do not correspond to any actual or possible principle in Being. And this enlargement of ontological space identifies new points of unfreedom in organized space. In a way of life defined according to principles of gender duality, for instance, the presumptive rights of the hermaphrodite become enhanced after we glimpse ways in which this demand of duality disciplines and represses a being whose body does not fit into either of its artificially defined slots. A new claim to freedom is introduced here, one that challenges the last refuge of teleology lodged in contemporary theories of the body, one that opens up suggestive possibilities in other domains and for intermediate cases in this domain, one that can make its case in contestation with other standards and restraints operative in the common life.

Thought in this way, the quest for freedom, though it does so obliquely and imperfectly, strives to create more room for difference to be by calling attention to the contingent and artificial dimensions of historically established identities. More particularly, it supports rethinking the late-modern standard of human life as a project within the modern project of world mastery. For the more the self must be organized by these projects the more difference must be converted into otherness in need of correction, normalization, punishment, or exclusion.

Most fundamentally of all, perhaps, it strives to respond to the necessity of contingency in life by at once affirming its inevitability and striving to contend with it in ways that do not magnify its potential for destruction and devastation. For the individual this might mean coming to accept the fact of death without demanding transcendental compensations, since those compensatory demands also generate transcendental standards of good that treat every serious resistance to it as an evil to be conquered or converted.[8] For the state as a collectivity this might mean admitting limits and dangers to the modern project of world mastery and affirming a mode of life that accepts the accentuation of microcontingencies to avoid producing the most destructive global contingencies; it means striving to reduce and redefine the world demands of the state we live in so that it has a better change of long-term cohabitation with other states and stateless peoples.

In general it means affirming the tragic element in life without dissolving it into some model of theistic redemption or secular compensation or lapsing into resigned passivity. It means treating freedom neither as simply mastery over a contingent world nor as attunement to a higher direction, but as strife and interdependence with a highly contingent world: a striving that seeks to leave its mark on life and an interdependence that properly limits those dreams of mastery and attunement, conquest, and conversion that magnify global contingency.

When thought becomes responsive to differences between human formations and that which deviates from them, it can also treat historical variations in forms of selfhood, normality, and otherness as signs of the element of contrivance and contingency in each historically hegemonic formation. It thereby multiplies sites at which the issues of freedom and unfreedom can be posed in late-modern life. The time of late-modernity itself (as a system of interdependencies without a collectively organized agent), the state (as a dependent center of collective agency and social discipline), the normalized self (as the center of individual agency and self-discipline) and whatever in the self that resists normalization (the internal other), all become potential sites of freedom and constraint.

It is impossible to bring each of these sites and its claims into neat alignment with the others. The idea of freedom is thus most fundamentally a political idea in which each of its sites enables and confines, complements and opposes, each of the others. A political theory of freedom now becomes one in which each claim is drawn into engagement with others, where priorities are contested in a setting where many participants understand in advance that the world is not designed to establish perfect alignment among these interdependent and contending elements. It is a theory in which the idea of freedom becomes intimately bound up with the idea of politics.

Today it seems to me that the first and last sites deserve special attention, partly because the middle two have dominated discourse to this point and partly because these polar sites together manufacture much of that generalized resentment plaguing contemporary politics. To focus the eye of freedom where world-systemic effects escape collective control and where difference resists normalization and organization is to look with new vision into the spiral of demands to improve, correct, aid, control, perfect, treat, test, or deter individuals in the name of self-realization or state rationality. It is also to rethink the perverse relation between the late-modern experience of global contingency and the modern drive to master contingency through the intensified organization of life.

NOTES

I would like to thank Jane Bennett, Valentine Daniel, Richard Flathman, Joan Scott, Barbara Hernnstein Smith, Stephen White, and Sheldon Wolin for comments on an earlier draft of this essay.

1. This compensatory code of secular reassurance is located less in the assertions and arguments of contemporary texts, more in the rhetorical structure of these texts. The theories swim in a rhetorical sea that provides ontological reassurance. I cannot review this topic here. But several examples are examined in chaps. 5, 6, 8, and 10 of my *Politics and Ambiguity* (Madison: University of Wisconsin Press, 1987). The essay by Michael Shapiro in this text, "Weighing Anchor: Postmodern Journeys from the Life-World," explores these issues in a thoughtful way that, I think, complements my thinking. Those discourses that he says are governed by the metaphor of the conversation are the ones that also adopt a rhetoric that tends to sink contingencies and resistances in life into social ontologies of mastery or attunement. That is, their critiques of the actual, however mild or militant these may be, are governed by their projections of a possible world susceptible to mastery or attunement.

2. *The Unbearable Lightness of Being*, trans. Michael Henry Heim (New York: Harper and Row, 1984), p. 222.

3. Ibid., p. 8.

4. In Heidegger, *The Question Concerning Technology*, trans. William Lovitt (New York: Harper and Row, 1977), pp. 115–54. "The essence of the modern age can be seen in the fact that man frees himself to himself. But this correct characterization remains, nonetheless, superficial. . . . Certainly the modern age has, as a consequence of the liberation of man, introduced subjectivism and individualism. But it remains just as certain that no age has produced a comparable objectivism and that in no age before this has the non-individual, in the form of the collective, come to acceptance as having worth. Essential here is the necessary interplay between

subjectivism and objectivism. It is precisely this reciprocal conditioning of the one by the other that points back to events more profound" (127–28).

5. I will take rational choice theorists, most American political
economists, and theorists such as John Rawls and Ronald Dworkin
to exemplify the first view. George Lukacs and Jürgen Habermas
can be seen as exemplars of the second. And Charles Taylor,
Michael Sandel, and Alasdair MacIntyre can be seen to represent
the third. How they differ from each other is clear enough; it is the
affinities between them that interest me here. One way of putting it
is that each invokes a social ontology that is, from the vantage point
I am defending, insufficiently attentive to the ambiguities residing
in the highest possibilities it recognizes.

6. This means that one of the possible slots—the individualist
who also seeks attunement to a higher direction in the world—is not
filled. Perhaps William James and Ralph Waldo Emerson best represent that position in American thought, though I have studied
neither enough to be confident of this.

7. Heidegger, "The Question Concerning Technology," *The
Question Concerning Technology*, p. 25. In the preceding sentence
Heidegger says, "all revealing belongs within a harboring and a concealing." As I read Heidegger the idea here is to respond to the
mystery of Being by striving in thinking to let difference be, to let it
be insofar as it can be in the Being–being relation available to thinkers at a given time. Heidegger is often read as if he fit into one of
the "attunement" positions identified previously. I do not read him
this way, and if that reading prevails, he will stand inside the frame
of late-modern discourse I have delineated rather than on its edge. I
am interested in that intersection of thought—inhabited by Nietzsche, Heidegger (as I read him), and Foucault—where the most
thoughtful thinking about the circumstances of late-modernity and
the affinities among opposing thinkers thinking within the frame of
modernity can occur. Perhaps the best defense of the reading of
Heidegger I endorse is offered by Reiner Schurmann, *Heidegger on
Being and Acting: From Principles to Anarchy*, trans. Christine-Marie
Gros (Bloomington: Indiana University Press, 1987). "The difference between the 'original' and the 'originary' then tells us something about presencing as such as opposed to its predominant
modes in the West; namely, that it is without principle, an-
archic. . . . But as long as one seeks to revert to the initial question
of Western philosophy without also subverting the focal points into
which that question has been crystallized, it will remain unintelligi-

ble why Heidegger can claim: 'finding the way into the truth of being' presupposes that we renounce 'instituting rules' " (p. 149).

8. To reach "beyond" good and evil is not to go beyond evaluation and the affirmation of standards. Rather it is to see that because there is no transcendental principle or telos in the world from
which the good is derived, every good pursued is likely to encounter
resistances within selves and the world to the organization it requires. It is to affirm, with Nietzsche, "the rich ambiguity of existence." Nietzsche is also the thinker who has done the most to expose
the internal connection between the insistent projection of a higher
direction in Being or predisposition to mastery in the world and
underlying resentment against the anarchy of Being. That is well
elaborated in "On Redemption," *Thus Spoke Zarathustra*, trans. Walter Kaufman (Harmondsworth: Penguin Books, 1954).

What can I say to those who will contend that my debt to Nietzsche is strange because of, first, his own stance of mastery to the
world and, second, his anti-democratic position? Although I have
tried to deal with these issues elsewhere, let me say here that a Nietzschean ontology helps to make sense of the globalization of contingency, and the contemporary globalization of contingency sets the
context in which a contestation of the modern project of mastery
can occur. The point, of course, is not to eliminate it (for that cannot
be done in a world that is not predesigned to fulfill our needs if
only we become attuned to its providential design), but to tame and
reduce its scope because of the dangers it brings. The case for the
contemporary affinity between a social "ontology of discordant con-
cordances" and a particular conception of democracy is made in *Politics and Ambiguity*. A preliminary attempt to draw sustenance from
Nietzsche in a political theory that emphasizes contingency and
seeks to curtail the project of mastery can be found in *Political Theory and Modernity* (New York: Basil Blackwell, 1988).

Finally, when I endorse a *social* ontology of discordant concor-
dances to emphasize the incorrigible character of contingency and
resistances in human affairs, I am not saying that I *know* the *world
itself* is a *chaos* that we cannot know. First, this social ontology is a
projection that competes with other projections at this level of
thought. Second, it does not speak of the world itself separate from
our engagements but of human organization of the internal and external world; it is an essentially relational perspective. Third, it does
not say that the world itself is chaos, but that every organization of
the self and the world meets with resistances (as well as with organ-
izability). The point is not to fall into one of the tacit perspectives

that postulate either the world's predisposition to some mode of mastery (capitalist or socialist) or some inner direction in the world vaguely available to those who will listen for it attentively. Much of modern political thought, in leaning over backward to avoid the second, premodern projection, falls over unthoughtfully into the first projection. To try to think late-modern politics with no social ontology would be, I think, to increase the extent to which one's thinking is pulled unconsciously by the two dominant currents of our age. We cannot avoid those currents altogether but thinkers can develop strategies to curtail their influence.

PART IV

Mapping the Terrain in Political Analysis: Normalization and the Other

THE POLITICS OF EXCLUSION: ON THE CHRONIC MENTAL PATIENT AND THE POLITICS OF COMMUNITY

James Glass

INTRODUCTION: DALLMAYR'S FRAME OF ANALYSIS

What I want to do here is to look at Dallmayr's concept of the life-world in the context of mental patients, their treatment, reflections, and specific practical approaches to integrating the self into forms of productive activity. I will have more to say about these approaches in a moment. It is in this sense that Dallmayr's reflections on "practical ontology," that is, ontology centered around action and intersubjectivity or cobeing, may be considered as a frame for the following analysis.

In Stephen White's view Dallmayr asks, "What is the point of human existence, what modes of intersubjectivity or 'co-being' should we foster?"—important questions and ones that provide unique perspectives for examining the plight of persons excluded from the benefits of civil society and the world of care. Community, intersubjectivity, the position of the other and otherness, the concept of connectedness: all these critical philosophical notions take concrete shape, form, and meaning when thought about in the context of persons for whom the practical world means survival or disintegration. White writes in his introduction:

> Dallmayr stresses repeatedly that there can be no simple derivation of practice from ontological or other theoretical insights.

At best such insights give one intimations for guiding political
life. Following the intimations of his own two-fold ontology,
Dallmayr endorses what he calls a "post modern pluralist polity". Such a polity would involve a more radical attentiveness to
the *agonal* quality of public life than the old "end of ideology"
pluralism. At the same time the orientation toward care would
be expressed in a renewed commitment to the "politically and
socially dispossessed."

And I would add, what more disadvantaged group than
the schizophrenic, for whom not only action but the very nature of thought itself is problematic: thinking, symbolizing,
the use of logic, place consciousness in a position of contra-
diction with the governing assumptions of the normalizing
society.

The language of disease, the medical language and paradigm, exercises a powerful hold over the mental patient's and
former patient's sense of identity and liberty. It reinforces the
self's knowledge of its own separateness, its essential and abiding alienation from the species, from community. It is that
alienation and its persistence that form the real threat, not
only to the psychically displaced, the homeless, but to the very
society that because of its neglect and willed blindness (in
René Girard's[1] sense of scapegoating the other) bears considerable responsibility for the tragedy of this situation.

It is necessary, then, to rethink the concepts of community, otherness, intersubjectivity; to recast the notion of place
and care; to reflect on the homeless and the psychically displaced as persons for whom a public mode of being might
contribute to their terribly fragmented concepts of self. The
possibility of connectedness, the establishment of some *concept*
of civic identity, may help to bring the withdrawn or schizophrenic consciousness out of its hermetic isolation. Foucault,
as I shall argue, demystifies the regime of psychiatric power,
but fails to provide an adequate response to the concrete
needs of persons the society discards because of their peculiar psychological alienation. E. E. Schumacher may offer a
theoretical orientation for accepting the notion that the psychically displaced *can* function as long as the holding environ-

ment creates a viable sense of community and belongingness and sustains a measure of economic productivity. I have a few comments about Schumacher's general theory, as an approach to holding psychic fragmentation, at the end of the chapter.

OUTSIDE AND INSIDE: PROBLEMS IN BEING A FORMER PATIENT

A growing body of evidence suggests that the chronic mental patient drifts from halfway house to run-down sections of large cities, to boarding houses, and frequently back to the hospital (the "revolving door syndrome"). "Deinstitutionalization," although emptying some of the more flagrant back wards of mental hospitals and replacing incarceration with management through medication and "community-based facilities," has created a whole host of new problems centering upon the former patient's ability, capacity, and need to discover a sense of place and community.[2] Although deinstitutionalization is to be preferred to the locked back ward, it is not a movement that has responded to the relation between the self's sense of its own *public* effectiveness and collaborative aspects of working in common (its "being with others"). What has emerged in the drearier areas of large cities is something akin to a psychological proletariat, living and (rarely) working in a social universe noticeably short on sympathy and empathy.[3]

Deinstitutionalization involves more than an ideological position or view of mental health and hospitals.[4] It has become a very real social fact on the level of community: how to provide community, how to prevent the isolation of the homeless, how to contain the very real alienation that such persons experience.[5] Although it is true that many patients return to the outside world and lead productive lives, the great majority find themselves trapped from two directions: from inside, an inner confusion and self-doubt, intensified by a lack of a sense of place; from outside, the suspiciousness of a social world that regards mental disorders with fear and anxiety. Former patients who are successful in reintegrating possess skills relevant to the complex technological society and also have access to effective support services. The least successful in adapting, on an economic level, are those whose labor is regarded as peripheral to any specific job-related activity and who, because of insufficient training and low skill levels, find it difficult to sustain a long-term work relation with the surrounding community. It is no exaggeration to say that the latter form the vast majority of the chronically mentally ill, particularly in economically disadvantaged populations.[6]

Even the halfway house becomes a transition point for unhappy individuals. Its connection with reality is not only tenuous but also threatened by an unresponsive and hostile competitive world.[7] Many former patients regard the halfway house as "halfway to nowhere," a depressing way station that offers little help. If the former patient is to have any kind of life outside the hospital, both private and public aspects of "being" require attention. Former patients, however, for the most part find themselves excluded from work that is anything more than drudge labor. Since it is not the function of the medical model to inquire into the relation between the private and public selves, the psychological impact of work, and the absence of community, these issues are generally not systematically explored as part of hospital treatment. This is a real limitation in what the medical model offers in the way of orienting the self toward the *public* demands of civil society.

The discussion that follows derives from several areas of research: open-ended conversations with former patients, over a ten-year period, at the Sheppard and Enoch Pratt Hospital in Towson, Maryland; interviews with former patients at a halfway house in Baltimore, Maryland; and field research in Belgium and Israel. What emerges as a compelling observation in conversations not only with patients and former patients but also with social workers, mental health professionals, therapists, and, in the case of Belgium and Israel, administrators, is the difficulty in formulating a sense of community that can be sustained in the face of overwhelming pressure and demand for *performance* from the outside "civil" society.

THE PRIVATE AND THE PUBLIC:
EFFORTS TO BRIDGE THE GAP

Part of the task of restoring the self's sense of place is to create environments where the expression of self, as a peculiar and idiosyncratic way of framing reality, is not regarded as "evidence" of some supposed second-class humanity or citizenship. The chronically mentally ill have performed usefully in sheltered workshops, in jobs that require cooperation and mutuality, work that involves some form of being in public, consensual actions. It is therefore not a foregone conclusion that the chronically disturbed can be expected to perform only at some menial or subhuman level; even the regressed schizophrenic may possess unusual and surprising capacities, depending on how those capacities are organized and the specific tasks the self is taught to master and learn.

Yet the whole issue of work and collaboration for the chronic mental patient is a thorny one. It is handled variously, depending on the social and cultural context. Yet no matter how disparate the cultural environment, the issue of the relation between the private and public selves remains critical. Consider two widely divergent cultural backdrops that shed light on this dialectic between the private and public: the dispersal of chronic patients within the town limits of Geel, in northeastern Belgium, and the treatment of chronic schizophrenics in Israel.[8]

Geel has a long history (dating back to the thirteenth century) of accommodating the mad and, even more important, of demonstrating sensitivity to the public needs of the chronic patient. The town's foster care program has a unique reputation in the history of the treatment of the mentally disturbed; accounts of Geel in American psychiatry, for example, can be found as far back as the midnineteenth century: Pliny Earle (1887), superintendent of the Northhampton [Massachusetts] Lunatic Asylum, wrote somewhat critically in his annual report for 1879 that the system of treatment in Geel, because of its effort to assimilate the mad to the way of life of the normal society through boarding in local homes and work on the farms, would be unsuitable to the American environment.[9] Geel is a "place," then, that has had an enormous impact on theories of foster care and ways to integrate the chronic patient into an ongoing community. It was therefore with some excitement that I anticipated my visit. In Israel I hoped to find data on the integration of the chronic patient by visiting kibbutzim and interviewing schizophrenics who had been members. Further, I thought that the Israeli emphasis on the collective (the talent of the kibbutzim for creating and sustaining vital collectivist organizations) would illuminate the particular difficulties of persons as private as schizophrenics in dealing with formal modes of organization and collective types of work.

In both countries I met with mental health practitioners and administrators; I visited hospitals, community care centers, sheltered workshops, residential care houses; I spoke at some length with patients and residents (in all kinds of mental health facilities) both with and without the aid of translators. In Geel, economic reality and technological advance appeared to be endangering this centuries-old tradition and radically altering the attitudes of the townspeople. In addition, the *practice* of care (the laissez-faire approach to psychosis through the absence of confinement) had come under attack from mental health professionals in other districts in Belgium, particularly in the south. Several people in Israel mentioned the need for a "kibbutz" for the chronically disturbed, staffed and organized by professionals and paraprofessionals committed to working with this population. Yet no one had a shred of hope that the idea would ever be accepted, much less funded, by the state, although there is a kibbutz for the mentally retarded.

Neither in Geel nor in Israel did I see treatment programs that offered any startling innovations. But the dedication of persons connected with these programs and their efforts to work in environments that were significantly underfunded and understaffed were enormously impressive. Ingenuity, adaptation, persistence, and making virtues out of necessities consistently distinguished the commitment of these workers. The following observations may shed some light on the broader issue of the relation between the private and the public self.

The Geel program consisted primarily of four interrelated areas: a central hospital handling acute and severe long-term cases; the foster care program for which Geel is primarily noted, in which residents are boarded in homes throughout the city; sheltered workshops and activities programs both in the central hospital and in buildings located elsewhere in town; and general acceptance of the idea that the residents are free to wander about the town as long as their behavior conforms to general canons of civility. The presence of foster care residents among the townspeople created no major problems. Historically, the residents had been assimilated in to what had been a rural farming economy. With Geel's increasing prominence as a center for high-tech industry, however, opportunities for their integration into the town's labor force have significantly declined. Except for a few sheltered workshops, housed primarily within the environs of the central hospital, work (or seeing the chronic patient as a complex factor in a political economy) did not figure significantly in Geel's therapeutic regimen. The consensus of those connected with the program seemed to be that the tolerance of the Geel citizenry had declined, largely as a result of the influx of outsiders for whom the tradition of coexisting with the mentally ill was either unknown (and a rude shock), or a vague and somewhat distasteful part of Geel's history.

Though the number consistently declines, in 1985 there were nine hundred foster care residents, mostly elderly persons living in homes scattered throughout the city. The median age of the residents was fifty-eight, some were as old as seventy. Criticism comes primarily from Belgian psychiatrists who regard treatment on the Geel model as unscientific, anachronistic, out of step with the times. Geel is also thought to be unresponsive to the needs of young chronic patients, who are becoming the largest segment of the chronically disturbed population.

The foster care program (the per diem cost in 1985 was six dollars) is among the least expensive forms of care in Belgium. The financial arrangement for sheltered workshops is an interesting one as well. The state pays, directly to the hospital, 60 percent of the cost; private industry, for whom the work is done—usually piece work of different kinds—

supports the remaining 40 percent. The hospital administers the workshops; patients or residents are paid on an hourly basis. Although such a system could obviously be open to abuse, it has not in Geel led to either financial chicanery or administrative corruption. It is justified and defended in the language of coproduction: not only do the workshops diminish the costs of mental health care through the contribution of private industry, but they also provide income for persons who otherwise would be wards of the state and virtually penniless. At least 90 percent of foster care residents and hospitalized patients have been abandoned by their families or have virtually no family life and receive no financial support from outside. The relation between the hospital and private industry raises, of course, the important question of potential exploitation, but both administrators and workers in these minifactories feel that the financial arrangements are, given the circumstances, fair.

Proponents of these programs argue that in mental hospitals, 80 percent of a patient's contact time is with other patients; in Geel, given the dispersal of patients throughout the town, 80 percent of contact time is with normal society. In this respect, community is a central aspect of treatment combined with the salutary effects of natural or noninstitutional environments. And the importance of the chronic patient's having a "public" space is considered a vital aspect of psychological well-being. The content of that public space is primarily defined as the right of the resident to walk about the town, frequent its bars and restaurants, and sit in the public squares; still, even this much public life is far better than wandering the corridors of a mental hospital, since the resident's experience is open to the community and occurs within its boundaries. Further, it is argued, keeping the chronic patient in the community allows the self to become something more than an object to be managed by science; rather, the self's human ecology constitutes the primary focus of treatment, although the foster care program does rely on science in using medications and making provision for their administration.

Two examples I found in Israel spoke compellingly to the relation between public and private. First was a small factory near Haifa in which work—particularly working in common—was an essential part of treatment. Second, the status of schizophrenics on the kibbutzim pointed up both the dilemmas of collectivist organizations in confronting the radical withdrawal of the schizophrenic and the peculiar loneliness and isolation of the schizophrenic within the kibbutz environment.

The factory, the Kirit Ata workshop for mental patients in the Haifa area, was quite remarkable: 60 percent of the workers were chronic; each would be considered schizophrenic. Yet each was participating in a complex production line that involved the reconditioning of used telephones: difficult, often intricate, labor that required both training and a certain level of skill. The factory occupied two large buildings in an industrial section of a Haifa suburb. According to its manager, the operation served as a vital structure in the worker's sense of what community entailed, its responsibilities, and the pride in maintaining a community centered on work. To be at the factory, to work with others within this kind of social environment became for many the link to a hopeful future and to actions that gave meaning to the sheer demands of day-to-day survival. In the manager's words:

> The workers would frequently show up two hours before their shift and sit outside waiting for their work assignments. It wasn't that they were confused about the time. When I asked them why they were there so early, they said it just made them feel good to sit outside the place where they felt they were making and contributing something useful to society and for themselves.

I visited the Kirit Ata Workshop in 1985; run by a local branch of the B'nai B'rith under the supervision of the local social welfare agency, it is still in operation, providing significant work experience for the chronic patient.

It was a different situation altogether on the kibbutzim. Resident schizophrenics generally refused to adhere to the group's conception of work and participation, and those who had been sent to residential care facilities in the city were very reluctant, if not adamantly opposed, to returning to a kibbutz.

They preferred the anonymity of the city, its heterogeneity, and its opportunities to find places to "hide." Their problems on the kibbutzim were compounded by the facts of collective and group behavior: the feeling and sensation that all "eyes" were directed toward the self, the sense of being exposed and vulnerable, the impatience of the group with crazy thoughts and ideas, the premium on "normality."

The schizophrenic, because of withdrawal to an inner world, fears highly public environments; thus, the collaborative structure of a kibbutz takes on frightening properties, whereas family-oriented systems of kibbutzim depend on conformity, normality, and public cooperation as forms of security. Further, a significant proportion of schizophrenics are children of Holocaust survivors; the kibbutzim therefore find themselves in the difficult position of feeling a moral obligation to care for these persons (relative to other sectors of Israeli society, the kibbutzim spend a great deal of money on mental heath care) yet also express impatience with their unwillingness to work on a regular and consistent basis. This is a real problem on agricultural kibbutzim during times of harvest.

The kibbutz speaks to the issue of collective behavior and action; it represents a homogeneous society acting collectively to attain shared goals. As a place to live and be, it graphically demonstrates the intricate and often delicate process of tying the individual into the group. It is in some respects a place that symbolizes both the possibilities of that relation and its dangers. The feeling of being absorbed into a demanding group will account for something of the fear that schizophrenics expressed about returning to their kibbutzim. Yet at the same time, many kibbutz members find the psychological withdrawal, so characteristic of schizophrenia, to be disturbing and frustrating.

I heard criticism of the retreat to privacy from several regular kibbutz members. To paraphrase their comments: "We feel torn about how to deal with any of our members who becomes mentally ill; we of course offer them the best care and treatment. But we still do feel resentment. You have to understand our position: at the harvest, as just one example of what we need to do, it is essential to pick the grapefruit, to pact it, to ship it. If the work is not being done, if a person refuses to leave his room because of imaginary conversations or depression or whatever, it means one less worker in the field, possibly longer hours for everyone else and so on. Do you see? The group will here means survival. If the work is not finished, we will wither; if the meals are not cooked, we starve; if the guard is not posted, we may be infiltrated by terrorists, and so it goes. Sometimes our members who are mentally ill simply are incapable of grasping these very real facts of survival. If every one of us here were to sink into our private worlds, the kibbutz would disintegrate."

It is not that the kibbutz is hostile to the individual. Quite the contrary: it shows extraordinary tolerance (at times) and forebearance. What develops within the kibbutz is an intense competition between the interests of the individual and the common welfare of the group. A schizophrenic, for example, speaking with voices or caught up in an endless succession of hallucinations becomes for this kind of group both an impediment and a threat because the psychologically impaired member reminds the entire group of its vulnerability not only to outside forces but to the pressures of internal emotional conflict. In the kibbutz the community's definition of what is general and common frames action and relationship; that interest represents members who psychologically inhabit prevailing notions of consensuality and normality. To be schizophrenic, however, in a kibbutz may be a terrifying psychological experience that reinforces the sense of aloneness and separateness. For persons suffering this intense alienation, the group will may in fact appear to be tyrannical and unjust.

It would be difficult to find, in a social context, a more dramatic example of "eccentric" action than that of the schizophrenic, even though that eccentricity is not motivated by a calculated, instrumental reason. It is a form of behavior and thought that by its very nature sets the individual away from the group; to be schizophrenic is to be separate, different. That sense of separation and exclusion finds itself intensified within the collective refraction of the kibbutz envi-

ronment. It is understandable that schizophrenics on the kibbutzim are terrified of eating in huge dining halls, sometimes
holding as many as a thousand people. To be so exposed is to
be destroyed, annihilated by a self-consciousness induced by
an infinitude of others. As one former kibbutznik, living in a
residential treatment facility in Jerusalem, put it: "I was the
promise of my kibbutz, one of its shining lights; and then I
got sick. It was terrible; everyone was so kind, but I knew I
had failed in their eyes. I never want to go back; I hate that
place." (In the competition between the interests of the individual and those of the group, the schizophrenic inevitably
fares poorly.)

Nevertheless, what I saw in Israel, and to a limited extent
in Geel, parallels a sentiment expressed particularly by those
associated with sheltered workshops in the United States: that
the chronic patient possesses the capacity to act on specific (if
not circumscribed) social and economic imperatives. In other
words, the level of psychological and emotional impairment
need not necessarily lead to an unproductive and miserable
life. The strictly clinical environment, however, the world that
ministers only to the internal, in the form of treatment and/or
management, is not set up either to accommodate or to focus
on the relation between political economy and chronic mental
states. The medical model, frequently insensitive to the demands of the public self, utilizes a theory of power as therapeutic intervention that moves toward the amelioration of
psychological pain, not to the construction of an alternative
view of being and action. It is not a function of the medical
paradigm to think of diminishing psychic pain as a product of
the links between public collaborative participation and underlying emotional conflict. Political economy, and the place
of the self in it, is often ignored or is seen as having no therapeutic significance. Yet, is not work, and the collective and
public quality of its basic action, a source of self-respect and
esteem?

Therapy of whatever kind becomes, in the medical approach, an escape from pain, a view consistent with much in
the classical liberal position that regards the flight from pain
as the critical psychological dynamic in the maintenance of relationships. Gardening, woodwork, social skills, art, dance,

recreation: all hospital therapies find themselves compart-
mentalized as moments in an activities program. It was
precisely this kind of compartmentalization, and its negative
effects, that motivated social workers in Haifa to found a factory operated for the most part by chronic mental patients.
Therapy in the medical model is action geared to what is seen
as a passive object, the self's psychological body—a phenomenon that has become even more pronounced with the increasing reliance on antipsychotic medications to treat what
are often regarded as the organic or biochemical origins
of illness. In the Haifa model, therapy also consists in encouraging the expression of self through public forms of
participation.

Although the psychotherapeutic treatment of the chronic
patient is a humane and sincere effort to respond to unbearable pain, the governing paradigm avoids an equally important issue: the connection between the inner life and the
"place" or "space" that might facilitate the self's integration
with a public sense of its own worthiness. It is frequently an
overwhelming task for the chronically disturbed to find toler-
ant places, particularly in the area of work, that involve collaboration between "normal" and "chronic" individuals. For
example, in Geel, barriers to local employment for the mentally disturbed came not from local employers—who expressed an interest in working with the central hospital and
the foster care program—but from town workers on the production lines, especially the new workers who had recently
moved to Geel and who objected to working side-by-side with
the "loonies." (Contrast this to the factory in Haifa where
"normal" and "chronic" individuals worked side-by-side, with
equal demands placed on both.) It is a sad story, Geel's decline
in tolerance, not only because of the demise of what in the
past was a humane form of treating madness but because of
what the town and its central hospital meant in times of political crisis: the values of tolerance were part of Geel's political
culture. For example, after the invasion of Belgium by the
Nazis, the Geelians resisted in a way peculiar to their own tradition: the townspeople hid Jews among the patient population of the central hospital and, to a lesser extent, in their own
homes as "foster" patients.

The medical paradigm moves to contain the internal; it intervenes in precisely those areas seen to be skewed in terms of prevailing social conceptions of normality and acceptability. But what gives the self a consciousness of its public identity lies for the most part outside the objectives and sense of purpose of the mental hospital (the agent of the medical paradigm). Since therapy labors on different parts of the self, since it is disconnected from the broader concerns of the self's public being, it is understandable that patients often feel confined, worked upon, and frightened of what faces them in the outside world (most of the foster care residents I spoke with in Geel, by contrast, did not feel confined or "hemmed in" by the system). And, on the outside, most local jurisdictions simply do not have the funding or resources to provide for the self's productive being. Whatever resources do exist are expended on necessities (food, shelter) and, if possible, therapies (usually group therapy) that will keep the self (client) in some kind of contact with mental health professionals.

POWER AND THE MEDICAL GAZE: LIMITATION IN SELF-DEFINITION

For Michel Foucault the self, as it is worked on by the professions, is a victim of power.[10] Although much in Foucault's critique illuminates the nexus of social relations in which the self is enmeshed, I do not accept the larger implication that therapy may be harmful precisely *because* it is an agent of social power.[11] Nevertheless, Foucault does highlight the importance of giving some consideration to the constituents of the self in its public mode of being.

A more limited and, I believe, realistic (as opposed to ideological) use of Foucault would be to suggest that although the disturbed self finds itself enmeshed in relations of power, those relations do not necessarily have to be harmful. To correct the imbalance in power relations (the private self "scrutinized" by the therapies), it may be necessary to provide the self with some sense of its place in a public world, to respond to the need for work in common, an existence involved in be-

ing with others—again, a sentiment that in Israel lay behind
the view (although not the majority view) that the interests of
the chronically disturbed may best be served by integration
into collective forms of organization and action.

In the modern mental hospital, what Foucault calls the
scrutinizing or "panopticon" mentality[12] (the Benthamite
model of control) has been transferred to a variety of methods: behavioral conditioning (token economies), medication
and electroshock therapy, therapies that move to normalize
behavior, expressive and social therapies pursued in isolation
one from the other (the self seen as a series of pieces to be
administered, whether in the form of language, art, dance,
family relationships, or group dynamics). The light that Jeremy Bentham so effectively proposed as a substitute for the
dungeon now appears as a technology of power that holds
psychosis through a variety of interventions into the internal
or hidden self, psychopharmacology being the most recent
and technological of the modern treatments. Physical constraint is no longer necessary except in rare instances of disruptive or assaultive behavior, since the power of the
panopticon extends, through medication, to specific synapses
and sites in brain cells. A Foucauldian analysis, however, does
ignore the very real fact that for the patients the therapies
diminish psychological pain, and medications alleviate some
of the more frightening symptoms in severe mental illness.

Even with the modern panopticon, in its form as power
containing the internal self, patients experience intense anxiety over the prospect of discharge. Returning to the world
means losing the security of the ever-present therapeutic
gaze. Whereas Foucault conceives professional intervention as
an exercise of power (domination), the patient may demand it
in the frantic search for relief from pain and for acknowledgment that the pain is real and terrifying. In the words of Eve,
at Sheppard-Pratt:

> Here I am speaking to you about my feelings and thoughts;
> and when I'm discharged, I'll have to be tremendously careful
> about who I speak to. . . . At least here there are any number
> of people who will listen. But outside the hospital, who is

> there? Maybe my boy-friend? But even he is frightened of
> what I am. . . . I often think about my discharge, where I will
> be put, who they'll put me with. . . . Do I have to go back home
> or to a halfway house? It's so confusing because I feel so home-
> less, without any place to go or maybe nowhere is a place. I just
> don't know. It makes me so sad; my life, I think, is like a leaf.

She was describing something of the despair patients feel in
their effort to come to grips with the feeling that they are not
part of any community, that they are grist in an institution in
which they are dependent clients. However, although she
could be quite bitter about what she perceived as real inequal-
ities, Eve also acknowledged and respected what the hospital
offered as containment for her own feelings of disintegration.
In spite of her anger at inequality she was grateful for the
relief:

> Why would I want to leave? So I can go back home and live in
> a little room or listen to the prattle of roommates who really
> care about nothing but getting ahead? At least here people
> want to understand all parts of who you are. Even though I
> hate being on a locked ward, I still feel a sense of unity with
> many of the patients, even the sickest.

Eve's observations are fairly typical. Such patients come
to respect and even feel comfortable within the hospital's
therapeutic world. Yet the feelings of placelessness, of being
nowhere; the dread of returning to previous lives they know
will be unresponsive; of not having jobs or not believing that
they even deserve one: these fears of the future account for
much in their pessimism and cynicism. As Andrew (also at
Sheppard-Pratt) put it:

> What makes it so difficult is that no one cares about the world
> we have to go back to . . . the therapists and nurses speak to us
> about discharge and we make "plans," but no one really asks
> questions about what we are going back to. They assume that's
> what we want or should want. Yet, if you're psychologically dif-
> ferent, out there, it can be deadly. They'll kill you for it, either
> with phony kindness or solicitousness or with disdain and hos-
> tility. Either way you lose and end up being a parasite. The

hospital, even with all its activities, is still a place to be sick, not a place to go to work.

The experience here has helped, although I was a bit concerned that few people cared about what my illness meant. I don't want to think it was all for nothing, or that my delusions only told me I was sick. I would hope there was at least some meaning in my craziness. . . . On balance, you ask, did the hospital help me? Sure; I opened up here; I felt safe. . . . I didn't have to rationalize my behavior or explain my feelings if I chose not to. . . . No one judged me; and there were a few moments when I felt good, peaceful inside.

Confinement cuts both ways. It encircles the self in definition; it names internal worlds in the language of illness; in some respects, it dominates the self through infantilization. But it also provides comfort, containment, and the place to express, represent, and work through often unbearable psychological pain.

This was Andrew's second hospitalization; after his previous discharge, he had lived for a few months at a local halfway house:

I hated it. . . . I disliked most of the other residents; they were all so into themselves. And we didn't communicate very much, only over trivial stuff like washing dishes or keeping the halls clean, or making our beds. It was like being in camp all over again; except instead of counsellors we had aides who treated us like children. My parents' lack of concern made it even more difficult because I sensed in them relief that I hadn't come home. My friends treated me like some animal from outerspace. I began to see dead ends, no way out; here I was in a halfway house that was notable only for the antiseptic smell of its halls, and the need for residents to stay glued to the T.V. every morning. I would go to my job, yet my colleagues would stay clear of me or treat me like a fragile piece of china. My supervisor reviewed my work; and I think he had some doubts that an "ex-patient" could really do the [computer] programs. But my life had no meaning; I got up in the morning, caught the bus to work, came home. It was depressing and the residents were more depressed than I was. At some point, I don't

know why, maybe a bad day at work or I was turned down by a
girl I wanted to date, whatever, I decided to cut my wrists. I
think, looking back on it, I wanted back in [to the hospital] and
that was the only way I knew how to ask.

THE INVISIBLE SELF: ON COUNTERVAILING
FORCES TO ELIMINATION

In an interview in *Telos* in 1974 regarding prisons,
Foucault argued that once the inmate enters prison, he becomes a nonperson to society. A process that excluded the
convict (generally for years if not the rest of his life) from a
political, social, and economic sense of place generally is initiated. Prison therefore serves as a mechanism to break down
the convict, to render him invisible to the social order, without hope for a viable social future. Although this is not true
in all cases, it is a direction that confinement reenforces.
The inmate begins a career that effectively shuts him out of
a productive social life. "Society eliminates by sending to
prison people whom prison breaks up, crushes, physically
eliminates."[12]

Obviously, the conditions are not so harsh in humane
psychiatric hospitals (although many state and veterans' hospitals certainly now and in the past have treated patients as
inmates or criminals). Even so, treatment invariably remains
isolated from the self's public being, from its collaborative potential as a person who works and produces. Constraint is still
present, not as an external force that works on the physical
body, but as a set of internalized moral regulations defining
the self's structures of perception. The mental patient as a
disruptive social influence is eliminated through therapeutic
controls.

It is not as brutal a phenomenon as what Foucault sees
as the crushing of prisoners:—"Once they have been broken
up, the prison eliminates them by 'freeing' them and sending
them back to society."—but like the prisoner, the former patient, even with the ever-present social gaze defining reentry

and adaptation, faces enormous troubles. In Geel, for example, therapy now primarily involves weekly visits to the foster home by a social worker and whatever the resident receives from contact with others at various workshops and activities programs (including a "social" club) scattered throughout town. The activities programs perform a useful function in allowing the residents some social dimension to what are, for the most part, hidden and dreary lives. The exclusion practiced by family, friends, and employers, however, never completely disappears, and the label "former patient" is a powerful one in this society. Many find themselves desperate and alone and think about life as simply a matter of survival, feeling that little exists for them in the surrounding community. Attempted suicide, incapacitating symptoms, intolerable delusions may force the former patient's caretakers—whether family, halfway house, or friends—to place the person back in the hospital.

Some hospitals are more efficient and brutal than others in the process of elimination, yet no matter how benign the hospital setting, social interest dictates the masking of what society defines as "mental illness." How that eliminative process works for the discharged patient, how the self fares in it depends on the extent of medical health coverage, the willingness of families to sustain the cost of decent treatment, the luck of having been in a progressive mental institution or therapeutic community, the support of friends, and so on. It is obviously a phenomenon that should be distinguished from the treatment of former prisoners or from the kind of confinement Goffman speaks about in his analysis of "total institutions."[13] But at what point does the mental patient become a prisoner? What is the "line" or boundary that separates prisoner from patient? And—a question Foucault raises in connection with prisoners[14]—to what extent does social interest dictate the severity and extent of the exclusionary process?[15]

In addition to exclusion for social or political reasons (from rights, responsibilities, jobs, adequate living conditions), many former patients—and this is especially true for the

chronically mentally ill—suffer from a way of looking at the
world that in important respects differs from the prevailing
social orientation.

If the former patient has been schizophrenic (putting
aside for a moment the many different manifestations of this
state of mind), it is more than likely that the self's theory of
knowledge will involve delusional definition and reference. A
delusional reading of reality, nonconsensual and often fantas-
tic, is typical of schizophrenic persons. What this means is that
the self's theory of knowledge refuses to allow it to participate
in conventional rituals, since those rituals and assumptions
lack the necessary perspective and tolerance to accommodate
the schizophrenic's worldview. Any kind of life for the schizophrenic outside the hospital not only involves a series of existential compromises and frequent disappointments, but also
means living with thoughts and ideas that others find bizarre,
weird, or downright crazy, even though the crazy thoughts
may be harmless and not interfere with social obligations.

For the chronic patient who is capable of living and functioning (more or less) outside a hospital setting, delusions may
not necessarily disrupt daily tasks and activities. But they may
create conflict and misunderstanding in environments insensitive to these representations of thought. In the words of
Ned (a resident of a halfway house), "I still have strange
thoughts. Sometimes they come out, and people look at me as
if I were a man from Mars." Even though the former patient
may have a number of options—day-care centers, sheltered
workshops, halfway houses, support groups, and so on—it is
still necessary to survive and deal with so-called normal people who have a discouragingly low tolerance for the peculiarities even of nonthreatening "crazy" imagery and behavior.
One of the great strengths of Geel, at least in the past, lay in
the fact that the foster care residents were treated as persons
who deserved to be and live in the town, and not separated
from its environs.

With very few exceptions, being schizophrenic or chronic
means falling into nonperson status, in Foucault's sense, a
state of invisibility that involves a lot of drifting and confusion. Support systems are often inadequate; those in Isra-

el, for example, were frequently improvised with almost no financial backing from the state. The effort to rejoin society, especially in economic contexts, usually fails; activity suffers, and mistrust and disappointment pull consciousness away from any relation to public values, whether in work or in social activity. What the schizophrenic self trusts are delusions, and the more stressful life becomes on the outside, the more the delusion functions as a source of refuge and self-definition—unless it is counterbalanced by a community or work*place* that functions as a holding or containing environment. As one former patient put it: "When things start to fall in around me, the crazy thoughts come back." When delusion invades consciousness, the self loses its social connections, its relations to social time and space. Delusional time and space replace the self's rootedness and identity in interpersonal and social situations; the result is a loss of the self's public being, a reversion to private knowledge systems, and, most important, a complete loss of the sense of community.

CONCLUSION: PERSONHOOD AND THE RECOVERY OF PLACE

What, then, might be a way out of the impasse, the limitation in the medical model's view of the public self? On the one hand, the medical paradigm focuses treatment primarily on the inner self; power encircles and inhibits action. On the other, community-based resources, however, in the postdischarge world are limited; the former patient faces hostility from economic forces and internal impediments in the form of social impairments, low skill levels, inability to master complex technologies, and so on. If the rapid rise in homelessness is any indication, not enough is being done to minister to the public self of the chronically disturbed, not to mention the persistent psychological torment and fear that constitute a large part of waking life for such an individual.

It is necessary, then, to rethink the concept of place and what it means for the chronically mentally ill. A human psychiatric environment makes a serious effort to recover the human in the depersonalized, delusional self. Its effort, however, is limited by the failure to think through completely the relation between psychotherapy, work, and an identity grounded in some sense of a life in common. Further, delusional patients resist attempts to root perception psychically in what Harry Stack Sullivan called "consensual reality." It is therefore quite difficult for the chronic mental patient to struggle toward personhood, given the strength and tenacity of delusional defenses. The struggle is complicated even more by the impact of what to the former patient are socially noxious and objectifying dynamics in political society. If reentry into society serves to prolong the self's alienation and aggravate feelings of worthlessness and despair, it might be useful to rethink place as a synthesis of the public and private, an environment that defuses the impact of internal alien objects and creates an awareness of work with the objective of enhancing the feeling of efficacy and the public recognition of community or ends in common.

It is not at all clear that even the most progressive mental hospitals succeed in recovering on a long-term basis the humane and productive potential of the self who, for whatever reason, has withdrawn from social life. If even now, former patients find themselves shunted to undesirable labor within society, if they see themselves on the margins of the economic marketplace, if employers are hesitant to consider them for employment or fellow employees refuse to work with them, if all these things are part of the contemporary economic landscape, it seems unlikely that prospects will improve in the near future. The economy has become increasingly dependent on complex rational skills, on computer and information services and technologies that require extensive education and adaptation to prevailing social and cultural standards. It is therefore essential to look toward new ideas in the very serious problem of keeping the homeless, the placeless, within the bounds of the social order and not creating an underclass of alienated who remain permanently excluded from the social system.

What E. E. Schumacher[16] has argued about economics on a human scale may provide an alternative way of looking at the connection between community and production, what might be called the functions of "place," as place relates to the chronic patient. Schumacher's humanism, his emphasis on collaborative activity, his discussion of scale and technology, and his respect for nature and production hold values that offer an alternative to the instrumental and highly complex institutions that become so perplexing and unnavigable for the chronically mentally ill. It might even be useful in this regard to reexamine the historical Geel, to explore the possibility of "coproduction" within manageable limits, to develop innovative organizational techniques and approaches in both rural and urban environments,[17] to encourage and fund small-scale enterprises that might be able to harness the *limited* but very real productive potential of the chronic patient. Such persons are not completely dysfunctional or untreatable. If the chronic patient is to have any kind of productive life, it is doubtful that such a life will, on a long-term basis, be found in bureaucratic centers of power and in technologies that confound the self's perceptual capacities. Much of the solution to homelessness may depend on society's being able to encourage a productivity and a *relation* to production that enhance self-respect and contribute to self-esteem. To solve the problem of place, understood as both productivity and community—what Schumacher calls the self's productive "habitat"—is to go a long way to relieving the psychological alienation of the homeless.

This is not to say that hospitals fail to provide useful and important services. I am not arguing against concrete and humane actions to alleviate the inner terror of the self—a problem, for example, in much of the French critique of psychiatry; to couch the argument only in terms of ideology is to obscure and minimize the very real suffering of persons with mental illness. I do suggest that there are structural limitations to the functions of the hospital precisely because it refuses to treat the connection, or lack of it, between the self's private being and its public requirements.[18]

I do not question the premises of psychotherapy or the expressive therapies (art, dance, recreation, social skills, and so on). Sensitivity to the self's internal needs is essential, and patients respond to concerned and committed therapists. I cannot emphasize too strongly that symptomatic relief of pain, which the psychotherapies offer, is better than no relief, and it is no easy task to defuse the delusional bases of knowledge and identity in the more psychotic patients. But it might be productive to think of place in a political langauge—the language of community and civility, productive activity and collaboration—and not only in the medical language and the paradigm of disease and hospitalization. If what is lacking in the chronic mental patient is a belief in the efficacy of some form of public life—life shared with others not in silent wonderment or, at the other end, paralyzing fear but in expressive work and discourse—then such efficacy might be stimulated by allowing the self to conceive of its own future in a place where productive activity is infused with participation.

Finally, the concept of treatment, under this view, would be more open to thinking about the relation between public and private, between the self's productive being and the self's internal world and its alienation from consensual reality. In most psychological and psychiatric theories the private or hidden, whether inside the unconscious or inside the brain or in behavioral and chemical dysfunctions, becomes the object of therapeutic intervention. But it is also the self's being in public, its work, its interpersonal relations, and the inevitable politics of persons, institutions, and bureaucracies that drive troubled individuals into feelings of failure and hopelessness, particularly if those individuals have already been funneled through mental hospitals and the professional mental health care network. After such a journey the self experiences itself as so sick that even to think of it as healthy and worthwhile requires an almost heroic movement from pessimism and dejection to at least some belief in the possibility of transformation. It is the feeling of fragmentation, placelessness, and loss of rights that the chronic patient strives to escape. Yet it is precisely these feelings that the self encounters when it faces the competition, complexity, and instrumentalism so characteristic of modern society.

NOTES

This essay appeared in a somewhat different form in *Private Terror/Public Life: Psychosis and the Politics of Community* (Ithaca, N.Y.: Cornell University Press, 1989). Reprinted here with the permission of Cornell University Press.

1. R. Girard, *The Scapegoat* (Baltimore: Johns Hopkins University Press, 1986).

2. For an analysis of this phenomenon, see H. R. Lamb, "Structure: The Neglected Ingredient of Community Treatment," *Arch. Gen. Psych.* 37 (1980): 1224–28, and L. L. Bachrach, "A Conceptual Approach to Deinstitutionalization," *Hosp. and Comm. Psych* 29: 573–78. Bachrach calls for a "reassessment" of the plight of those persons who have "largely been lost to the service delivery system" (p. 575). Also see her article "Is the Least Restrictive Environment Always the Best? Sociological and Semantic Implications," *Hosp. and Comm. Psych.* 31 (1980): 97–103.

The federal government has sponsored a number of studies; one of the best is "Report of the Last Panel on Deinstitutionalization, Rehabilitation and Long-Term Care," in *Task Panel Reports Submitted to the President's Commission on Mental Health*, vol. 1 (Washington D.C., 1978). See particularly pp. 356–75.

3. See R. F. Mollica, "From Asylum to Community: The Threatened Disintegration of Public Psychiatry," *N. Engl. J. Med.* 308 (1983): 367–73. Mollica points to the serious problems of treating lower-class patients, that in fact "universal entitlement" for the mentally ill does not mean or translate into plentiful facilities. Also see H. Goldman, N. H. Adams, "Deinstitutionalization: The Data Demythologized," *Hosp. and Comm. Psych.* 34 (1983): 129–34.

4. The literature is copious on this theme; for general overviews see L. L. Bachrach, "An Overview of Deinstitutionalization," in *New Directions for Mental Health Services: Deinstitutionalization*, ed. L. L. Bachrach (San Francisco: Jossey-Bass, 1983); J. A. Talbott, *Chronic Mental Patients: Treatment, Progress, Systems* (New York: Human Sciences Press, 1981); J. A. Talbott, ed., *The Chronic Mental Patient* (New York: Gruen and Stratton, 1981).

5. There is an increasingly influential argument in the literature that suggests it may be time to rethink the role of the state hospital in caring for the chronically mentally ill. For example, Leona Bachrach argues that 50 of every 100,000 people in the United States reside as patients in state mental hospitals, "Deinstitutional-

ization: What Do the Numbers Mean?" *Hosp. and Comm. Psych.* 37 (1986): 118–221. H. R. Lamb points to the increasingly desperate situation of the homeless on the nation's streets and in urban centers, "Deinstitutionalization and the Homeless Mentally Ill," *Hosp. and Comm. Psych.* 35 (1984): 899–907. Several commentators note the utility of the state hospital as a place where "multiple functions" can be carried out humanely and with consideration of the welfare of the patient. The argument suggests novel forms of organizing services and programs within the state hospital physical setting. See H. H. Goldman, C. A. Taube, D. A. Reiger, et al., "The Multiple Functions of the State Mental Hospital," *Am. J. of Psych.* 140 (1983): 296–300. T. J. Craig and E. M. Laska call for "communitizing" the state hospital, "Deinstitutionalization and the Survival of the State Hospital," *Hosp. and Comm. Psych.* 34 (1983): 616–22. For a discussion of "custodialism" versus "communitizing," see J. K. Wing, "From Institutional to Community Care, *Psych. Quar.* 53 (1981): 139–52. For a fascinating symposium on the *psychiatric* rehabilitation of chronic mental patients, see *Schizophrenia Bulletin* (12, No. 4, 1986) NIMH publication, Rockville, Md. Cf. particularly John Strauss's rejoinder to the symposium; he argues that rehabilitation may in fact be considered a form of therapy. There has also been a extensive debate in Italy involving political and ideological arguments on both sides of the state hospital versus the "return to the community" issue. For a detailed examination of this debate, see the August 1986 issue of *Hosp. and Comm. Psych.* 37.

6. For a discussion of this aspect of the plight of the homeless, see *Positive Aspects of Long-Term Hospitalization in the Public Sector for Chronic Psychiatric Patients* (New York: GAP, 1982); D. A. Treffert, "Sane Asylum: An Alternative to the Mental Hospital," *Curr. Psychiatr. Ther.* 17 (1977): 309–14; E. Baxter, K. Hopper, *Private Lives/Public Spaces: Homeless Adults on the Streets of New York City* (New York: Community Service Society of N.Y., 1981); B. Pasamanick, F. R. Scarpitti, S. Dinitz, *Schizophrenia in the Community: An Experimental Study in the Prevention of Hospitalization* (New York: Appleton-Century-Crofts, 1967). The argument here is that conventional services are inadequate to the enormous demands and needs of the chronically ill. Also see M. E. Hombs, M. Snyder, *Homelessness in America: A Forced March to Nowhere*, (Washington, D.C.: Community for Creative Non-Violence, 1982).

7. Alice Miller, in *For Your Own Good: Hidden Cruelty in Child-Rearing and the Roots of Violence* (New York: Farrar, Straus and Giroux, 1986), is considerably more sanguine than, for example, Lamb

regarding the capacity of community services to handle effectively the plight of the chronic mental patient. Also see J. E. Gudeman, M. F. Shore, "Beyond Deinstitutionalization: A New Class of Facilities for the Mentally Ill," *N. Engl. J. of Med.* 311 (1984): 832–36; C. A. Kiesler, "Mental Hospitals and Alternative Care," *Amer. Psychol.* 37 (1982): 349–60; J. F. Borus, "Deinstitutionalization of the Chronically Mentally Ill, *N. Engl. J. of Med.* 305 (1981): 339–42.

8. Several persons in Geel and in Israel generously contributed their time and effort in arranging this research. In Geel, I am indebted to Dr. H. Matheussen, Medical Director of the Central Psychiatric Hospital, to Dr. J. Schrijvers for his efforts in facilitating the visit and providing a translator, and to Frans Vaneynde, Administrator of the Central Hospital. In Israel, I am grateful to Dr. Michael Avrouskine of the Public Health Service for arranging interviews and setting up contacts. In Haifa I would like to thank Dr. Yacov Naisberg of the Ramdam Medical Center in allowing me to accompany him on his rounds to local kibbutzim and Zalmon Sher of the Kirit Ata Shop; also, Muriel Dominitz, a social worker at Kibbutz Matsuva; Dr. Stanley Schneider, Director of the Summit Institute in Jerusalem; Dr. Eric Moss, Director of a community mental health center outside of Tel Aviv; Toby and Judy Hammerman, social workers in a suburb of Tel Aviv, and Dr. Y. Bar-El, Director of Kfar Shaul Mental Hospital in Jerusalem, who were all extremely helpful. Finally, I am much indebted to Dr. Uri Lowental for his kind hospitality and informative conversation.

9. P. Earle, *The Curability of Insanity* (Philadelphia: Lippincott, 1887). Reprinted by Arno Press (New York, 1972).

10. M. Foucault, *Language, Counter-Memory, Practice: Selected Essays and Interviews*, ed. Donald F. Bouchard (Ithaca, N.Y.: Cornell University Press, 1980), p. 201.

11. For a critique of Foucault's conception of the hospital, particularly in terms of its function in providing a sense of place and constancy, see A. Rosenblatt's discussion of the York retreat and Samuel Tuke's conception of moral treatment, "Concepts of the Asylum in the Care of the Mentally Ill," *Hosp. and Comm. Psych.* 35 (1985): 244–50.

12. M. Foucault, *Discipline and Punish* (New York: Vintage, 1979).

13. E. Goffman, *Asylums* (New York: Anchor, 1961).

14. M. Foucault, "On Attica: An Interview," *Telos* 19 (1974): 154–62.

15. M. Foucault, *Telos*, pp. 155, 161.

16. Schumacher has had a profound influence on reassessing the relation between technology (its size and scale) and the sustenance and maintenance of human life. He has consistently argued for small-scale technologies adapted to place and need, and he further sees a connection between such technologies (and their use) and the pursuit of community. Further, it is conceivable that his theory could be useful in thinking about the theory of community and its relation to the chronically mentally ill (with special emphasis on economic structure and technological implementation). See E. E. Schumacher, *Small Is Beautiful: Economics As If People Mattered* (New York: Harper & Row, 1973).

17. Rural Spring Lake Ranch in Cuttingsville, Vermont, and urban Fountain House in New York City provide useful models for a workable and sensible theory of coproduction between an institution and chronically disturbed persons. Fountain House, providing post-hospital care, is a club run chiefly by former patients which serves meals and functions as a meeting place and community center. But it is known primarily for its success in training former mental patients for effective work relationships: its transitional employment program has been a model for more than 240 similar programs throughout the country and abroad. The paid staff is quite small; the work in the club, from housecleaning to meal preparation to office duties, is performed by the members. Further, an outreach program involves agreements with local employers whereby members may work in the club for a time, then be placed—generally for a six-month period—in an "outside" entry-level position. Currently, 600 to 700 members participate in the day programs, and some thirty local employers have agreed to employ 140 members part time. One member, who was a patient in a mental hospital for twenty years, says that the program has allowed her to "be with others" and, in her words, gives "you the pride of making your own money . . . being on your own." Fountain House, then, providing its members with training and the chance of gainful employment is an alternative to long-term hospital care.

For a comprehensive approach to this question (particularly from a psychiatrist quite familiar with modern theories of political economy) see R. Warner, *Recovery from Schizophrenia* (New York: Routledge & Kegan Paul, 1985).

18. For some pioneering studies of the effect of compartmentalization on treatment and relations within the hospital, see A. H. Stanton, M. S. Schwartz, *The Mental Hospital* (New York: Basic Books, 1954); W. Caudill, *The Psychiatric Hospital as a Small Society*

(Cambridge, Mass: Harvard University Press); M. Greenblatt, D. J. Levinson, R. H. Williams, *The Patient and the Mental Hospital* (New York: Free Press, 1957). It should be mentioned that these works accept the hospital as a useful therapeutic environment and, unlike Goffman's global critique, each author accepts the fundamental and abiding legitimacy of the hospital as an institution.

ANTIGONE'S DAUGHTERS RECONSIDERED: CONTINUING REFLECTIONS ON WOMEN, POLITICS, AND POWER

Jean Bethke Elshtain

Why Antigone's daughters? In an earlier essay I appropriated the evocative and complex luminosity and transgressive yet restorative words and deeds of Antigone as worthy of consideration by feminists skeptical of state organization of social and political life, hence determined to position themselves against a public identity confined to the normalizing terms of the juridicopolitical apparatus. My original aim was "to define and to defend a female identity and a feminist perspective that enables contemporary women to see themselves as the daughters of Antigone."[1] American feminists were already the political and discursive daughters of some thinker or school of thought, whether daughters of J. S. Mill, or Karl Marx, or the intrepid few who traced their parentage to a long buried matriarchal past or proclaimed parthenogenetic birth.[2] Sophocles' Antigone dies childless and alone. Yet she has spawned, engendered, if you will, countless progeny in Western literature, art, and thought. "Why a hundred 'Antigones' after Sophocles?" queries George Steiner.[3]

No maternal figure, Antigone seems unsisterly as well. When the cautious Ismenê shrinks from joining Antigone in open defiance of Creon's edict forbidding anyone from enacting his or her familial obligation to bury and honor Polyneicês, brother to Antigone and Ismenê, Antigone sends her away with harsh words. Ismenê pleads with Antigone, reminding her that women cannot fight with men nor against the law. Ismenê has no stomach for a rebellious act undertaken in obedience to a solemn, unwritten obligation; instead, she asks the dead to forgive her. Antigone's determination flows from her conviction that Creon's order must not be allowed to efface the honors "due all the dead." She goes forth to bury her brother, to claim her fate. Reverence and care invite, indeed require, conflict and strife. So it begins.

THE PLAY RECALLED

The reader knows the bare bones of the story. But an interpretive gloss is useful to refresh memories and to frame reflections.[4] Polyneicês, brother to Antigone and Ismenê, has been denied the burial honors bestowed upon a second slain brother, Eteocles, by Creon, king of Thebes, who is as well uncle to Antigone and her siblings. As a member of Creon's family, Polyneicês is one toward whom Creon has incurred a burial obligation. But Polyneicês is a traitor, an enemy to the city. For Creon the latter is all that counts. He exhibits no visible signs of a tug between his moral obligations as an uncle and his civic duties as a king as he lurches arrogantly toward a harsh version of the latter. Notes Steiner, "Creon's world is that of masculine immanence, of a willed at-homeness in a sphere of political action and futurity."[5]

Contrary to all expectations, most startlingly received standards of male and female *public* behavior, Antigone violates Creon's orders by throwing dirt over her brother's rotting corpse. Brought before Creon, she affirms her deed, insisting on familial love and piety as a superordinate moral obligation that must be honored no matter what the consequences. Her words and actions are crystallized in adversity as she confronts "the other," Creon as king-uncle, a protagonist who embodies an alternative ethic. Antigone knows she will suffer for her steely stance. And the city itself may be in peril, too, given the king's impiety. Creon fends off Antigone's challenge by construing her actions as symptoms of mental incapacity or moral derangement, hence a threat to civic order. Antigone's fate is sealed. She must die.[6]

But the embattled Creon's troubles have only begun. His son, and Antigone's betrothed, Haemon, implores his father to reconsider his intransigent course, informing him that "the people" support Antigone's devotion to a supreme law shared by all blood kin. The Theban Chorus nags at Creon, warning him that he has made things too easy for himself. Where are the tears that should accompany a terrible decision, and few could be more terrible than condemning a member of one's family to die, after having prevented another from receiving an honorable burial? Something is wanting in Creon's moral makeup.

Martha Nussbaum argues that, hoping to simplify conflicts between duty to family and requirements of civic order, Creon achieves this end by diminishing the familial pole of his human obligations and feelings. Insulated against all entreaties, having pared his understanding of what is good and necessary down to a few rigid imperatives, Creon is fated to suffer the hard lessons of repeated tragic blows. Only when he has lost nearly all he loves does he acknowledge sadly that his view of the city has been wanting, as the doomed Haemon and the Chorus suggested all along. Perhaps civic piety and justice cannot be severed from private duty and its solemn demands: that is the lesson Creon finally learns as he stands surrounded by the havoc his relentlessly one-sided view of political necessity and patriarchal privilege has wrought.[7]

THE ESSAY REVIEWED

A second reprise is necessary before I reenter the debate over whether interpretations of the *Antigone* carry, or should, any authoritative weight from the standpoint of political theory and feminist concerns. "Antigone's Daughters" issued a warning to and about American feminism as part of a lively debate within feminist discourse. Thus the essay offered up brief critiques of mainstream liberal, radical, and Marxist feminisms insofar as each either privileged the state with too little mistrust of increasingly unaccountable and ever-more-pervasive centralized authority or held forth the promise that the state (or some unspecified future feminized order) would be a wholly benign force once it was purified of centuries of phallocentrism.

Along with many others, I was unconvinced by the "oppressed group model," analyses that saw in women's traditional identities only victimization, thereby denying women historic agency, culture, and authority. Those who accepted this view found themselves valorizing the statuses and identities of the dominant male as normative for the subordinate female—an unwittingly ironic posture for a feminist as it would, if played out, further rationalize the extant order with substitutions of personnel in the absence of genuine transformative possibilities as ways of being in the world. What was at stake, then, was a particular sort of ready-to-hand public identity, a historical form of masculine domination that bore the weight and logic of the contemporary status quo. The *Antigone* helps to clarify these lines of fault, serving well any thinker concerned with the complex cominglings of revolt and restoration, of anticipative and reverential attitudes, of care and conflict in human identity and practice. The narrative defies easy construals that see women either entering the public world or remaining stuck in the company of pots, pans, toddlers, and soap operas.[8]

The critical point, then, was the claim that to construe the contemporary "public world as the only sphere within which individuals made real choices, exercised authentic power or had efficacious control" meant that the "private world, in turn, automatically reflected . . . powerlessness, necessity, irrationality."[9] Just as the darker realities of the public world were unexplored, the powers and dignities of women's private sphere were ignored by those who denied any lineage with Antigone as a figure of representation. Moving from this critique to intimation and tentative affirmation, I noted "difference feminism," then beginning to make an impact, and linked it to a feminism that poised itself *knowingly* on the

boundaries of irony and paradox, embracing rather than eschewing conflicts and tensions, hence a stance that required
moving back and forth between complicated and not easily re-
solvable public and private commitments. Positioning women
as social actors in the world, I aimed to pit them simultaneously against imperious public power and petty private demands even as they sustained a public identity, as citizens, and
embraced worlds of intimate obligation.

Both worlds, public and private, are social locations,
strikingly at odds, if one treats them concretely rather than
abstractly, with much of the theorizing in the Western tradition that features a very thin notion of human social worlds.
Breaking out of a rigid public and private dichotomy, even as
one recognizes and seeks to preserve some version of a public-
private distinction, "social feminism," as I tagged it, challenged received categories and promoted a feminism at once
more historical, more interpretive, in its approach.[10]

THE ARGUMENT REPRESENTED

The power of Antigone is such that rich interpretations
by contemporary commentators, including Steiner and Nussbaum noted earlier, continue to emerge and to put pressure
on one's own reading. Confronted with such challenges,
whether tacit or implicit, one is often tempted to retreat to
previous formulations, to grow wary of embracing an
Antigone-for-one's-time or for explicitly polemical purposes.
For political theorists this means enhousing one's own version
of the narrative within the dominant encoding in the canon of
Western political thought: Hegel's strong reading.[11] Any representation of Antigone for political theorists must move
through Hegel. But it cannot rest there, as Fred Dallmayr's erudite consideration of "Life-World: Variations on a Theme"
(in this volume) helps to make clear, or so I shall argue briefly
below.

First, a brief Hegelian recursus. Hegel discusses Sophocles' *Antigone* in the *Phenomenology* and the *Philosophy of Right*,

structuring the drama in a way that enables him to reassert the essentiality and limits of women's ethical identity as the carrier of familial ethical life. Hegel contends that the family

> as the inner indwelling principle of sociality operating in an unconscious way, stands opposed to its own actuality when explicitly conscious; as the basis of the actuality of a nation, it stands in contrast to the nation itself; as the *immediate* ethical existence, it stands over against the ethical order which shapes and preserves itself by work for universal ends; the Penates of the family stand in contrast to the universal spirit.[12]

How can the family take its ethical importance from "universal ends" even as it "stands over against" those ends?[13] Hegel's answer takes shape as one considers his differentiation of family members on the basis of their relationship to the familial and universal spheres. The sister bears or embodies a "feminine element" or form. She cannot, by definition, actualize a full ethical life: "the law of the family is her implicit inward nature, which does not lie open to the daylight of consciousness but remains inner feeling. . . . " Her devotion to the Penates of the family is positioned "in contrast to the universal spirit."[14] In the male alone the family has a member "in whom its spirit becomes individualized and enabled thereby to turn towards another sphere towards what is other than and external to itself and pass over into consciousness of universality."[15]

Antigone and Creon, on Hegel's reading, can do little more than exemplify the ontological commitments of this prior construction. Hegel uses Sophocles to reinforce his insistence that familial ethical life is natural, limited, and "female" and that only in overcoming or transcending the opposition between particular and universal can universal ethical life be achieved. Hegel's universal moment is embodied in the male for he alone is individuated from the family and concretized as a citizen in the "actuality of the ethical Idea," the life of the state. This means that Hegel misses—that he must miss— what is most powerful and poignant about Antigone. Her rebellion requires that she abandon the traditional standpoint of woman, forsake the temerity and withholdingness of Ismenê, and force herself into the civic arena, there to face the consequences of her rebellious action.

The family is, as I argued in "Antigone's Daughters," her entry point into the civic. But she goes on to force herself upon the stage, to step into the public arena: not under some description of abstract or universal personhood but in and through a particular encumbered identity. This Antigone, in contrast to Hegel's, must dare to "challenge public power by giving voice to familial and social imperatives and duties." Hers is a "robust voice, a bold voice." Her defense of particular obligations is a simultaneous reincoding of a shared communal (one is tempted to say "universal") ethical obligation. Hence Haemon's words to his insensitive father: the people sympathize with Antigone. They share her commitments, commitments that are constitutive of the city itself. Patricia Mills seems to me right when she insists that Antigone's position is not "an unconscious intuition of her ethical duty as Hegel would have us believe. Rather, it is a noble stance consciously taken."[16]

Antigone embraces a course of action knowing that it will have tragic consequences. Ironically, a mode of "letting be," the playing out of "familial usage and codes of sentiment," demands of her a move toward active positioning against Creon's "new public rationality." She becomes a "forward imaginer" in invoking the unwritten laws, "summoning up futurities of conscience."[17] It is Ismenê who does not act on her beliefs and who embodies "traditional womanhood" (if such a locution can reasonably be deployed in a discussion of Greek tragedy). To retain intact his overarching schema, Hegel not only ignores Antigone's knowingness but keeps her sealed up in his sphere of intuited ethical particularity. She cannot "break out," yet that, of course, is precisely what she does, otherwise the play loses its power as a narrative of tragic civic conflict.

Not surprisingly, Hegel never mentions Ismenê. To do so would have required a discussion of the differences between the stances of Ismenê and Antigone and made it more difficult for Hegel to confine Antigone. Indeed, Mills argues that Hegel goes so far as to change Antigone's final words in order to make them square with his interpretation of the play. He does so by altering her insistence that "I have done no wrong/ I have not sinned before the gods. Or if I have, I shall know the truth in death," to which Antigone adds that if guilt lies upon Creon "his punishment should equal my own," to read as if it were a straightforward acknowledgment of guilt for the "crime" of burying her brother.[18] Contrary to Hegel, then, Antigone embodies a civic revolt, action undertaken in the public sphere in defense of exigencies that emerge from the private sphere. The entire history of feminism is in part a story of such forms of revolt.[19]

Antigone does not seek the institutionalization of a narrow private good, the instantiation of some insular, privileged purity; nor does she aim for deliverance from private/public, particular/universal conflicts. As I have argued, she recognizes that her action will deepen and make public conflict between differing understandings of human good and civic necessity. Her pursuit of virtue is her own, rooted in the sustaining features of communal tradition. Her preparedness to take the consequences of her actions is bracing and poignant because she is clearly torn by the conflict. Her understanding of the community and its values is deep, involving an explicit acknowledgment that unwritten obligations are part of a stock of constitutive civic necessities and cannot be arrogantly set aside by decree.[20]

Fred Dallmayr's unpacking of the concept of the life-world helps one to appreciate the fullness of Antigone's position and brings to a reading of Sophocles a greater depth in our understanding of the standpoint of *Antigone* in the modern world. Working within a Hegelian tradition, broadly construed, Dallmayr might be expected to reinscribe Hegel's reading of the Antigone. But his phenomenological roots take him in a different direction, beginning with his discussion of Husserl's discursive centering of "the living body" and its unique concreteness and givenness as that through which I act; that which is never not-present; that which can be acted upon. We must pay this living body heed; it is not a taken-for-granted. Thus the "life-world emerges as the universe of embodied experiences and complementary life situations."[21]

Husserl, however, gives in to strong Hegelian temptations as we learn from Dallmayr's challenge to Husserl's notion of the ego as a "distant" spectator, teleologically propelled toward a reflexive standpoint "above" the pregivenness of the world. In Schutz's notion of the life-world, a domain of everyday life "permeated . . . by preconstituted social meanings and typifications," Dallmayr finds a fertile correction to abstractedness.[22] Rounding out his discussion, Dallmayr (following Heidegger and Merleau-Ponty) reminds us that body and world are not simply externally related but internally entangled, making of the life-world a "multi-layered arena fraught with ruptures and discontinuities."

What Dallmayr offers to a reading of Antigone is this: we behold her life-world in disarray. She responds not by retreating to a point of safety but by advancing to a point of no return. Her actions are transgressive: confronted with rupture, she carries the discontinuities further and deepens the perils and possibilities of an already fraught situation. Drawn into a discursive frame with Antigone, the notion of life-worlds reminds us that we are preeminently spatial beings, not airy creatures lofting upward on the winds of pure thought. Nor, Dallmayr suggests, should our moral reasoning take the form of universalist grandiosities, booming code words that enable us to override the concreteness of *this* event, *this* individual, *this time and place*.

The questions posed by Antigone are problematic, then, in ways I recognized in earlier considerations and in ways I did not. There are numerous perils in operating under the description I urged, and my answer to a question I posed for myself in "Antigone's Daughters" is not so straightforward as I then claimed. I wrote: "But how does one hold on to a social location for contemporary daughters of Antigone without simultaneously insisting that women accept traditional terms of political quiescence? The question answers itself: the standpoint of Antigone is of a woman who dares to challenge public power by giving voice to familial and social imperatives and duties."[22] The question does not "answer itself." The answer emerges from political struggle and the by-now-centuries-old battle over the meaning and implications of the Antigone story.

WHOSE ANTIGONE IS SHE ANYWAY?

With other great representations of the human spirit at once particular to a time and place, yet transcendant, vibrantly recalled in any time that tries the souls of men and women, Antigone resists simple capture. Meanings are mobile. Readings are never fixed once and for all. As this rereading draws to a close, I am haunted by two representations. The first is drawn from Steiner's *Antigones*:

> In his diary for 17 September 1941, the German novelist and publicist Martin Raschke recounts an episode in Nazi-occupied Riga. Caught trying to sprinkle earth on the publicly exposed body of her executed brother, a young girl, entirely unpolitical in her sentiments, is asked why. She answers: "He was my brother. For me that is sufficient." In December 1943, the Germans descended on the village of Kalavrita in the Peloponnesus. They rounded up all the males and did them to death. Against explicit orders, in peril of their lives, the women of the village broke out of the school in which they had been imprisoned and went *en masse* to lament and bury the dead.[23]

These episodes detail a primordial (not primitive) set of urgencies at work, not in the form of an articulated political philosophy but, instead, of exigent imperatives: one cannot do otherwise. No explanation is required. One level of Antigone is made concrete here in a terrible and sublime modern allegory: women acting to preserve something in the midst of unbearable destruction, to honor obligations that cannot be annihilated by brute force.

But there is a second haunting, a political parable drawn from more recent years that evokes, then carries through and out, possibilities that lie immanent within Antigone representations. This is a story of the Mothers of the Plaza de Mayo in Buenos Aires, Argentina. The mothers, by their public presence and courageous action, shattered the systematic deceit that had surrounded the disappearances, torture, and murder of their children; they transgressed official decrees by marching publicly. Just as Creon aimed to portray Antigone as mentally deranged, the Mothers were labeled "las locas," the madwomen—beyond the pale, outside the boundaries of legitimate politics. Reversing the strategy of the authorities by turning it on its head, the mothers fashioned a powerful political weapon. The language they spoke was double: the language of a mother's loss and the language of human rights, moving back and forth from intensely particular, yet universally recognized, imperatives of love and terror, to what has become a universal and potent political discourse.

I asked several of the Mothers how they found the courage to act publicly and to persist and whether they would go on indefinitely. One, the mother of three *desaparecidos*, told me that the Mothers would always be prepared to "watch and to denounce every violation of human rights. Because, you know, at the beginning, we only wanted our children. But, as time passed, we got a different comprehension of what was going on in the world. Today I was listening to the radio and there was somebody who sings very well who was singing about children, about babies starving. This is also a violation of human rights. Perhaps it is not much that we can do, but people for human dignity and human rights must realize justice where they can." All the Mothers were insistent in their characterization of their struggle as they described it to me during long hours of conversation. It always had a "clear moral purpose" and had "always been non-violent and carried out with dignity."

Acting out of individual grief and conscience but in behalf of a common morality and to a shared end: that is how these latter-day daughters of Antigone understand themselves and require that we, in turn, appreciate them. One of the Mothers, to whom I gave a copy of "Antigone's Daughters," read it and offered her reactions (in English). She said:

> We *are* your daughters of Antigone. I did not get to bury my children, as Antigone buried her brother. But I have risked my life to make public their suffering. Now, somehow, I must find the strength to go on living. I can do this because if I do not my children will have died twice, once at the hands of their tormenters and a second time from my silence. Thrown into the sea, tossed like garbage into mass graves, where are my children? I cannot bring flowers, nor pray, nor visit their final

resting places. Like the Mothers, the Disappeared are every-where, wherever a single person is abducted, tortured, killed unjustly. Like Antigone, we will endure beyond our lifetimes. This is what we recognize. This is our hope.

Why Antigone's daughters? When I was marching with the Mothers in the Plaza on a bone-chilling, drizzly afternoon in Buenos Aires, the answer was stunningly clear. I witnessed suffering redeemed through moral courage and political defiance exemplified through knowing and purposeful action. With the Mothers of the Plaza de Mayo, all contemporary daughters of Antigone must resist and, in their resistance, reject both revenge and self-sanctimony. This is a remarkable achievement in "normal" circumstances; it is astonishing in situations of torture and terror, individual and communal helplessness and humiliation. Yet something of this sort is called for in the Nietzschean hope Dallmayr reaffirms at the conclusion of his essay, the hope that human beings might be delivered from revenge.

NOTES

1. Jean Bethke Elshtain, "Antigone's Daughters," *Democracy* April, 1982, pp. 46–59, especially p. 47. Rhetorical considerations played a role in entitling my essay. During a question and answer period following a talk I delivered at a university in the Midwest, one questioner asked, "Why Antigone? Why not Ismenê, whose caution is perhaps worthy of emulation?" And I responded not, I trust, flippantly, this way: " 'Ismenê's Daughters' just doesn't have a ring to it, does it?" True: reminding us of the controversial luminescence of Antigone as compared with the rather dull aura surrounding her sister.

2. A bizarre mimesis of the Greek male autochthony myth, a belief in self-sufficient generation that represses "the biological role of the female and therefore the family in the continuity of the city." See Martha Nussbaum's discussion in her masterful work, *The Fragility of Goodness* (New York: Cambridge University Press, 1986), p. 40.

3. Steiner moves to answer this question in his erudite exploration, *Antigones* (New York: Oxford University Press, 1982). Steiner's

discussion appeared after my essay. His sweep through centuries of
Antigone reappropriations in great works of art and thought and
direct acts of human courage offers a rejoinder to Mary Dietz's suggestion that my use of Antigone "as an archetype for feminists of
the 1980s" is "odd or anachronistic." It is unclear from Dietz's discussion why turning to Antigone is odd but to Aristotle entirely normal, not at all anachronistic. Suffice it to say that immersion in representations, puzzling over ongoingly reinscribed texts and myths,
is what political thinkers do. We are (Montaigne was right) "the interpreters of interpretations." Dietz's critique is part of a longer discussion in "Citizenship with a Feminist Face: The Problem with
Maternal Thinking," *Political Theory* 13, no. 1 (February 1985), pp.
19–38.

4. My current reading draws upon Nussbaum and Steiner as
well as several years of lecture notes and student comments and
questions. Nussbaum's exploration of Antigone comprises chap. 3 of
The Fragility of Goodness.

5. Steiner, *Antigones*, pp. 185–96.

6. As I reread the play in preparation for writing this essay, I
detected intimations of a dynamic whose origins I had previously
located with Aristotle's *Politics*. I refer to what became, with modernity, a socially structured and reinforced double bind for women, a
conundrum along these lines: concerns arising from women's position in the family, including the health, education, and welfare of
children, were construed as private expressions of essentially apolit-
ical sentiment. But any hard-nosed talk about power by women, or
public displays of its use, meant they had forfeited the right to represent to the public sphere a private world they had presumably for-
saken. This was never the whole story but it is one important part of
the story. The collisions and collusions evident in modernist con-
structions are presaged by Creon's reaction to Antigone: he attempts to deny her a public voice and, failing that, to delegitimate
her voice. Having become a public person and in light of necessities
Creon refuses to acknowledge as they do not mesh with his stringent
vision of civic necessity, Antigone becomes, by definition, a civicly
bad woman, an outlaw. See my *Public Man, Private Woman: Women in
Social and Political Thought* (Princeton: N.J.: Princeton University
Press, 1981), pp. 14–16.

7. Thus Steiner: "and it is Creon, not Antigone, who will de-
stroy the city, an act the more transgressive as it contradicts the cus-
todianship, the instruments of conservation, inherent in legitimate
sovereignty."

8. For example: is compulsory military service really central "to the concept of citizenship in a democracy," as a National Organization for Women *amicus* brief (1981) claimed? Does resisting the view that women's traditional lives and identifies were so many handicaps to be overcome make one guilty by definition of nostalgia for the past? And so on.

9. "Antigone's Daughters," pp. 49–50.

10. In light of the fact that "Antigone's Daughters" offers an explicit criticism of an "overly schematic" public/private dichotomy and laments the fact that much of what goes into making a person "what he or she is falls outside the frame of formal, abstract analyses," it is puzzling to note Dietz's claim that "Elshtain envisions a world divided naturally and abstractly into dual realms and human beings as either virtuous private or arrogant public creatures." See Dietz, "Citizenship with a Feminist Face," p. 30.

11. I did not take up Hegel in "Antigone's Daughters" because I was, at that point, more interested in the pressure a social feminist reading of Antigone might bring to bear on alternative feminist positions than in challenging or reconfirming Hegel's Sophoclean moments.

12. G. W. F. Hegel, *The Phenomenology of Mind*, trans. J. B. Baille (New York: Harper and Row, 1967), p. 50.

13. Portions of the Hegel material are drawn from *Public Man, Private Woman*, pp. 170–83.

14. Hegel, *Phenomenology*, p. 476.

15. Ibid.

16. See her essay, "Hegel's Antigone," in *The Owl of Minerva* 17, no. 2 (Spring 1986), pp. 131–52, especially p. 141.

17. Steiner, *Antigones*, pp. 182–83.

18. Ibid, p. 140.

19. This makes feminist critiques of the standpoint of Antigone seem particularly strange, coming as they do from those committed to the notion that the "personal is political."

20. Once again, Nussbaum's discussion of all of this is wonderfully rich: must reading.

21. All citations are drawn from Dallmayr's essay in this volume.

22. One need not share Schutz's strong theory of intersubjectivity to appreciate his insistence on the density of the world we inhabit, the fact that it presses in upon us even as we act on it.

23. "Antigone's Daughters," p. 55.

24. Steiner, *Antigones*, pp. 108–9.

SELECTED BIBLIOGRAPHY
OF FRED R. DALLMAYR

A. BOOKS

Freedom and Emergency Powers (with Robert S. Rankin). New York: Appleton-Century-Crofts, 1964.

Beyond Dogma and Despair: Toward a Critical Phenomenology of Politics. Notre Dame, Ind.: University of Notre Dame Press, 1981.

Twilight of Subjectivity: Contributions to a Post-Individualist Theory of Politics. Amherst: University of Massachusetts Press, 1981.

Language and Politics: Why Does Language Matter to Political Philosophy? Notre Dame, Ind.: University of Notre Dame Press, 1984.

Polis and Praxis: Exercises in Contemporary Political Theory. Cambridge, Mass.: MIT Press, 1984.

Critical Encounters: Between Philosophy and Politics. Notre Dame, Ind.: University of Notre Dame Press, 1987.

Margins of Political Discourse. Albany: State University of New York Press, 1989.

B. EDITED BOOKS AND VOLUMES

Materialienband zu Habermas' Erkenntnis und Interesse (Essays on *Knowledge and Human Interests*), edited with introduction and epilog. Frankfurt: Suhrkamp Verlag, 1974.

Understanding and Social Inquiry (with Thomas A. McCarthy). Notre Dame, Ind.: University of Notre Dame Press, 1977.

From Contract to Community: Political Theory at the Crossroads. New York: Dekker Publishing Co., 1978.

"Foucault Memorial Issue" (with Gisela J. Hinkle). *Human Studies,* vol. 10 (1987), pp. 3–170.

The Communicative Ethics Controversy (with Seyla Benhabib). Cambridge, Mass.: MIT Press, 1989.

236

C. BOOK CHAPTERS

Thomas Hobbes, *Staatslexikon*, 6th ed., vol. 6 (Freiburg: Görres-Gesellschaft, 1960), pp. 108–12.

"Hobbes and Existentialism: Some Affinities," in Reinhart Koselleck and Roman Schnur, eds., *Hobbes-Forschungen* (Berlin: Duncker & Humblot, 1969), pp. 259–85.

"Equality and Social Change," in Carl Beck, ed., *Law and Justice: Festschrift for Robert S. Rankin* (Durham, N.C.: Duke University Press, 1970), pp. 181–206.

"Empirical Political Theory and the Image of Man," in Glen Gordon and William E. Connolly, eds., *Social Structure and Political Life* (New York: D. C. Heath and Co., 1973), pp. 168–91.

"Phenomenology and Marxism: A Salute to Enzo Paci," in George Psathas, ed., *Phenomenological Sociology* (New York: John Wiley & Sons, 1973), pp. 305–56.

"Phenomenology and Social Science: An Overview and Appraisal," in Edward S. Casey and David Carr, eds., *Explorations in Phenomenology* (The Hague: Martinus Nijhoff, 1974), pp. 133–66.

"Phänomenologie und Marxismus in geschichtlicher Perspektive," in Bernhard Waldenfels, ed., *Phänomenologie und Marxismus: I, Konzepte und Methoden* (Frankfurt: Suhrkamp Verlag, 1977), pp. 13–44.

"Genesis and Validation of Social Knowledge: Lessons from Merleau-Ponty," in Joseph Bien, ed., *Phenomenology and Social Science* (The Hague: Martinus Nijhoff, 1978), pp. 74–106.

"Fragen an Habermas und Apel," in W. Oelmüller, ed., *Transzendental-philosophische Normenbegründungen* (Paderborn: Schöningh, 1978), pp. 27–37.

"Response" (to MacIntyre and Braybrooke), in Maria J. Falco, ed., *Through the Looking-Glass: Epistemology and the Conduct of Inquiry* (Washington, D.C.: University Press of America, 1979), pp. 83–90.

"Critical Theory and Public Policy," in Ernest R. House, ed., *Evaluation Studies, Review Annual*, vol. 7 (Beverly Hills: Sage Publications, 1982), pp. 740–52.

"Kommunikation und Gemeinschaft," in W. Kuhlmann and D. Boehler, eds., *Kommunikation und Reflexion: Festschrift für Karl-Otto Apel* (Frankfurt: Suhrkamp Verlag, 1982), pp. 191–220.

"The Theory of Structuration: A Critique," in Anthony Giddens, *Profiles and Critiques in Social Theory* (New York: Macmillan, 1982), pp. 18–27.

"Introduction," to Michael Theunissen, *The Other: Studies in the Social Ontology of Husserl, Heidegger, Sartre and Buber* (Cambridge, Mass.: MIT Press, 1984), pp. ix-xxv.

"Comments on Giddens," in Gary Shapiro and Alan Sica, eds., *Hermeneutics: Questions and Prospects* (Amherst: University of Massachusetts Press, 1984), pp. 231–38.

"Phenomenology and Marxism in Historical Perspective," in B. Waldenfels, J. M. Broekman, and A. Pažanin, eds., *Phenomenology and Marxism* (London: Routledge & Kegan Paul, 1984), pp. 3–30.

"Life-World and Communicative Action," in Bhikhu Parekh and Thomas Pantham, eds., *Political Discourse: Explorations in Indian and Western Political Thought* (New Delhi: Sage Publications, 1987), pp. 152–78.

"Political Inquiry: Beyond Empiricism and Hermeneutics," in Terence Ball, ed., *Idioms of Inquiry* (Albany: State University of New York Press, 1987), pp. 169–185.

"Heidegger, Hölderlin and Politics," in Joseph Buttigieg, ed., *Criticism Without Boundaries* (Notre Dame, Ind.: University of Notre Dame Press, 1987), pp. 111–28.

"Praxis and Reflection," in Alan Blum, Michael Brown, Fred Dallmayr, Maurice Roche, and Kurt Wolff, *Self-Reflection in the Human Sciences* (Edmonton, Alta.: University of Edmonton Press, 1987), pp. 1–15.

D. JOURNAL ARTICLES

1956

"Proudhon et la coexistence," *Revue internationale d'histoire politique et constitutionnelle*, pp. 205–17.

"Studie über Norberto Bobbio," *Archiv für Rechts- und Sozialphilosophie*, vol. 42, pp. 403–28.

1958

"Epimeteo Cristiano o Prometeo Pagano?" *Revista Internazionale de Filosofia del Diritto*, vol. 35, pp. 657–79 (on Carl Schmitt).

1961

"Public and Semi-Public Corporations in France," *Law and Contemporary Problems*, vol. 26, pp. 755–93.

1966

"Heinrich Rickert und die amerikanische Sozialwissenschaft," *Der Staat*, vol. 5, pp. 17–46.
"Strauss and the 'Moral Basis' of Thomas Hobbes," *Archiv für Rechts- und Sozialphilosophie*, vol. 52, pp. 25–66.

1967

"Functionalism, Justice and Equality," *Ethics*, vol. 78, pp. 1–16.

1968

"Political Science and the Two Cultures," *Journal of General Education*, vol. 19, pp. 269–95.

1969

"Bilanz der amerikanischen Politikwissenschaft," *Politische Vierteljahresschrift*, vol. 10, pp. 149–53.
"Hobbes and Existentialism: Some Affinities" (revised version), *Journal of Politics*, vol. 31, pp. 615–40.

1970

"Empirical Political Theory and the Image of Man," *Polity*, vol. 2, pp. 443–78.
"History and Class Consciousness: Georg Lukács' Theory of Social Change," *Politics and Society*, vol. 1, pp. 113–131.

1972

"Reason and Emancipation: Notes on Habermas," *Man and World*, vol. 5, pp. 79–109.

"Critical Theory Criticized: Habermas' *Knowledge and Human Interests* and Its Aftermath," *Philosophy of the Social Sciences*, vol. 2, pp. 211–29.
"Ingens Sylva: Begegnung mit Vico," *Philosophische Rundschau*, vol. 19, pp. 74–82.

1974

"Plessner's Philosophical Anthropology: Implications for Role Theory and Politics," *Inquiry*, vol. 17, pp. 49–77.
"Toward a Critical Reconstruction of Ethics and Politics," *Journal of Politics*, vol. 36, pp. 926–57.

1976

"Beyond Dogma and Despair: Toward a Critical Theory of Politics," *American Political Science Review*, vol. 70, pp. 64–79.
"Marxism and Truth," *Telos*, no. 29, pp. 130–59.
"Expérience du sens et réflexion sur la validité: K.-O. Apel et la transformation de la philosophie," *Archives de philosophie*, vol. 39, pp. 367–405.
"Natural History and Social Evolution: Reflections on Vico's 'Corsi e Ricorsi'," *Social Research*, vol. 43, pp. 857–73.
"Phenomenology and Critical Theory: Adorno," *Cultural Hermeneutics*, vol. 3, pp. 367–405.

1977

"Hermeneutics and Historicism: Reflections on Winch, Apel and Vico," *Review of Politics*, vol. 39, pp. 60–81.

1978

"Sinnerlebnis und Geltungsreflexion: K.-O. Apels Transformation der Philosophie," *Philosophische Rundschau*, vol. 25, pp. 1–42.
"Vico and Herder," *Review of Politics*, vol. 40, pp. 140–45.

1979

"Knowledge and Commitment: Variations on a Familiar Theme" (review essay), *Polity*, vol. 12, pp. 291–302.

1980

"On Critical Theory" (review essay), *Philosophy of the Social Sciences*, vol. 10, pp. 93–109.
"Between Theory and Practice" (review essay), *Human Studies*, vol. 3, pp. 175–84.
"Heidegger on Intersubjectivity," *Human Studies*, vol. 3, pp. 221–46.

1981

"Critical Theory and Public Policy," *Policy Studies Journal*, vol. 9, pp. 522–34.
"Frankfurt School: An Essay," *Review of Politics*, vol. 43, pp. 141–46.
"Life-World and Politics" (review essay), *Research in Phenomenology*, vol. 11, pp. 256–63.

1982

"Conversation, Discourse, and Politics," *Phenomenology and the Human Sciences*, vol. 1, pp. 49–88.
"Agency and Structure" (review essay), *Philosophy of the Social Sciences*, vol. 12, pp. 427–38.
"Language and Praxis" (review essay), *Human Studies*, vol. 5, pp. 249–59.

1983

"The Relevance of Relevance: Comments on McBride," *Philosophy in Context*, vol. 13, pp. 71–75.

1984

"Response" (to Rasmussen and McCarthy), *Philosophy and Social Criticism*, vol. 10, pp. 121–29.
"Is Critical Theory a Humanism?" *Boundary 2*, vol. 12–13, pp. 463–93.

1985

"Continental Perspectives and the Study of Politics," *News for Teachers of Political Science*, No. 44, pp. 15–17.

"Pragmatism and Hermeneutics" (review essay), *Review of Politics*, vol. 47, pp. 411–30.

1986

"Heidegger, Hölderlin and Politics," *Heidegger Studies* vol. 2, pp. 81–95.
"Tradition and Modernization in India" (review essay), *Review of Politics*, vol. 48, pp. 621–26.

1987

(with Gisela Hinkle) "Foucault *in memoriam* (1926–1984)," *Human Studies*, vol. 10, pp. 2–9.
"Democracy and Post-Modernism," *Human Studies*, vol. 10, pp. 143–70.
"Praxis and Reflection" (review essay), *Phenomenology and Social Science*, vol. 12, pp. 2–9.
"Politics of the Kingdom: Pannenberg's *Anthropology*," *Review of Politics*, vol. 49, pp. 85–111.
"Politics against Philosophy: Strauss and Drury," *Political Theory*, vol. 15, pp. 326–37.
"Public or Private Freedom? Response to Kateb," *Social Research*, vol. 54, pp. 617–28.
"Politics and Conceptual Analysis: Comments on Vollrath," *Philosophy and Social Criticism*, vol. 13, pp. 31–37.
"The Discourse of Modernity: Hegel and Habermas," *Journal of Philosophy*, vol. 84, pp. 682–92.
"Hegemony and Democracy," *Philosophy and Social Criticism*, vol. 13, pp. 283–96.

1988

"Understanding Nietzsche's Anti-Politics" (review essay), *Review of Politics*, vol. 50, pp. 133–39.
"Heidegger and Marxism," *Praxis International*, vol. 7, pp. 207–24.
"Habermas and Rationality," *Political Theory*, vol. 16, pp. 553–79.
"Reading Horkheimer Reading Vico," *New Vico Studies*, vol. 5, pp. 57–62.

CONTRIBUTORS

WILLIAM E. CONNOLLY is Professor of Political Science, The Johns Hopkins University. He is editor of the journal *Political Theory*. His books include *The Terms of Political Discourse, Politics and Ambiguity,* and *Political Theory and Modernity.*

FRED R. DALLMAYR is Packey J. Dee Professor of Government, University of Notre Dame. His major works are included in the Selected Bibliography in this volume.

JEAN BETHKE ELSHTAIN is the Centennial Professor of Political Science, Vanderbilt University. Among her many articles and books about political theory and feminism are *Public Man, Private Woman* and *Women and War.*

JAMES M. GLASS is Professor of Government and Politics, University of Maryland. He has published widely in the area of political theory and psychology and is the author of *Political Delusion* and *Private Terror/Public Life.*

JOHN O'NEILL is Distinguished Research Professor of Sociology, York University. He is coeditor of the journal *Philosophy of the Social Sciences.* Among his books are *Sociology as a Skin Trade, For Marx against Althusser,* and *Five Bodies.*

243

CALVIN O. SCHRAG is George Ade Distinguished Professor of Philosophy, Purdue University. He is coeditor of the journal *Man and World*. His most recent books include *Radical Reflection and the Origin of the Human Sciences* and *Communicative Praxis and the Space of Subjectivity*.

MICHAEL J. SHAPIRO is Professor of Political Science, University of Hawaii. His most recent books are *The Politics of Representation* and *International/Intertextual Relations* (coedited with James Der Derian).

BERNHARD WALDENFELS is Professor of Philosophy, University of Bochum. He has been a visiting professor at The New School and is the author of a number of books in philosophy and phenomenology, including *Phänomenologie in Frankreich*, *In den Netzen der Lebenswelt*, and *Ordnung im Zwielicht*.

STEPHEN K. WHITE is Associate Professor of Political Science, Virginia Polytechnic Institute and State University. He has published in the area of contemporary political theory and is the author of *The Recent Work of Jürgen Habermas*.